MIND FROM CONSCIOUSNESS.

EMPIRICAL PSYCHOLOGY;

OR,

THE HUMAN MIND AS GIVEN IN CONSCIOUSNESS.

FOR THE USE OF COLLEGES AND ACADEMIES.

By LAURENS P. HICKOK, D. D.
UNION COLLEGE.
AUTHOR OF RATIONAL PSYCHOLOGY, MORAL SCIENCE, ETC.

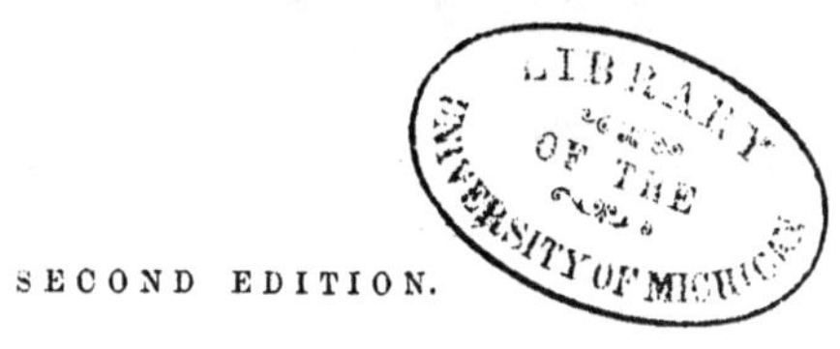

SECOND EDITION.

SCHENECTADY:
PUBLISHED BY G. Y. VAN DEBOGERT.

1855.

RIGGS, PRINTER,
Schenectady.

VAN BENTHUYSEN, STEREOTYPER,
Albany.

PREFACE.

It is the design, in the present work, to represent the human mind as it stands in the clear light of consciousness. We go to our own inward experience to find the facts, both of the single mental phenomena and of their connection with each other. An *Empirical* Philosophy is here alone attempted, and in which we cannot proceed according to the order of a *pure* science. The necessary and universal Ideas, which must determine all mental activity in every capacity, in order that these capacities may become intelligible to us in their conditional laws of operation, are not now first assumed, and then carried forward to a completed system by a rigid *a' priori* analysis and deduction in pure thought. Such a work has already been accomplished in a thoroughly Rational Psychology. The subjective Idea which must condition and expound all Intelligence has been attained, and then the objective Law which controls all the facts of an acting Intelligence has been determined to be in exact accordance. But in this work we wait upon experience altogether. We use no fact, and no combination of facts, except as they have already been attained in the common consciousness of humanity. It is rather a description of the human mind than a philosophy of it; a psycography rather than a psychology; and should not assume for itself the prerogatives of an exact science.

Still, with this renunciation of all claim to a pure science, the attempt has been made to find the human mind as it is, and all its leading facts as they combine to make a complete whole. The aim has been to present all the constituent parts in the light of their reciprocal adaptations to each other, and to show how all depend upon each one, and that each one exists for all, and thus to give the mind through all its faculties as a living unity, complete and consistent in its own organized identity. When a system is thus matured from conscious experience, having all the symmetry and unity of the acting reality, it may be known in a qualified sense, as a philosophy, and be termed a science of mind. It is a science, as Chemistry, Geology and Botany are sciences; the study of facts in their combinations as nature gives them to us, and thus teaching what is first learned by careful observation and experiment. It assumes not to have found those conditioning principles, which determine that the facts *must* have been so; but it may and does from its own consciousness affirm, that the facts *are* so.

Such a method of studying the human mind should precede that which is more purely philosophical, and thus more truly metaphysical, and is, perhaps, the only method to be attempted in an Academic or a Collegiate course. It is universally essential, as a portion of that applied discipline which is to prepare for vigorous and independent action in all public stations, and cannot be dispensed with in any learned profession without detracting from both the utility and the dignity of the man. It equally applies to the full process of Female Education, and both adorns and refines while it also expands and strengthens. This empirical exercise, thus indispensable for every scholar, is also a preparative and incentive to the study of the higher Metaphysics in more advanced stages of philosophical enquiry.

The present work has been written with the eye constantly on the class for whose study it is designed, and indeed mainly while the daily instruction with my own class was in progress, and the care has been to make it intelligible to any student of considerable maturity, who will resolutely and faithfully bring its statements to the test of his own clear consciousness. No instruction in Empirical Psychology can be given by mere verbal statement and definition, nor by attempted analogy and illustration. If the Teacher does not send the pupil to the fact as he has it in his own experience, there will be either an inadequate or an erroneous conception attained. The phenomenon within is unlike any phenomenon without, and all ingenious speculation and logical deduction will be empty and worthless without close and direct introspection. With such habits of investigation, it is fully believed that the following delineation of mental faculties and their operation will be readily apprehended, and consciously recognized as mainly conformed to the person's own inward experience.

UNION COLLEGE, 1854.

CONTENTS.

SECOND DIVISION.

THIRD DIVISION.

FOURTH DIVISION.

INTRODUCTION.

Psychology is comprehensive of all the necessary principles and the developed facts of mind. The necessary principles determine the possibility of an intelligent agency, and reveal in the reason how mind must be constituted in order to any cognition of a nature of things as existing in space and time; and is thus distinguished as *Rational* Psychology. The developed facts of mind are taken as they reveal themselves through an actual experience in consciousness, and when combined in systematic arrangement they give the specific science known as *Empirical* Psychology. It is this last only which comes within the field of present investigation.

Empirical Psychology is thus inclusive of all mental facts which may come within human consciousness. The being of mind, with all its faculties and their functions; every phenomenon in its own manifestation, and its law of connection with other phenomena; all, indeed, about which an intelligent enquiry can be made in reference to mental existence and action, come within the province where this philosophy should make itself thoroughly and familiarly conversant. As an empirical science, it is demanded that all the facts be collected, and that they be orderly arranged according to their known connections and dependencies. All that belongs to mind must have place, and each element its right place, in the system.

Mental Philosophy has not thus, as yet, attained its consummation. All the facts of mind are not probably yet found; many that have been attained are not clearly discriminated; and what have been used have never appeared in any system with exact order and perfect harmony. Much more labor of observation, analysis and combination is to be expended on this field, before it can be said to be fully in possession, and all its parts completely subjected to science. Peculiar difficulties and special hindrances lie in the way of mental investigation. The subject itself is for many reasons obscure, demanding the most patient and profound study. The most subtile analysis and the most comprehensive generalization are at times necessary, and in addition to the acuteness of the perception and the intensity of the thinking which are called into requisition, there are various liabilities to error from certain sources of deceptive bias and delusive influence. These operate at the present as they have done in the past, and a preliminary examination cf them may best facilitate an entrance upon this investigation, and prepare the student the most effectually to resist all perverting tendencies, and attain the truth by holding the facts in a clear light and looking at them in the right direction.

Among the more prominent difficulties and sources of error, are —

1. *The inverted method of the mind's operation in attaining its facts.*

The elements for Empirical Psychology are the facts of mind which come within every man's own experience. We may not assume what the facts are from any presumption of what they should be, nor take them upon trust because others have said what and how they are; we must find them within ourselves, and clearly apprehend them in our own consciousness, or they may prove utterly false and thus wholly worthless. Others may have observed the same facts, and used them in their way in their philosophy, and their statement of them may direct our minds to them and greatly facilitate us in the attainment of them; but their descriptions and assertions must not be allowed to stand valid, except through our own conscious apprehension and conviction. A fact, that has not been held in the clear light of my own consciousness, can truly be no fact for my philosophy. All the facts I use must come within my cognition, or I can make nothing but a borrowed science out of them.

But, from its first conscious apprehension, the mind has been accustomed, in its agency, to turn its attention outwardly to the phenomena of nature, and gain its facts in the perception of the objects of an external world. It has steadied itself in its operations upon the organs of sensation, and thus long habit has made it to be easy and pleasant for the mind to increase its knowledge, in the attainment of new facts through sensible observation. The facts we now need lie in altogether another direction, and are to be gathered from an entirely different field. The old habit of throwing the attention outwards is now to be broken up, and an entire inversion of the mental action is to be practised. The mind is to make its own phenomena its study, and turn the attention inward upon its own action. It is, as it were, to hold itself out to its own inspection, and turn itself round on all sides to its own observation. This position of the mind is always at first difficult to assume, and the perpetual counteraction of its wonted course is ever, in the beginning, painful to sustain. The effort, steadily to look in this unaccustomed direction, induces a weariness that destroys the capacity for clear perception and patient investigation. Repeated attempts, and decided and perpetuated effort, which shall ultimately habituate the mind to give this intro-version to its attention, can alone secure that there shall be any deep interest and delight in this order of mental operation. A fixed and prolonged observation and examination of the phenomena of the inner mental world is, on this account, the agreeable and chosen employment of comparatively very few minds, probably less than one in a thousand in our more enlightened communities.

The perpetual tendency from this is to induce impatience and haste in the induction of mental facts, and to leave the whole philosophy of mind to a superficial examination. The assertions of one, hastily made, are taken upon trust by others; specious appearances are carelessly assumed to be veritable realities; complex operations are left unanalyzed, and erroneous conclusions drawn from partial inductions; and then the whole is put together through the connections of mere casual or fancied resemblances; often even mingling contradictions and absurdities in the system; thus making the result to be a spurious and worthless philosophy. Certainly many doctrines, which falsify the very distinctions between mind and matter, and the grounds of all responsibility, and the order of discipline and culture, are left to spread themselves among the people, and influence opinion and practice, solely because the common mind is unaccustomed to accurately note the daily experiences in its own consciousness.

This difficulty is to be overcome, and the liability to error thereby avoided, only by a resolute perseverance in overcoming the old habit, and learning the method of readily reading the lessons from our own inward experience. The organs of sense must be shut up, and the material world shut out, and the mind for the time shut in upon itself, and made to become familiar with its own action. The man must learn to commune with himself; to study himself; to know himself; to live amid the phenomena of his own spiritual being. When this habit of intro-spection has been gained, the investigation of mental facts becomes not only possible, but facile and delightful. It should not be anticipated by any student, that this difficulty will be overcome without rigid and persevering self-discipline; nor that any satisfactory progress will be made in mental science, until this difficulty is thus surmounted; but all may be assured that the narrow way may be passed into spacious and pleasant fields of truth, by fixing a manly resolution, and persisting a while in its execution.

2. *The ambiguity of language.*

Language is the outer body of thought. Words, without thought, are empty; and thought, without words, is helpless. The common speech is thus the outer expression of the common thoughts of mankind. Philosophy attains the necessary principles, and determines the rules for the grammatical construction of language; but philosophy does not make nor change language. The working of the human mind within determines for itself its own outer expression, and, as an inner spirit and life, builds up its own body, and gives to it a form according to the inherent law of its own activity

But the great mass of mankind are conversant mainly with the objects of the sensible world. They think, and thus speak, of little else than those phenomena which meet them face to face through the organs of sense. Daily experience fixes their habits and limits their mental action, while few only turn their minds in upon themselves, and think and speak of the facts of their spiritual being. The common language of mankind is thus only an expression of what they find in their daily experience. When man begins to reflect, and philosophize concerning himself and nature around him, he needs a new language for his new thoughts; but his first reflection and philosophizing is about natural objects, and physical science occupies his study and opens the way to mental and metaphysical investigations. His philosophical terms are such still as give expression to his reflections upon nature, and his whole technical phraseology is readily referred, for its interpretation, to the outer objects of which it is the symbol, and thus gives little ambiguity, or mistake and confusion in apprehending the thought. And when mathematical science is studied, the conceptions are pure numbers and diagrams, and can be constructed as pure objects alike by all mathematicians, and thereby all mathematical language comes readily to possess a definite meaning, and can at once be referred to its pure figure as an exposition of the thought, and preclude all possible obscurity in the apprehension. Physical and Mathematical Sciences give little occasion for verbal ambiguities.

But, in mental science, the case becomes quite different. The thought must have its word, and the science its philosophical phraseology; but the thoughts, as elements of mental science, are quite peculiar—even thought itself, and all the inner faculties and functions of a spiritual existence. The word, as symbol, cannot be explained by any reference to sensible objects, but must carry its meaning over to another mind, only by inducing the conception of the same mental fact in his own consciousness. All these distinct and peculiar mental facts call for their expressive terms in language, and the science of mind cannot proceed until the words for mental phenomena are appropriated. To give to all these new thoughts entirely new words, would be laborious in the invention and burdensome to the memory. The mind naturally and readily accommodates the language, already appropriated to sensible objects, in application also to these inner spiritual phenomena. Where there was apprehended some striking analogy between the outer and the inner fact, the word for the outer was used also by accommodation of meaning for the inner, and thus often the same word came to possess its two meanings; one in reference to the physical, and the other to the metaphysical world of thought. The mind, though wholly spiritual, unextended and illimitable by any of the forms of space, is thus said to be *fixed* or to *wander*, to be *dull* or *acute*, *narrow* or *comprehensive*. The names for tangible qualities in nature are also transferred to the intangible characteristics of the spirit, and the feelings of the human soul are said to be *frigid* or *ardent*, *lax* or *intense;* and the heart *cold* or *warm*, *hard* or *tender;* and the will to be *firm* or *weak*, *stable* or *flexible;* according to such supposed resemblances. The mind as well as matter has its *inclinations* and *impressions;* and many words taken from the outer come at length to have an almost exclusive application to the inner; as *disposition*, *induction*, *conclusion*, *abstraction*, etc. Very many words in all languages have thus their primary and secondary significations; and in the science of mind we are perpetually thrown back upon the analogies of matter. Ambiguous words and equivocal expressions repeatedly occur, and thus a constant liability is induced to mistake and confound things which greatly differ. The thought is widely misapprehended, in the illusion from the two-faced symbol that conveys it. Sturdy controversies have been often mere logomachies;

the philosophy alike, and only the phraseology differently apprehended.

The errors from this source are to be avoided, not by excluding all such ambiguities, which will be wholly impracticable, but by universally bringing the fact within the light of consciousness. By whatever symbol the mental fact may be communicated, the conception must be known as that of some phenomenon within us, and not some quality from the world without us. The analogy must not be permitted to delude, but the fact itself must be found amid the conscious elements of our own mental experience. The truths we want in psychology are not to be sought in the heavens above, nor in the depth beneath; but they are nigh us, even in our own being, and amid the hourly revealings of our own consciousness.

3. *Inadequate conceptions of mental being and development.*

The complete conception of a plant includes far more than its sensible phenomena of color, shape, size and motion; or that of all its separate parts of stock, branches and leaves. It must especially include its vital force as an inner agency which develops itself in a progressive and orderly growth to maturity. This is widely different from all conceptions of mechanical combinations, in which the structure is put together from the outside, according to some preconceived plan of arrangement. There is, both in the plant and the machine, the conception of some law of combination, and in this a rational idea which expounds each its own structure; but in the plant it is that of an inner living law, spontaneously working out its organic development, while in the mechanism it is an artificial process for putting dead matter together. The former conception is far more difficult adequately to attain than the latter.

The conception of animal life and development rises quite above that of the vegetable, and includes the superadded forces of an appetitive craving, an instinctive selection of its peculiar food, with the faculty of locomotion to bring itself to it; and the capacity for mastication, digestion, assimilation and incorporation into its own substance, and thus a growth in the whole system of the body and its members. Superior in *degree*, in man, is the faculty of judging from sensible experience, and thus acting from the dictates of prudence; and the distinctive and far more elevated endowment in *kind* of rational faculty, in its artistic, philosophic, ethic and religious capacities, gives to him the prerogatives of action in liberty and moral responsibility, thereby lifting him from the bondage of all necessitated things into the sphere of personality. All this complexity of superinduced faculties, from mere vital force up to rational being, has its complete organic unity, constituting but one existence in its own identity, and its own inner spirit works out a complete development of the whole, through all the manifestations of growth and mature activity. One life pervades the whole, and one law of being makes every part reciprocally subservient and accordant with all other parts.

If then, an adequate conception of merely vegetable organism, as distinct from the combinations of mechanism, be difficult to attain, how greatly is the difficulty augmented in attaining the full conception of humanity with all its included capacities and exalted prerogatives! From these inadequate conceptions of humanity, must necessarily originate very faulty systems of psychology. All resting in the analogies of mere mechanical combinations and movements must be widely erroneous; and any failure clearly to discriminate between the animal and the rational, must necessarily fail in the attainment of a spiritual philosophy; and any complete conceptions of man's spirituality, which do not at the same time recognise the modification therein given from its combination with the material and the animal, will also necessarily render the person incompetent to study and attain the science of mind as it dwells in a tabernacle of flesh and blood. An exclusion, in fact, of any one of the superinduced powers and faculties in humanity, and their reciprocal dependencies and modifications, must so far vitiate the system of philosophy which is thus attempted to be constructed. Liabilities to error here are greater than from all other sources.

The only way to obviate these difficulties, and escape these liabilities to error, is by cultivating the intellect and elevating the conception to the essential spiritual being of the subject to be investigated. The use of any mechanical analogies or animal resemblances must not be allowed to delude the mind, and induce the conclusion that the rational and spiritual part of humanity can be at all adequately apprehended through any such media. The mind must be studied in the light of its own conscious operations, and the perpetual interactions of the sense and the spirit, "the law in the members" and "the law of the mind," must be accurately observed, and while the philosophy thus knows to distinguish things that differ, it must also know to estimate the modifications which these different things make reciprocally upon each other. All material and animal being has a law imposed upon it, while all spiritual being has its law written within it; the first moves wholly within the chain of necessity, the last has its action in liberty and under inalienable responsibility; and all philosophy is falsely so called, which does not adequately discriminate between them.

4. *The broad comprehension necessary to an accurate classification of mental facts.*

The mind is a unit in its existence, through all its varied states of activity and all its successive stages of development. It is moreover a living unity, growing to maturity and maintaining the integrity of its organization, by the perpetuated energy of one and the same vital principle. When, then, we have attained all the single facts of mind which can be given in any experience, and know how to analyze every fact to its simple elements, we have not yet completed our mental philosophy. The philosophy truly consists in the combination of all these discriminated facts into one complete system. But there are very many ways in which a classification of the facts found may be made, and thus systems from the same facts may be as various as their varied combinations may admit. Merely casual relationships may be taken, or even fancied or arbitrary connections assumed, and made the principle by which the facts are brought into system; or a blind imitation of another man's system may be followed, with no independent examination and determination of what the true order of classification may be.

The liabilities to such faulty classifications find their source in the difficulty of attaining comprehensively what is the living order of arrangement, as found in the mind itself. Single facts can much easier be found, than the right place for them in combination with all others. To put each fact in its own place demands a knowledge of its relationship to all others, and thus no classification of it can be known as correct, except through a knowledge of all others with which it must stand in connection. The entire facts in the system must thus be known, each in its own control over others or dependency upon others, before they can be put together in any valid order of systematic arrangement. Such a comprehensive view is not readily attained. Few minds are willing to take the labor necessary to reach such a standpoint, where they may overlook the whole field and accurately note every division and subdivision within it. The several faculties and functions of mind are facts, as really as the phenomena which come out in their particular exercises; and the whole mind, with all these faculties, is itself a fact, to be accurately known in its completeness as really as any one faculty, or any one act of any faculty. The whole mind can be so known only by knowing all its component elements, and psychology can be consummated only by such induction of every element, and such complete combination of them in a system, accordant with the comprehensive fact in the human mind itself; and only by such comprehensive knowledge can the liability to faulty systems in mental science be excluded.

Thus forewarned of the difficulties in the prosecution of the study of mind, and the liabilities to error thereby induced, the student is better prepared to enter upon the necessary investigations, and to guard against any delusive influences that may assail him. His task is to attain the facts of mind and classify them, exactly as they are found to be in the clear light of conscious experience.

ANTHROPOLOGY.

THE CONNECTIONS OF MIND AND BODY.

MAN holds within himself a combination of elements from the material, the animal, and the spiritual worlds; and while he is to be studied as existing in his own unity, it must still be in the full apprehension of all this complexity of being. The material elements which enter into the composition of the human body are perpetually changing, and are themselves in reality no part of that which is essentially the man; and yet, both the animal and the rational in man are much modified, by the influences which come in upon them through the body. The mind is the distinct subject for present investigation, but not mind as pure and disembodied. The psychology we attain must recognize, through all its facts, the existence of a rational spirit, which dwells in a tabernacle of flesh and blood.

Physiology would contemplate man solely as *living body*, excluding all the peculiar endowments and prerogatives of a spiritual life; and while the study of man in such a limited view would find facts of much interest, as bearing upon the welfare of his physical constitution, yet would they be only remotely subservient to the investigations of psychology.

Anthropology, on the other hand, contemplates man in his *entire being*, physically, intellectually and morally; recognizes the connections of mind with matter, and the influences of one upon the other; and expounds the modifications which mind undergoes, from the action of the external world upon it through the body. The facts attained in such a science have an important bearing upon psychology, where mind is regarded in its own unity, and with all its different faculties and functions of operation relatively to itself. The mind itself, viewed exclusively in its own inherent relations, is not in humanity as mind would be separately from all bodily connections. The psychology of angels must differ much from that of man, inasmuch as pure spirit must exclude many facts which belong to an existence as incarnate spirit. Preliminary and auxiliary to the study of psychology is, thus, a summary recognition of some of the more prominent facts of anthropology. We need to take mind and body as one living organization, and learn the modifications of the former which are made by its connections with the latter.

Life is a spontaneous force, which collects its materials from the elements of surrounding nature, and assimilating them to its own uses, builds up thereby the organism of its own body. Matter is variously modified by mechanical, chemical and crystaline forces; but in no way does it take on the forms of an organized existence, except as thus vitalized and constructed into a corporeal dwelling for some living spirit. The crystal may seem in many respects but a little remove from the plant; yet is the former the same in quality through every part, and as perfect in the smallest portion as in the whole; while the latter has all its parts different from others, and no portion is in perfection without the whole. The crystal is still dead matter, and has no organs which reciprocally exist for each other; the plant is alive, and its root, stock, branches and leaves live each for the others, and all for each.

In the plant we have the lowest forms of living organization, and the life always working outwards to the surface. The growth of the stock and branches is on the outside, and every perpetuated bud successively develops itself only as a perpetual repetition of what has gone before it. A higher force is superinduced upon vegetable life, and in this we have the animal, in whom every part grows simultaneously. The life is internal; digestion and assimilation are carried on within the body; and a sentient capacity enables the animal to feel itself and the outer objects which come in contact with itself. Through the appropriate organs of sensation, perception is effected; and the faculty of locomotion is guided, and the power of selection directed to its objects.

Every individual life has its own law of working, and builds up its own body after its own pre-conditioned order. The forms are not in the matter, but already given in the vital force itself; and every plant, tree and animal, grows out after that shape which its own inherent law has determined for it. External conditions may force modifications of the primitive form, but it is still easy to find the original pattern, after which the inner life is struggling to shape its corporeal being. The life-force can only develop its own rudiments after its own forms, and can neither give to itself any new faculties, nor work after borrowed patterns. The conditions being supplied, each individual life works out its own organic forms to maturity. It also prepares and perfects the spermatic germs for perpetuating the race; separating these from itself, and leaving them to begin anew, in their distinct identity, the same work of development according to the old inherited type of existence.

Superinduced, again, upon the animal is the far higher force of a rational existence. The capacity for thought and liberty is given; and the spiritual is imparted, that is to restrain and control the animal; and in this we have the human, with its intelligent and responsible agency. The man has his life-force, with its own abnormal type of being and development, as has the plant; and the capacity for inward digestion, assimilation, and nutrition; for locomotion, perception, and selection, as has the animal; but far above all these is his spiritual endowment; in which is rationality, personality, and the responsibilities of an immortality. Thus man is not merely life, like the vegetable; but animal life: and not alone animal life, like the brute; but a spiritual life, which enthrones the rational upon the animal, allying him to the angels, and putting on him the likeness of the Divine. The one life, modified by all these superinduced forces, each distinguishable from the others, builds up for man his outer tabernacle from the dust, and develops all his mental faculties to their maturity, and thus presents us with that humanity which is the subject of our philosophy, and all the facts of which, in its purely mental relations, are to be combined in our psychology.

The connections of mind with the body, and thus with the agencies of an external world, are mediately through the nerves, and their origin is in the brain and its elongation in the spinal-cord. These nerves, as they go off from the brain and vertebral-column, branch out to all the members, and over the whole body. They thus carry their communications each way, from the mind to the muscles, and from the outer world to the mind. These functions are performed by distinct fibres of the nerves; those which communicate with the mind, from the outer world, are termed *afferent*, or sensation fibres; and those that communicate from the mind, outward, are termed *efferent*, or motor fibres. Sometimes a fasciculus of nerves may form a plexus with another having quite a different origin, and an inosculation may thus occur, by which the powers of sensation or motion may be given to such nerves as had been before destitute of one or the other. A distinct system of nervous communication is employed for the digestive and nutritive functions, and also for the respiratory operations. The communications of some are voluntary, others involuntary; some are in consciousness, others in unconsciousness. A perpetually open medium of communication is thus given between the mind and body; and, through the bodily organization, between the mind and the external world. It is thus to be expected that the mind will itself be affected by its bodily connections, and in this respect it is, that it has been said above, the prominent facts of anthropology have an important bearing upon psychology. A few such may be given under the following heads:

1. *Modifications from external nature.*

Both plants and animals are greatly affected from the surrounding agents in external nature. The soil, the water, the air, the general climate, all modify the vegetable and the animal life, and give the peculiarities of their locality to all living things within the range of their influence. Some plants and animals are indigenous in certain regions, and may be cultivated as exotics over a wider territory, but beyond certain limits, no care can make either the plant or the brute perpetuate themselves. The tropical, the temperate, and the frigid zones, all have their peculiar flora and fauna, and the limited adaptations of circumstances restrict many to a special locality. The cedar has its place on Lebanon, and the hysop, or the ivy, springs out of the wall. The rush does not grow without mire, nor the flag without water. The camel traverses the desert, the wild goat inhabits the mountain crag, and the pelican gathers its fish and feeds alone in the wilderness. Man is far less restricted in his home, than any other living creature on the earth. Though less protected by nature, he can yet feed and clothe himself, and so bend nature to his use, that he may live in any clime, and people every isle and continent. The earth has but very limited regions which man has not traversed, and few localities so inhospitable where he may not make his home. But though thus truly a cosmopolite, yet is man every where subject to changes from the external influences which act upon him. The variations of climate and season, and even sudden changes of the weather, often induce, in the same man, a wide difference of mental states; and he is made energetic or enervated, feels elasticity or lassitude, cheerfulness or gloom, and passes through very varied emotions, by only passing through varied scenes and circumstances. So, moreover, the influence of food and dress, employment and society, indoor confinement or outward exposure, will very much modify his mental experience, and make the same man exhibit quite other physical and mental characteristics, by taking him out from the action of one, and putting him under the operation of another regimen.

Let any one of such influences, or a combination of several, operate long upon a man, and this will secure in him fixed habits and traits of disposition; and let this operate upon many men, and it will assimilate them each to each, and give to them all, in comparison with others, the peculiarities of a class; or, in broader limits it will secure the distinctive marks of national character. Such influences, from deeper and stronger sources in nature, operating upon some of the people in early ages, and passing down in hereditary succession over long and widening generations, have divided the one human family into several distinct races; and given to such as are the prominent types of their race, a marked discrimination from others. Perpetuated external influences, and the inherent law of propagation that 'like tends to the production of like,' has kept these lines of demarcation quite prominent, and the races shade off and run in to each other, only as the external influences become blended, or the amalgamation in the parents combine and assimilate their peculiarities in their offspring. The physical form and features, and the mental facts, are all diverse in this diversity of races amid the family of mankind.

There has been little uniformity in the estimation of the distinct races of mankind, some numbering more and others fewer distinctions. If there be considered three races, whose type and characteristics differ exclusively of each other, and all other varieties be considered as a blending of these and their peculiarities as sub-typical only, and not indicative of distinct race, the most satisfactory account may be rendered. We shall then have the Caucasian, the Mongolian, and the Nigritian races, as distinctively marked types in our common humanity. There is, in the geography of Asia, two elevated plateaus, stretching from west to east quite across the continent. The western commences in Turkey, and has the Caucasus on the north, and the Taurus and Kurdistan on the south, and passes on through Persia to the Indus, having the table-lands of Iran at its eastern extremity, and declining to the plains of the Tigris and Euphrates on the south, and of the Caspian and Bactriana, with the rivers of Sihon and Gihon on the north. Then commences a far more elevated table-land, having the Himmaleh on the south, and the Celestial and Altai mountains on the north, and stretching eastward to the sea of Ochotsk on the Pacific, descending to the great peninsular plains of Hindoostan, farther India and China on the south, and the frozen plains of Siberia on the north. This eastern Asiatic elevation contains Mongolia and Chinese Tartary. If we call the first the Caucasian, and the second the Mongolian table-land, we shall have the cradles of the three races of mankind, and the names for two of the most distinguished and the most numerous.

The Caucasian race is that of the most perfect type of humanity, and may be said to have its center and most distinguished marks in Georgia and Circassia, and to be modified by distance and other circumstances in departing from this geographical center. The peculiarity of the Caucasian type is that of general symmetry and regularity of outline. The head oval; the lines of the eyes and the mouth dividing the whole face into three nearly equal parts; the eyes large and their axis at right angles with the line of the nose, and the facial angle about 90 degrees, with a full beard covering quite to the ears. The complexion is white, and the stature tall, straight, and well proportioned. The Caucasian race can be followed through various migrations from the central home, as peopling south-western Asia, northern Africa, and almost the whole of Europe. In south-western Asia, we have had the Semitic families of the Hebrews, Assyrians and Arabians; in Egypt and Mauritania, the Mitzraim stock; and in Europe, the old Pelasgic tribes of the Mediterranean, with the successive Scythian irruptions; the old Celtic, Teutonic and Gothic branches of southern Europe, and the Scandinavian and Sclavic tribes of the north of Europe.

The Mongolian race differs widely from the Caucasian, and is quite inferior. Their home is in a more cold, hard, and inhospitable region. The highest mountains in the world environ and run through this immense plateau of western Asia, covered at their tops with perpetual snow, and especially at the south, fencing off all the warm and moist gales of the Indian Ocean, and with only few and distant openings for any communication with the vales below on either side. The primitive type of the Mongolian is a triangular or pyramidal form of the head, with prominent cheek bones; the eyes cramped, and standing far apart, with the outer corners greatly elevated; the facial angle 80 degrees; the nose small; the hair coarse, black, and hanging lankly down; with scanty beard, which never covers the face so high as the ears; and a bronze or olive complexion. The expansions of this race have passed down and peopled the peninsulas of India and China on the south; Tartary and Siberia on the north; and have extended westward in the old Turcomans, the Magyar or Hungarian people, and the ancient Finns and Laps in the north-west corner of Europe; and to the north-east of Asia in the Yacontis, the Tschoudi, and the Kamtschatkadales. The Tartars once overrun and subjugated the Sclavic tribes in European Russia, but a combined resistance drove them to return to their own family in Asia.

The Nigritian race, which in Central Africa becomes the full-typed Negro, has a less distinctly marked central origin. Circumstances, however, determine the region which must have been the cradle of this race. At quite the eastern portion of the Caucasian table-land, or perhaps in the valley of the Indus and at the foot of the Himmalehs must have been their origin. There are now black people in this region, and of a wholly different type from the Caucasian or Mongolian. But the branching off of the propagations from this stock, from this point, is the surest evidence. The characteristic marks of the Nigritian are a dull sallow skin, varying in all shades to a sooty and up to a shining black, with a crisp woolly hair, and nearly beardless, except upon the end of the chin, and more scanty on the upper lip. The head is compressed at the sides, the skull arched and thick, the forehead narrow and depressed, and the back of the head elongated. The facial angle 70 degrees, the nose flat and broad, the lips thick and protruding, and the throat and neck full and muscular. A strong odor is constantly secreted from the bilious coloring matter beneath the epidermis, and from numbers, under a hot sun, becomes intolerable to a European.

They have passed on to the south-east, and been wholly, perhaps, displaced in Hindoostan and farther India, but were the primitive inhabitants of Australia, and still survive in the Papuas of New-Guinea and the more degraded savage of New-Holland and Van Dieman's Land. They also are found in the neighboring South Sea Islands, and where there is an admixture of the Mongolian blood, among other modifications, the woolly hair becomes a curling, crisping mop, springing out on all sides of the head. To the east, they are still found in Laristan, southern Persia, and, as a mixture with the

Semitic stock, in the black Bedoueen of Arabia. But it is only as they have crossed into Africa, either by the Straits at the south, or the Isthmus at the north of the Red Sea, and passed down into the interior of the continent, that we find them in their most congenial and abiding lodging place. In Abyssinia are found natives almost black and with crisp hair, but in Senegal and Congo the full negro type is completely developed. From hence, they have been violently and cruelly transplanted as slaves to other continents, and especially to America. The Maroons, escaped from Spanish and Portuguese masters in South America, have formed independent communities in the congenial swampy regions of Guiana, and farther on upon the banks of the Amazon, and in the absence of other races are rapidly multiplying.

In addition to these, Blumenbach has the Malay and American races as equally exclusive and distinct. But the Malay is manifestly a hybrid stock, and is no where marked by a distinctive type that is expansively homogeneous. The peculiarities of the Mongolian always more or less appear in the pyramidal head, prominent cheek bones, and scanty beard, but other modifications abound as the mixture of the Nigritian or Caucasian is the more abundant. They are usually inhabitants of the coasts and parts of islands, but are seldom the controlling people of any region. Their most central locality is the peninsula of Malacca, but they are found also on the Indo-Chinese coast, in the island of Madagascar, in the Pacific Archipelago, and indeed it would seem that the extreme South American and Patagonian were expansions of the Malay stock. The American, again, is pretty manifestly the Mongolian, having crossed over Bhering's Strait and thence spreading its propagations over the continent. The high cheek bone, the scanty beard, and copper complexion, bespeak the Mongolian parentage; and except in the Esquimau of the north, or the Patagonian of the south, there appears no particular characteristic demanding the supposition of any blending of races, and the Esquimau may be only the lowest degradation of the Mongolian, as the Hottentot and Bushman is of the Nigritian. The extremes from the central home seem, in all cases, to present the greatest deterioration.

The three races may in this way be made to include the human family, and any other broad and long continued distinctions may be considered rather as sub-typical, and indices of amalgamation, rather than exclusive typical divisions of race. But an exact delineation and separation of the races is of less importance, than the determination of the enquiry, if all races were originally from one parentage? It is the theory of some very learned and able philosophers, that man, though of one genus, is of several different species, and that each species had its separate ancestry in its own central locality. This is not a favorable place for such investigation, nor can the main design now admit of an extended discussion, but the following considerations may be found sufficient to sustain the position, "that God hath made of one blood all the nations of men to dwell on all the face of the earth."

Among animals, there is at least as great a distinction between such as are undoubtedly of the same species, as in any difference of race among men. There are wide differences of race in neat cattle, horses, and especially dogs, where there is no ground to suppose that they sprang from an originally distinct created ancestry. In the case of swine and sheep, peculiarities have arisen within very authentic tradition, from some great change in a single case, and which have been perpetuated with all their typical marks, in a variety so broad as to make them henceforth properly distinct races. Domestication in fowls, as well as animals, has produced such remarkable changes, and which perpetuate themselves from generation to generation, that we ought not to be surprised at the distinctions which circumstances may work among mankind, even to so great a degree as to be truly separations of race. Individual differences and peculiarities, and class and tribe distinctions, are greater among men than among the same species of animals; it ought, then, to be anticipated that human races may be broadly discriminated.

But, while there is this broader diversity in different portions of the human family, there is also, on the other hand, stronger indications of unity, linking all the typical races into one common brotherhood. The common powers of speech and language; the kindred emotions, sympathies, and appetites; the convictions of responsibility to law, and the establishment of political governments; the sense of dependence upon an Absolute Spirit, and the propensity to some religious worship; the similarity of capacity in forming habits, coming under discipline and receiving cultivation; and the sameness of times in the age of puberty, menstruation, and gestation, except in the modifications of manifest causes; all determine that mankind of every race are yet the children of one family. In addition to all this, there is the great fact, that the races amalgamate and propagate from generation to generation, which is in contravention of the law between wholly distinct species. A few only can at all produce a hybrid offspring in a cross-generation, and when they do, the progeny is wholly sterile. The conclusion from this is certainly quite sound, that the distinctions of race among men are adventitious, and that all are the descendants of one original parentage.

The argument for different species through a distinct original ancestry, from any supposed different centers of propagation, is altogether inconclusive. At the widest distance apart, it is still wholly practicable that all should have been cradled in the same region. The Patagonians or the Esquimaux may have an ancestry who wandered from Central Asia, and such a supposition involves no improbability. Indeed all tradition, so far as any is found among the scattered tribes of humanity, as well as all other indices, point to a common locality whence all have departed. The substantial facts of the Mosaic account are the most probable, and the most philosophical, of any theories that may be adopted. There are two strong objections to the vague popular notion that the first peopling of the earth, as now inhabited, radiated from the Armenian Mount Ararat. The old

Celtic, Teutonic, and Sclavic tribes of western Europe, historically emigrated from a region much farther to the north-east, and this would make them to have first emigrated eastward, up high mountain ranges, only to have returned on the old track, in their passage to a permanent home in Europe; and the fact that the Armenian Ararat is an almost inaccessible peak of a single mountain, springing from a comparatively limited base and with precipitous sides, makes it exceedingly unlikely that the ark, which, divinely directed, had survived the deluge, should have been there stranded, demanding a miracle to bring its enclosed animals safely down upon the plains below. It is said that the Circassian word Arak signifies solely a peak, and thus Ararat may very probably be a generic word for the high summit of any mountain. Others affirm it to be the name of a region, without any reference to any particular mountain. The greatest amount of probability is attained in supposing that the cradle of the human family, after the deluge, was in the region of the sacred rivers Sihon and Gihon, which are now confluent into the sea of Aral, as the Araxes and the Oxus. This plain of the Aral, as that to which the primitive patriarchs, with their posterity already somewhat multiplied, "journeyed from the east," and which was "in the land of Shinaar," would indicate that it was some of the high mountains which surround the table-land in Eastern Asia, and by far the most elevated points on the face of the globe, on which the ark rested after the deluge. The great dispersion of the human family, from this point, in the confusion of tongues at Babel, would very readily accord with all the facts of different races, and all the indicated centers of their typical peculiarities.

Those emigrating eastward would enter the mountain defiles, and spread themselves upon the high table-lands of Tartary and Mongolia, and assimilating from marriage, climate and other circumstances acting in common, would become the grand Mongolian stock, sending off its successive tribes, and pressing each other farther onward, down the southern Asiatic plains and peninsulas, and off to the northern streams which empty into the Arctic Ocean. Those going southerly would come upon the mountain steps of Iran, and others round the Caspian would reach the more western portions of the Caucasian plateau, and the like assimilations would originate the Caucasian race, having a common center where its typical marks received their most complete development. At the foot of the Koosh and Himmaleh mountains, within the valleys of the Indus, might be generated a dark-skinned, crisp-haired family of children, which should propagate their peculiarities, and carry abroad their typical marks, and emigrate to more southern and tropical climes, instinctively indicated as most favorable for the perfect development of their intrinsic characteristics, and actually find this great center only as they reach the interior of the African continent.

It is not probable that distinctions of race at all took their rise in the three sons of Noah. Nor is it to be supposed that any three different pairs of the human family, at any age, originated the three great distinctive races, and then, excluding and exhausting all others, at length came to people the world between them. Strong typical peculiarities somewhere began, and absorbed and assimilated all others within them. And thus, taking intrinsic germ and extrinsic circumstances, as given in humanity and outward nature, we find the fact to be, that mankind has worked its propagations in the three different fundamental types of the white and bearded, the olive and beardless, and the black and crisp-haired races. All other varieties may readily be reduced to some blending of these generic peculiarities. These distinctions of race are older than history, and the combination of Egyptian, Assyrian and Hindoo sculpture may give us the whole, as complete in unknown centuries backward, as any living specimens of the present age can furnish.

2. *Modifications of mind from constitutional organization.*

Both the animal and rational forces, as originally superinduced upon the life-force, may be different, in proportion and degree, in different individuals; and thus a different mental development may be secured, in the differences of rudiment in the original germ. But that which is more manifest in experience is here of more importance: viz. that differences of bodily organization make corresponding modifications of mental development.

The difference of *sex* manifests its influence through all the anatomical structure, and physiological characteristics. The bones, muscles, skin, hair, and the venous and nervous systems, are all modified from the constitutional peculiarities of the particular sex. But the bodily development is not, perhaps, any more strongly marked by sex than is the mental. There is a radical and abiding difference between male and female intellect, and no culture can change the one to be as the other. Oftentimes the mind of the man may be more feminine, and that of the woman more masculine than the generality of the sex, and thus it may also be with the physical constitution; and yet the one is never found to have made its leap quite over into the province of the other. In emotion and sympathy, intellectual adaptations and inclinations, together with entire mental propensities, the male and female mind have each their own type, manifestly discriminated the one from the other. They may each become distinguished, in the public observation, for the same pursuits; and whether of art, literature or science, there may be the products of both male and female industry which stand out prominent in excellence; but perhaps never will the case occur, in which an experienced and philosophical critic will not at once determine, from the inherent characteristics of the productions themselves, that which the man and that which the woman has originated. The nature of the case makes the peculiar province of each separate from the other, and the law of nature has fixed the constitutional organization of the one unlike to the other; it is thus to be expected, that in the ongoings of nature, she will keep the openings of mind in each, perpetually discriminated the one from the other.

The different *temperaments* among men present their peculiar facts quite as prominently as those of the distinctive mental characteristics of the sexes. Every person has some prevalent type of mental activity induced by his constitutional temperament, and this temperament finds its source in the peculiar arrangements and functions of bodily organization. The body, as an entire system, has within itself different subordinate systems, which minister together for the growth and preservation of the whole. Conspicuous among these subordinate systems are the nervous, the muscular, and the digestive organizations; and any peculiarity of their agency might be expected to mark their results in certain constitutional states of the entire bodily system. They are, in fact, the source of the distinguishing temperaments among men, and throw their influence upon mental action in such a way as to secure permanent traits and habits of human life. The vitality and energy, which gives to one of these subordinate systems a special control in the whole body, will mark its effect in the whole organization; and according to the measure of its controlling force, will be the temperament effected in the constitution. There may be frequent cases in which no one of these so prevails as to exclude all traces of some other; and yet, in perhaps all cases, some one will be found manifestly predominant, and thus give to the man the peculiarities of temperament which belong to its class. Rarely shall we find such a blending of all, as to leave the distinguishing temperament doubtful.

Where the life gives a predominating energy and activity to the nervous system, there will be induced the *sanguine* temperament. In the nervous system, there is made provision for animal sensibility and motion; and where there is a rapid and augmented supply of blood, the animal sensibility and activity is thus proportionally quickened. The whole nervous system is thereby made preeminently vigorous, and prompt to respond to every excitement. In this is the peculiarity of the sanguine temperament. Such a constitution will readily wake in sudden emotions, and be characterised by ardent feeling, quick passions, impetuous desires, and lively but transient affections. There is a strong propensity to mirth and sport, and it easily habituates itself to a life of levity and gaiety. If sudden calamities occur, the sanguine temperament is readily overwhelmed in excessive grief, and melts in floods of tears for every affliction; but soon loses the deep sense of its sorrows, and springs again buoyant to new scenes of pleasure.

In literature, this temperament prompts to the use of figures, and abounds in striking expressions, glowing imagery, strong comparisons, and perpetual hyperbole. Its style is always highly ornamental and florid, and its prose abounds in all the metaphors of poetry. Whatever awakens emotion will be agreeable, and it opens itself readily to the excitement of music, or painting, or eloquence; especially when the appeal is made to the more lively and sprightly sensibilities. There is a perpetual propensity in all things to excess and exaggeration, to intense feeling and passionate excitement. The action is impulsive; the resolutions suddenly taken, and immediately executed; and before unexpected difficulties, or long resisting obstacles, easily disconcerted and turned off in other directions.

This temperament is often found strongly marked in individual cases, and sometimes gives its controlling peculiarities to national character. It is the temperament widely prevalent in the French nation; and, though much modified in the form of its action, is still also the prevalent temperament of the Irish people. Single persons, among both the French and Irish, are characterised by other temperaments; but the controlling type is that of the sanguine, and appears in their habits, their literature, their eloquence, and their military exploits.

Where the digestive organization is vigorously active, and the vital force goes out strongly in the process of assimilation and nutrition, there will be the *melancholic* temperament. This is named, perhaps, from what may be rather the extreme point of the tendency of vigorous digestive functions; but such a constitutional habit naturally disposes to rest and quietude, inducing to solitary meditation; calm, serious, and often sad reflection; and thus tending to gloomy and melancholy contemplations. Moderately controlling, such a temperament gives a sedate and serious habit of mind; and when more strongly prevalent, induces sadness and gloom. The prevalent distinctive type is, a meditative, moralizing state of mind; a tendency to live in the past, and hold itself strongly conservative; lamenting the departure of former goodness and greatness, and afflicting itself with the mournful convictions of present degeneracy. There may often be a less sad and gloomy habit of meditation, and then the mind delights to lose itself in fond dreams and romantic fancies, and live in a world of ideal creations. There will be a passive longing after imagined scenes of angelic purity and perfection; discontented with the realities passing around him; and withdrawing from the actual, to absorb himself in the tranquil and serene enjoyment of his own ideals.

This is rather the temperament for particular persons, than for collective communities; and can, perhaps, in no case be said to have constituted a national peculiarity. It may be found the most frequently, in the contemplative and speculating German; but its clearest exhibition is in scattered individuals among all ages. Jeremiah in Judea; Homer in Greece; Dante in Florence; Cowper in England; and Goethe in Germany; are all, in different forms, examples of the melancholic temperament.

Where the muscular system is strong and of quick irritability, and the connected arterial action is full and rapid, there will be given the *choleric* temperament. The direct tendency of this controlling muscular vitality, is to prompt and sustained activity; enlarged plans and hardy, patient endurance in execution; difficult enterprises, and courage and resolution in meeting difficulties and conquering all opposition. It differs from the sanguine temperament, in that its action is from deliberate purpose, and not from impulse; and is sustained in persevering decision, and not by violent passion. Its aims are high, and its ends comprehensive; demanding plan and calculation for their success, and time and combined instrumentalities for their accomplishment. With a bad heart, the enterprises may be malignant, and their prosecution shockingly cruel, bloody and ferocious; and with a good heart, the undertakings will be benevolent, and urged on with a generous and noble enthusiasm; but in each case, there will be determination, self-reliance, and invincible decision and persistence in attaining the object. Magnanimity, self-sacrificing chivalry, and exalted heroism, will compel admiration for the actor, even in a bad cause, and secure lasting respect and veneration for the dauntless champion of truth and righteousness; and the choleric temperament may be found in each of these fields so different in moral estimation, but direct, determined and persevering in both. Vindictive and selfish, or humane and philanthropic; the choleric man will be bold, comprehensive and effective. The energy of muscle stimulates to enterprise of mind.

The old heroes of Lacedemon, and the Spartan band; the intrepidity and firmness of old Roman generals and armies; these may stand as examples, of numbers together, who have been prompted by the influences of a constitutionally choleric temperament; but in quite opposite moral scenes, we may find the most striking instances in separate cases. It has revealed itself in the ambitious and the benevolent; the usurping tyrant and the strenuous resister of tyranny. Cæsar and Brutus had each a choleric temperament. Buonaparte and Howard, Hampden and Laud, Herod and Paul, all were choleric.

On the other hand, if the muscular system is less energetic and irritable, and the vascular system more quiet and the circulation calm and equable, there will be the *phlegmatic* temperament. This, again, is named from the extreme indices of its class, and when the temperament is emphatically phlegmatic, it is meant that the mind is heavy and torpid, and the man sluggish and approaching to the stupid. But when only moderately phlegmatic, this temperament is of all the others the most favorable for well directed, long sustained and effective mental activity. The quiet and orderly movement of the vital functions, and the well tempered muscular energy, give occasion for clear self-possession, and the direction of the mental action to any point, and for a long period. With the same original talent, this temperament will best conduce to eminence and influence, and secure the most lasting reputation. It will escape the passionate excitements and impulses of the sanguine; the meditative, dreamy, and sometimes gloomy inactivity of the melancholic; and the impetuous and often irritable and violent enterprises of the choleric temperaments. In the even flow of the vital force through all the nervous and muscular organization, the entire mental energy finds its opportunity to go out full and free to any work, under the control of a sound and calm judgment. Where the sanguine would be impulsive and fitful, the moderately phlegmatic will be self-balanced and stable; where the melancholic would be visionary, and either romantic or dejected, this will be practical, judicious, and cheerful; and where the choleric might be strenuous and obstinate, self-willed and irascible; this will exhibit equanimity, patience, and calm self-reliance. The consciousness of complete self-possession, and the capability of entire self-government, enables the man steadily to apply any required faculty, and stedfastly to persevere in any undertaking.

The Dutch, as a nation, approach the extreme phlegmatic point; the philosophic German mind is phlegmatic, tempered with the melancholic; and the practical English mind is phlegmatic, modified by the choleric. The Dutchman plods, the German speculates, the Englishman executes. The New-England mind is more intensely inventive and executive than its parent Anglo-Saxon stock, in that the Yankee temperament is less phlegmatic and more choleric. The moderately phlegmatic temperament has given the world some of the most noble specimens of humanity. The patriarch Joseph, the prophet Daniel, the philosopher Newton, and the patriot Washington, all were moderately phlegmatic. More than all, the temperament assumed in the man Christ Jesus was the perfection of the phlegmatic.

Every man is thus, constitutionally, under the perpetual bias of some prevailing temperament. The putting forth of the mental activity is, readily and spontaneously, in the line prompted by the constitutional temperament, and the man, thus, possesses a natural character—a constitutional disposition—in the bias given to the mind through the bodily organization. This does not by any means determine the radical moral character, which is wholly from the spiritual disposition and not from constitutional bias. Peter was sanguine, Paul was choleric; whether as men, or as Christian Apostles. A change of moral character makes no change of constitutional character, inasmuch as only the state of the will, or moral disposition, changes, and not the constitutional temperament. The temper is to be governed and held in subjection by the firm good will, and the peculiar temperament will demand its peculiar discipline, and the man must be held responsible for his self-control with any temperament; but every man needs to know his own constitutional bias, that he may discipline himself intelligently and not blindly.

3. *The effect of bodily weakness upon mind.*

The rational, the animal, and the vital are so connected in man that they make up the one mind; and the body is so built up by it, and developed with it, that all goes to make up the one entire man; and thus it must be that an intimate sympathy shall ever subsist between the mind and the body. In the thousand cases of bodily weakness or defect, the mental activity must thereby become modified. Experience teaches that one cannot suffer, without the other suffering with it.

In the *immaturity* of bodily development in youth, the mind also is immature, nor can any intellectual culture hasten, very much, the mental faculties to maturity beyond the growth of the body. An earlier and better course of instruction may give to one child's mind much greater attainments than to another, but at the widest practicable difference, it will still be one child's mind differing from another child's, and neither will have the manly mind until the body also has its manly stature. And thus also in the decline of life through growing years; the body does not long pass its maturity, and begin to experience the infirmities and decrepitude of age, but the corresponding fact appears also in mind, that its vigor and activity suffers a similar decline. The steps are not always, nor indeed often, exactly equal between the body and the mind; and thus manifesting that, although in the same organic unity, the mind is not to be confounded with the body; still the steps tend ever in the same direction; and while one may hasten at times faster than the other, they cannot very long at the same time be going the one opposite to the other. From the cradle to the grave, the body and mind reciprocally affect each other.

The *sickness* of the body, at any period of its development, works its effect also in the mind. The mental faculties are ordinarily paralyzed, in the languor and weakness of bodily disease. Instances are sometimes given of feeble health and bodily suffering with much mental activity and power, as in the cases of Richard Baxter, Robert Hall, etc. But such cases are rare, and though perhaps occasionally giving examples of great energy of mind, which resists and to a great extent conquers the tendencies of a sickly body; yet, unless preternaturally quickened by the very excitement of bodily distress, the strong probability is, that those very minds would have been more vigorous and active, had they been lodged in sounder bodies. They can hardly constitute exceptions to the general rule, that the sound mind must have a sound body. The dismemberment or derangement, of any particular organ of sense, affects at once the power of perception through that organ; and a given degree of violence to the bodily structure, and especially of percussion upon the brain, immediately arrests all consciousness, and leaves a blank in all the operations of the mind. Sudden shocks, given to the bodily frame, are often attended by the distressing mental phenomena of swooning, syncope, delirium, etc.

A still more remarkable affection of the mind, in connection with bodily exhaustion, is found in the state of *sleep.* When the body has used a given amount of its nervous and muscular power of irritability, and thus become enfeebled in its own action, there must be the recurrence of a state of sleep, in order to recruit and restore the exhausted energy. Urgent claims and exciting exigencies may drive off sleep for a time, and protract the period of wakefulness; but at length there comes the limit, beyond which no effort nor exigency can prevent sleep. The fatigued soldier sleeps amid the carnage of battle; the exhausted sailor sleeps upon the top of the mast. Mind and body both come under a partial suspension or paralysis of their ordinary functions; self-consciousness is lost, or only partially and confusedly retained, in the reproductive imagination of dreams; the control of voluntary agency ceases; and the mind shuts itself up from all communication with the outer world. When the man again awakes in clear consciousness, he finds both his bodily and mental faculties revived and invigorated.

Plants do not wake, and thus plants cannot be said to sleep. There may be in some a folding of the leaf, from the withdrawment of light, but nothing that is analogous to the sleep of animals. It is the function of sensibility, and its origination of motion, which demands sleep. The animal, and man as animal, sleeps; but though rationality may be suspended in unconsciousness, it cannot be said that the reason sleeps, nor that reason dreams. Our dreams may simulate the experience of sense, or the judgments of the understanding; but the mind never truly philosophizes, and builds up systems of science in its dreams.

4. *The reaction of body and mind upon each other.*

Physicians have long known, and very carefully regarded the fact, in their medical practice, that there is a reflex action of the mind upon the body, which is both certain and strong. Confidence, cheerful anticipation, and the stimulus of hope and expectation of happy results, are almost the necessary conditions of any very favorable effect from any prescribed remedies. Not unfrequently, most remarkable cures of chronic diseases occur from the strong excitement of intense expectation; while at other times, diseases prove fatal from an irritable or a desponding state of mind, which might otherwise, to all appearance, have been readily cured. Diseases, also, become epidemic, and spread sometimes through large communities, from the general prevalence of a panic, or diffused sympathy over the region; and such prevalent diseases cease when the panic subsides, or the public attention becomes directed to other objects.

Strong mental agitations, in any way, especially violent passions, have their immediate effect upon the body; and these consequences are so invariably connected with their peculiar mental antecedent, that we at once determine the inward emotion from the outward bodily affection. Joy, grief, anger, fear, etc., when strongly active, are as readily apprehended in the countenance, and the external bodily affections, as they could be by a direct communication with the spirit itself.

Remarkable cases, of mental emotion reacting upon bodily organization, are sometimes given in the effects upon the unborn infant, from strong maternal excitement. There seems to be strong evidence, from the conscious experience of the mother, and her apprehension and expectation of such results to appear in the child after birth, that the maternal emotion and the marks of the offspring are truly connected as cause and effect. At one time, slight peculiarities only are induced; at others, permanent marks appear in the skin; impressions are made upon the features, or modifications of the members or of the body occur; and indeed, in extreme cases, there are monstrous malformations and shocking deformities. In the general fact of such reactions of mind upon body, these peculiar cases are readily explicable. The life of the infant is still one with that of the mother, as the bud and fruit are one with the parent tree while growing upon it, and while the organization of the embryo is in its forming state, it is more susceptible to impressions than any portion of the parent's already matured organism. The action of the mental emotion is more readily upon it, and the effects more lastingly produced in it, than in any part of the maternal constitution. The adult body is sometimes strongly and permanently affected, from the reaction of powerful mental excitement. Lasting distortions of the muscles, and a changing of the hair to permanent whiteness, have been induced by extreme paroxysms of mental agony and sudden fright or shocks from some imminent danger.

Bodily habits also arise and become confirmed, through the action of some permanent mental peculiarities. A peculiar train of thought, or course of study, or any special channel through which the intellectual activity is made to move, will give the outward characteristic in the air and general manners and demeanor of the person. Hence different professions and employments in life, where strongly engrossing, give their distinctive peculiarities, and form well known classes of men in their general appearance. So the members of the body become habituated to certain movements, by the long control of the mind over them, and thus are made skilful in many employments. The limbs move almost spontaneously from such habits, while formerly the action could scarcely be effected by the most painful attention. So in mechanical trades, playing on musical instruments, especially in penmanship, and the use of the organs in speech; the muscular movement is so habituated in its course, that the man loses all consciousness of his voluntary control over it.

Strong mental effort often indicates itself in external bodily changes and motions, and the kind of inner action marks its struggling energy in the appropriate outward expression; the eyebrows are raised, or the lips contracted, or the nostrils dilated, or the shoulders shrugged, or even the whole form expanded and elevated, from the mental energizing. A player at bowls or quoits involuntarily distorts, and turns his whole body awry, when that which is thrown is seen moving wide from the mark; while the body is as spontaneously made erect, and rigidly straight, when the thing thrown is moving direct to hit its object. When striving to communicate in an imperfectly understood language, the mind, in the same way, reacts upon the body. Unconsciously, every limb and muscle is made to gesticulate and express, and the whole body takes on those attitudes which help the mind to give over its thoughts to another. Particular and permanent expressions of countenance are thus naturally induced. The inner emotions have energized to give their outward expression, and the frequent action has brought the muscles under their controlling forms, and this has been perpetuated so long that the marks have become firmly set upon the features, and the face is made to look the full reflection of the inner prevailing disposition. The old proverb, "Handsome those who handsome do" is thus founded in truth; and the general principles of physiognomy have a truly philosophical basis. The law of mental action is enstamped on the bodily organization.

EMPIRICAL PSYCHOLOGY.

CHAPTER I.

THE GENERAL METHOD OF EMPIRICAL PSYCHOLOGY.

IN entering upon the study of the human mind, as given in experience, we have no conditions, in any determining ideas of how the mind *must* be and act, to guide us in our progress; and we can determine our general method, therefore, not from any previous conceptions of the subject mind, but only from the manner in which we are to investigate it. This is by direct observation in the inner sense, and attaining whatever can there be found; vindicating the accuracy and completeness of our observation; and putting all our elements into one whole, according to their ascertained relations. Whatever statement or illustration we may give, the end in view must be, not so to paint an image or express a conception, that another mind shall take the fact wholly from verbal representation; but that, in going direct to his own consciousness, our representation shall help him to find the fact already there, among the mental phenomena in his own experience.

The elements to be used are thus the facts which experience gives us, and which are to be found only in the consciousness that the mind has of its own faculties and phenomena; and such elementary facts must *first* be attained. It not unfrequently occurs that certain alleged facts are disputed, and one affirms of some phenomena in mental experience that which another denies; it is thus necessary to attain and apply some ultimate criterion, which shall be conclusively and universally decisive in settling all contradictions; and such authoritative test must be a *second* requisition. The facts, as collected and made valid beyond dispute, must arrange themselves into an ordered system, and the whole at last stand out in our combined psychology, as the exact and complete counterpart of the thinking, feeling, active mind in its own reality; and this systematic arrangement is the *third* result to be accomplished. The whole field is completely filled by these three operations:—

I. THE ATTAINMENT OF THE MENTAL FACTS.

II. THE RECOGNITION OF A CRITERION IN DISPUTED CASES.

III. THE CORRECT CLASSIFICATION IN A SYSTEM.

This general method has itself a certain order by which it may be best completed, and this makes it desirable to occupy this chapter in determining some of the particulars by which this general method may best be carried forward.

I. IN THE ATTAINMENT OF FACTS.

That mind is, and *what* mind is, will include all the facts which belong to our subject, and these are to be obtained in the readiest and surest manner. The more general and comprehensive facts will be first needed, in order that by their light the leading divisions in mental classification may appear, and thus the more particular facts may be found and noted, each in the order and place they ought to assume in the completed system. And as the best process for finding the facts, whether more general or more particular, the following directions will be found serviceable.

1. *Fix the attention upon single facts.*

Begin, by holding the apprehension steady and clear, to some one and simple phenomenon of your inner mental being. Overcome, in this, and reverse the old habit of ever looking outward, and resting upon organic sensation for distinct and definite perception, and constrain yourself to a facility of inward attention, and clear apprehension of that which is going on in your own conscious activity. Take up some one mental fact by itself—a thought, an emotion, or a volition—and examine it so closely and accurately, that you henceforth are fully competent, in the knowledge of the fact in itself, to distinguish it completely from any other mental fact that may afterwards be apprehended. When one is thus known, take another, and then another, in the same way and with the same result of ready discrimination, until you have fully excluded the liability to confound any one fact with others that may be like it. It is not meant that the mind should be detained in this inspection of single facts, successively, until the entire mental elements have been examined in detail; such a perpetuated process would weary and overload the memory, and the former facts be crowded out as later facts were acquired. But take facts, thus, one by one, until you have made yourself quite familiar with mental phenomena, and habituated yourself to the process of intro-spection, and learned to define inner appearances as accurately as outer objects. Just as the painter must accurately distinguish colors and know them in their single being as separate one from others, before he can blend them into his combined forms of beauty, so must the student of the human mind get its facts singly and distinctly, before he can put them together in one harmonious system of psychology. When he has habituated himself to this, he may go on with his system—building safely and pleasantly.

2. *Compare single facts with each other, and find their true relations.*

Each mental fact is elementary in the completed mental system, and must stand in unity with every other fact as component part of the same mind. There must, therefore, be that in each fact which determines its relation to others; and that which thus determines its connection is itself a part of the fact, and as necessary to be apprehended as any thing else which appears in it. Its true place in the system cannot be found, except as this determined relationship is fully apprehended. The wheels of a mill, with their pinions, and cogs, and bands, will never come together and go, except according to the law of conformation in each part; and no more will a mind than a mill become an acting whole, except as each part finds and observes its determined relationship. When we examine separate grains of sand, we can find nothing which determines their mutual relationship in one mechanical combination; for they have not thus been adapted to each other by any reciprocal conformation. But not thus with any single element of mind. Each has that in it which marks its relation to others, and all must be found and put in connection accordingly.

3. *Complex facts must be carefully analyzed.*

Many single facts of the inner as well as of the outer world may at first appear also to be simple, but which a careful analysis determines to be compounded of several elements. In the whole study of mind, there is nothing which demands so keen a penetration and acute discrimination as this accurate analysis of the facts which come up in our consciousness. Some of the most perplexing points of controversy in morals and theology originate, either in the neglect or the incompetency to see a distinction in things which differ, and thus putting as one thing, that which should be known as a combination of several things. Mischievous errors long keep their control, and are maintained and enforced as fundamental truth, solely because some analysis of a mental fact has been incomplete or faulty. The capacity for accurate and complete analysis is to the metaphysician, what the scalpel is to the anatomist, and the retort and solvents to the chemist.

II. The ultimate criterion for disputed facts.

We shall find some facts that are themselves preliminary to, and conditional for experience, and which can not thus be given in experience, and for which our consciousness can only testify *that* they are, without being able to reveal *what* they are. But the special elements, which go to constitute an Empirical Psychology, must be given in experience, both as to the fact and the manner of their being; it must thence follow, that we have no need to make any enquiries, which shall carry us out of the proper field of human consciousness. If we would determine the necessary and universal principles, by which experience itself must be conditioned and expounded, we should thereby wholly leave the province of Empirical, and go over into that of Rational Psychology.

To each man, therefore, his own consciousness must be the test of his facts. If he cannot find it within his own consciousness, the phenomenon to be used in a system of psychology can, in reality, be no fact for him. That mental state or exercise, which has not been within his own experience, cannot be so communicated by any use of language, that he can attain an adequate conception of it. He who was never conscious of a sound, or a color, can never be made to conceive what these are by any description or attempted analogous representation. And so of any purely mental phenomenon; it can be apprehended only as it is made to appear in the man's own consciousness. A cognition or feeling, for one man, is not that also for another, except as it has alike been within the experience of both. And when the testimony of consciousness is given for any fact, this must be conclusive to the man himself. For, should any one pretend to doubt the being of a fact clearly given in consciousness, he might at once be asked, by what authority he could affirm that he doubted? His doubt must be a phenomenon given in consciousness. And if the consciousness is valid for a fact of doubting, so also must it be for the fact which he pretends to doubt. A denial of the conclusiveness of consciousness for the person himself, would preclude the possibility of any valid affirmation of his own scepticism. If the question be one of experience, simply, the testimony of consciousness is final. It is not competent for us to enquire into the determinative principles of consciousness itself, and thus show how *any* experience is valid; for this must take us at once into the higher sphere of reason, and give a philosophy *for* consciousness and not a system founded *in* consciousness. Implicit faith in the distinct revelations of a clear consciousness, is the basis of all empirical science; and any questions that would reach higher, and unsettle this confidence in consciousness, can be met only in the higher light of a Rational Psychology.

But, while the consciousness of the man must be valid for himself, it may not unfrequently be alleged that there is a discordant consciousness in reference to the same mental phenomenon. The same man at different times, or different men at the same time, may affirm that the testimony of consciousness is contradictory. To each man, at all times, his consciousness must be conclusive; but here comes a case of direct contradiction, and both cannot be valid. Is then all experience at a stand, and on this point can nothing be determined as fact in our psychology? or, shall we say that both are alike good, and each man's fact competent to become an elementary part of his own system, and thus leave psychological systems to differ from each other, as each man may determine in his own case? This cannot be permitted; for we must have the one system of psychology for universal humanity. Here, precisely, arises the demand for some valid universal criterion, which must settle all disputed cases.

This criterion is given in *the common consciousness of mankind:* or which may, in other words, be termed COMMON SENSE. Let it be here fully noted, that a philosophy of common sense can never go beyond empirical facts, and conclusions drawn from them in the logical understanding. All principles that are above a nature of things, and which condition nature in a supernatural, must be wholly foreign and entirely impertinent to such a philosophy. If such necessary principles are at all recognized and used, this can be only as mere assumption, and solely because the philosophy finds the need of them and cannot progress without them; but not at all because common sense can know anything about them, nor know anything by them, except altogether through the sophism of a *petitio principii.* Eminent names among the philosophers of the Scottish school, feeling the restrictions of the system of Locke, have assumed to use *a' priori* principles under the name of common sense, and to call the work, the philosophy of common sense, yet is it easy to convict the system of assuming much more than common sense can vouch for. The common consciousness can never reach beyond the series of condition and conditioned, and thus common sense can know only "within the conditioned;" and therefore it is wholly incompetent for this philosophy to be using absolute truths and necessary principles. There is the conscious need of such principles on which to hang its conditioned facts, and find a true beginning for its philosophy, but common sense can no other wise attain them, than by making the *want* of a thing to be an evidence of the *valid possession* of the thing; and in this way no use of first principles can be legitimate.

Common sense can vouch for only that which comes within the common consciousness, and we have here need to use it as ultimate criterion for nothing more. Our present system receives only the facts of experience, leaving all necessary principles to be determined in a higher philosophy, to which the application of the term 'common sense' would be wholly a misnomer. But within the field of experience, the test of common sense is final. It determines for us all that Empirical Psychology can use, and can stand as umpire in all disputed cases that can arise. In any occurrence of an alleged contradiction in consciousness, we need to find that which is the common consciousness, and this must exclude all else. If any man allege a consciousness different from that of mankind in general, this can be no matter of any farther concern to us; for if it were true, it would only prove that he was *alterum genus*, and that any facts, which were peculiar to him, would be of no account in a system which embraces those only of our common humanity. Rightly used, the test of common sense is conclusive, for only that which common sense sanctions can have any place in our psychology.

But this appeal to common sense must, in all the process, be legitimately pursued. Three important rules must be observed in order to insure a safe decision.

1. *The facts must lie within the range of common consciousness.*—There are many questions which may be raised about facts that are quite beyond human experience, and many facts which have come within the experience of but few of the human family. No such facts are needed in a system of empirical psychology, and for such facts, a criterion of common sense would be unavailable. Any facts in the experience of disembodied spirits must lie wholly beyond the range of mortal consciousness; and such facts as the experience of a miracle, a resuscitation from a drowning state, or a balloon ascension, have come within the consciousness of too few of mankind, to make any general appeal practicable. The test must be attempted only in such cases as manifestly fall within the range of common experience.

2. *The decision given must be general.*—Not the decision of a few in any age, or of one age amid successive generations; but so universal in all ages, as to prove for itself the general assent of the race of man. This may be gathered from the history, the laws, the languages and the common customs and popular proverbs of the world; inasmuch as in all these ways is embodied the conscious experience of ages.

3. *The decision must be unbiassed.*—The great mass of mankind do not give an unbiassed decision in relation to human guilt for general ingratitude to God; the obligation of immediate repentance; or the fact of constant divine dependence; inasmuch as common depravity darkens or perverts the common consciousness. But general decisions, where no bias appears, or especially where manifestly the decision is against a general bias, may well be trusted.

These three requisites in the application of common sense, the *competency*, *generality* and *honesty* of the decision, will give validity to any fact that may so be sustained.

III. THE CLASSIFICATION OF THE FACTS.

Our system cannot here be built up, as in an *a' priori* science, by the carrying of one necessary principle through every fact, and thus binding them all in unity by it. Nor can it be properly inductive, in the sense of assuming some general hypothesis, and selecting and arranging the facts by it as they may be found in nature. We have simply to find the human mind as it is, and attain and classify its facts, just as these facts are given and connected in the consciousness.

There are two methods in which a classification may be conceived as progressing; one, where the order of nature is followed, by beginning at the center and working from thence outward; the other, by taking nature as already a product, and beginning at the outside and working within, as far as practicable. The first may be called the *order of reason;* inasmuch as the reason would so take the moving force, or conditioning principle, at the center, and follow it out to the consummation: the second may be called *the order of discovery;* inasmuch as in experience, the thing is already given, and we begin on the outside and follow up the discovery, as far as we may, to see how the product was effected. The genius that first created the idea of a watch, would begin, in the thought, with the moving power at the center, and carry this force, in its development of forms and connections, outward, till in his completed conception, he had the whole in its unity, from the main-spring to the moving-hands over the dial-plate. But the discoverer, of how a watch already in experience had been invented, would begin his examination at the hour-index, and go backwards toward the central force in the main-spring. Both get the science of the watch; one *makes* it, the other *learns* it.

In empirical philosophy, we can only be learners. We must study what is, not project what may be. Nature began at the center and worked outward. She had her vital force in its salient point, and carried that out to the mature development. The germ expanded to the ripened plant; the embryo grew to the adult stature. But the empirical philosopher can take nature's products only so far as already done, and study as he may how has been nature's process. He is shut out from nature's hiding-place at the center, and cannot say what it is that lies potential there, and determine in the primal cause what the effects must be. He can only learn nature, as she has already made herself to be; and cannot project nature in her primal laws, and thereby determine how she must be.

So we must study the human mind. We are to attain the facts in completed system, just as mind in reality is, and not form some ingenious theory, nor adopt some other man's theory, which we strive to maintain without nature, or in spite of nature. Valid facts, classified according to their actual connections, will give a psychology which proves itself. In it, all confusion will be reduced to order; it will expound all anomolies, and expel all absurdities, and stand out the exact counterpart of the living actual mind itself.

The general order of classification, thus determined to be that of discovery; there need only be added the following general directions:

1. Permanent and inherent relationships between the mental facts are alone to be regarded.

2. Homogeneous facts only may be classified. Nature never mingles contraries together.

3. The system must find a place for all the facts.

4. When completed, the system must be harmonious and self-consistent.

CHAPTER II.

GENERAL FACTS OF MIND.

THERE are certain facts relative to the mind as a whole, and which appertain to it comprehensively in its own being, and which as thus generally inclusive of all the other subordinate facts of mind, it will be better to attain primarily and separately. In these general facts and states of mind, may be apprehended the true order of arrangement for bringing all subordinate facts into a completed system, and we shall, therefore, in this prepare the way for an intelligent classification of all the elements of the system that may subsequently be attained.

1. *The general fact of the existence of mind.*

The doctrine of true and valid being, which determines and settles all dispute between idealists and materialists, nominalists and realists, constitutes the distinct science of *Ontology*, and which can be made to rest only on the conclusions of Rational Psychology. In all empirical science we begin with the assumption that the facts exist, and having thus begun with experience, it is not competent from experience to prove the validity of those facts which are conditional for it. The qualities of substances and the exercises of agents alone appear in consciousness, and thus all that experience can vouch for is the quality and the exercise, and not the essential being in which the qualities inhere and from which the exercises spring. Permanent, substantial being, as the ground of all attributes and the source of all events, is assumed and not given in consciousness; and there is thus an occasion for scepticism to come in, modified in various ways, and which can be excluded only through the most profound investigations of transcendental science. It is not the place in Empirical Psychology to state these sources and varied forms of scepticism, much less philosophically to exclude them; suffice it to say the sources exist, and are exceedingly prolific of sceptical theories, and which must all be put over into the field of Rational Psychology. But passing all attention here to the appropriate investigations of an ontological science, we may give those particulars that come within experience, and on which an Empirical Psychology must rest for the actual being of that mind, which is put as the agent of all those exercises that appear in consciousness.

We are not conscious of what mind is, as we are conscious of what an exercise is; we know a thought, an emotion, and a volition, as we do not know the mind which thinks, feels and wills. The mind itself cannot appear in consciousness, as does its acts. But, while the mind itself does not appear in conciousness, and the different exercises are successively appearing and disappearing, there is that which does not come and go as the exercises arise and depart. One consciousness remains, and holds within itself all these fleeting appearances of thoughts, feelings and choices. There is also, in this one consciousness, the additional testimony that these exercises are not thrown in upon its field, as shadows passing over a landscape, but that they come up from some *nisus* or energy that produces them from beneath; and that when the thought appears, there has been a conscious energizing in its production; and when the thought vanishes and an emotion or a volition appears, there has been something which did not pass away with the thought, but energizes again in the emotion or the volition; and thus that there is some entity as opposed to non-being, which abides and energizes in consciousness.

And now, this fact of a permanent, perpetuating itself through all these changing exercises, is the first which we wish should be apprehended and noted. Something is, while the varied exercises successively come and go upon the field of human consciousness. *What* this something is, the consciousness does not reveal; but *that* it permanently is, in its unchanged identity, the consciousness does testify. It is as if the mirror could feel itself, and its repeated throes of reflection, while it can by no means envisage itself, but only that which stands before it. This conscious perduring of somewhat, as opposed to non-entity, we now take as a fact in experience, and call it MIND. We do not attempt to determine what it is, though negatively we may say in many things what it is not; all we need is to affirm, that it is; and we then have permanent being which does not arise and vanish with its acts.

2. *This existence is not phenomenal nor ideal.*

The phenomena appear and disappear, arise and vanish; this does not appear, nor does it lose itself when they depart; but it holds them, though successive, still within its own unity, and determines them all to be its own. It perpetually is, in all its phenomena, and these phenomena are all from it.

An *effervescence* is a result from chemical combinations; a *spark* is produced in the collision of two hard bodies; but the effervescence and the spark come and go, as the modified states of what previously was, and are wholly phenomenal. The mind gives out its own phenomena without its own appearing, and itself originates in no previous phenomenal compound. *Motion* is continued alteration in space of some permanent thing, and is only a peculiar state of that thing, and thus merely phenomenal. Mind is not a state of some other thing, but a somewhat that has its own successive states, while it perdures through them. A *mathematical point*, or *line*, is an intuition in pure space, and the product of the mind's own agency, and is thus wholly ideal. But the mind perdures while its energizing may construct a thousand lines, or posit a thousand points in pure space, and remains the same through all its constructions.

In this conscious permanency of being, that somewhat, which we have called mind, is taken wholly out from the list of fleeting phenomena; and as perduring through all its ideal constructions, is not itself ideal. Though we cannot say what it is, yet we may say that it is neither phenomenal nor ideal.

3. *It has its conscious identity through all changes.*

The exercises of the mind arise and vanish, and are each separate and distinct from others in their appearance, but the same mind is in, and through, them all, and holds them all in its one consciousness. The thought which was yesterday, or last year, in consciousness, and the conscious thought of to-day, are both recognized as being in the same self-consciousness. The self-consciousness has not changed, while the exercises have been continually coming and departing. The mind, thus, remains in its own identity, yesterday, to-day, and onward in to the future, perpetually the same mind. Through all development of its faculties; in all its states; the mind itself neither comes nor goes, but retains its self-sameness through all changes. Its phenomenal experience varies *in* time, but itself perdures *through* time.

4. *Mind is essentially self-active.*

All matter is essentially inert, except as acted on by outward forces. Its inner constituting forces are balanced in exact counteraction, and hold itself in its own position, with a *vis inertiæ* that resists all action which would displace it. The movement of matter must be traced up, through all its propagations, to some first mover in a mind; and out of this mind only, could the impulsive moving energy have originated. Nature, thus, acts upon nature, in its different parts, mechanically, as its different forces balance themselves in their own action, or in unbalanced movement obtrude one upon another. One portion of matter, impinging upon another, is a *percussive* force; when suddenly expelling others that surround its own center, is an *explosive* force; and when coming in combination with another, and giving off a third, is an *effervescive* force. But when we have superadded to all the forces in matter, whether gravitating, chemical, or crystalline, a proper *vital* force—which takes up matter, penetrates it, assimilates, and incorporates it, and thus builds up about itself its own organized body—we have an existence self-active, self-developing, spiritual; which originates motion from itself, and spontaneously uses inert matter for its own ends. When this vital force rises from simple spontaneity in the plant, to that of sensation in the animal, and from this to distinct self-consciousness in man, we have the higher forms of the spiritual; and, in the human mind, attain to a manifest discrimination of it from all that is material, in its inherent self-activity.

The human mind has the consciousness of this self-energizing. Its agency is properly its own, and originates in its own causality. As a created being, the original ground of the mind's existence is in God its Maker. It is dependent upon its Creator both, that it is, and for what it is; but as created by God, it is endowed by him with a proper causality. It originates its own thoughts, emotions, and purposes; and needs only the proper occasions for its activity, and this activity is spontaneously originated by it. This activity is circumscribed within given limits, and in its sphere of action it must have, also, certain occasions for action; yet within this sphere, and supplied with these occasions, it originates its own acts, and is conscious of its own *nisus* as it goes out in exercise. The occasions for thought do not cause the thinking; the mind thinks from its own spontaneous causality. Within such limits, and under such occasions, it is cause for originating thought and feeling.

This is quite a different conception from what is sometimes termed *passive power*, and which may be predicated of all matter. This means merely capability of being moved; excluding the conception, altogether, of self-motion. It does not imply that there is properly latent power—a force possessed, but for the time lying dormant—the meaning is solely, capacity to receive the action of some efficient cause. This, we have said, may be predicated of all matter; but precisely in this, is mind discriminated from matter. The movements of matter are communicated to it, the actions of mind may originate in it. Consciousness testifies, not that there is such an agency of another as brings thought and feeling within it, but that *my mind* thinks, feels and wills. Mind may receive an action from without, and be the subject of influences imposed upon it, and even undergo changes to which itself is merely passive; but it may also act from its own causality, and spontaneously originate its own changes.

5. *The mind discriminates itself from its objects.*

We say nothing here of the particular facts in the process of discriminating one object from another, and all objects from the mind itself; and nothing of the awakening in self-consciousness, which is consequential upon such discrimination; but only mark the general fact itself, that the mind separates itself from all its objects of action. All mental action is conditioned to some object or end of action. We cannot think, without some content of thought; nor feel, without some object of emotion; any more than we can see, or hear, without something to be seen or heard. There must be the agent acting, and the object as end of action; and between these, the mind discriminates, and assigns to each, its own distinct identity. The object is known as other than the agent; and thus the mind has the fact that it is, and that some other than it is, and that there is a separating line between them.

Of itself, as acting being, it affirms that it is the *subject* of the activity. The mind *lies under* the act, and is a ground for it. Of that which is the end of its action, it affirms that it is the *object* of the action. It *lies directly in the way* of the act, and meets it face to face. The act springs from the mind itself, as subject, and terminates in its end, as object. In this discrimination, we have occasion for the frequent use of the qualifying terms, *subjective* and *objective*. In the investigations which belong to psychology, we have so perpetually to refer to facts which relate to the mind, and those which relate to its ends of action, and such constant necessity to mark the characteristics which belong, in this relation, to the facts themselves, that we cannot dispense with these terms, except in the inconvenience of much circumlocution. Subjective applies to all relations in the mind itself; and objective to all relations in its ends of action. Thus, the gratification of the appetite, the prudential consideration of health, or the claims of duty, may be subjective motives to eat; the article of food, as end of the act, and which is to consummate the subject's intention in it, is the objective motive. When the mind is the end of its own action, as in all self-observation, it becomes both subject and object. The mind, then, in all that relates to its own agency, is subjective; and in all that relates to itself, as end of its action, is objective; and the mind itself, spoken of in both relations together, is termed subject-object.

CHAPTER III.

PRIMITIVE FACTS OF MIND.

We now have the one self-active mind, existing in connection with its organized body, and proceed to gather the specific facts which may be found in reference to it. A few of these specific facts are preliminary to all action in consciousness, and must first be found as conditional for all the phenomena that come within a known experience. Inasmuch as these facts must precede all conscious activity, and that without them no awakening in self-consciousness would be possible, they are termed PRIMITIVE FACTS. In finding these, we shall have prepared the way for a specific method in attaining all other facts. These primitive facts embrace the following particulars: 1. Sensation. 2. Consciousness. 3. The Mental States, as Capacities for knowing, feeling, and willing.

What these are, and that they are primitive facts, will be manifest in the process of investigation.

I. Sensation. The several distinct organs of sense, the eye, ear, nose, tongue, and the outer surface of the body in the skin, are connected by various appropriate nerves to the great receptacle of sensation in the brain. These serve as media of communication between the inner and the outer world. The living organism is perpetually penetrated with a sentient energy, and all affections in any part give their notice in the common sensorium, and these are respectively modified in their particular channels of communication, so that the sensations differ in coming through the different organs. The action of the outer world upon the living organ may be known as an *impression*, and such impression, met by the reaction of the living organ, constitutes what we now term *sensation*. It is fully completed within the living organism, and is not yet at all a perception. It is quite antecedent to the perceiving act, and a preliminary condition for it.

To describe it more fully, we may note, that the rays of light from some outer object meet the eye, and make their impression in this living organ; or, the undulations of air from the percussion of some sonorous body strike upon the tympanum of the ear, and make their impression, also, in this living organ. In such a meeting of the outer and the inner, there arises a reciprocal affection; each is modified by the other, and neither is as it was the moment before the contact. There has been action and reaction, and both that which has come into the organ and the organ itself have become changed. The ray of light has gone into the eye; that ray is no longer a ray of light, and that eye is no longer an empty organ. So with the undulation that has gone into the ear; it is wave of air no more, and it is empty ear no longer. The mutual modification has become completely a *third somewhat*, and which can have no name so appropriate as a *content* in the sense. It is not matter; it is not object; it is not anything yet perceived; it is solely a content in the organ, out of which a perceived phenomenon is to be elaborated by a farther mental action. This identification of the reciprocal modifications, of both the recipient organ and that which has been received, is precisely what is meant by sensation. In the eye, it is no longer ray of light, nor is it yet color; in the ear, it is no longer wave of air, nor is it yet sound; it is solely a content in the eye or the ear, out of which an intellectual agency will produce a color or a sound. As yet it stands wholly in the living organism, and has not at all come out in the consciousness, and is the same thing for either blind instinct or a clear perceiving. The same holds true with all the other organs of sense. As living organism, an impression is made upon it from without, and both outer and inner are modified in the contact, and this is sensation, and is a content out of which is to come the particular phenomenon of the smell, the taste, or the touch.

Sensation, thus, precedes and is not given in consciousness. We do not see the contact of the rays of light with the eye, nor hear the percussion of the undulating air upon the ear, nor do we perceive the mutual modifications which are thus induced; they give only the content in sensation, which is subsequently brought to be a distinct and definite phenomenon in consciousness. Still, these are facts which may be verified from the deductions of experience. A vivid flash of light or a stunning percussion injures and pains the organ, and too intense and protracted use wearies it, and a dissected eye gives its image, and a detached ear, with its organic elements, gives its movements and percussions to our observation. We learn that the affection occurs, from what we otherways know; and from the facts thus attained, it is competent to infer the whole fact of this sensible content.

It is important to distinguish sensation, as a primitive fact, from all conscious feeling which comes in subsequently, and by occasion of the sensation. The impression upon the organ of sense may be termed a feeling, but inasmuch as it is antecedent to all consciousness of it, such feeling can be blind only and operate solely as an instinct. The feeling that comes after the sensation, and by occasion of it through a perception, is wholly in consciousness, and influences the mind as an intelligent motive. It is properly an *emotion*. Thus, music excites a peculiar feeling as an agreeable emotion; but such feeling is completely separated from all blind feeling in sensation. The moving air, which propagated the instrumental vibrations to the ear, on coming in contact with that organ, made its impression on it and induced an affection in it, and by reason of the mutual action and reaction of air and organ a content for a sound was given. But, as yet, this is not perceived. The sensation is in its chaotic state, without form and distinctness, until the spiritual intelligence brood over it, and construct it into a definite tone in the consciousness. All the tones and their relation in harmony must be so perceived, and a deeper insight into the harmony of tones must apprehend the tune that is being carried along in them, and then the living sentiment which this tune expresses must be clearly caught by the mind; and only till such a long process has gone on beyond the feeling as sensation, can the agreeable feeling as emotion from the music come out. The blind feeling as sensation, and the distinct feeling as agreeable emotion in consciousness, are wholly unlike, and in the processes of mental activity are far apart from each other.

This discrimination is more specially important in the sense of touch, as the sensation and emotion are more liable to be here confounded. We say of a certain body, it feels smooth, or hard, or warm. But such smoothness, or hardness, or warmth, is already completed perception, giving distinct quality in the consciousness, and for which the sensation, as content in the organ, must have been an antecedent condition. The smoothness here is a perception, and not at all a proper feeling; and we only say of the body, it *feels* smooth, to indicate that the perception is one of touch, and not that the perception is at all an emotion. This perception of smoothness is the occasion of an agreeable feeling as emotion. Thus, my fingers come in contact with a piece of velvet, and the action and reaction is a content as a blind sensation. By the proper intellectual activity, I bring the sensation into complete perception, and I have then the distinct phenomenon in consciousness of the quality of smoothness; and to mark the perception as that of the touch, I may say of the velvet, not that it *looks* smooth, but that it *feels* so. But as yet we have not reached any feeling as emotion. It is only as I find the perceived smoothness of velvet to be agreeable, and thus the perception awakening an emotion, that I come to the consciousness of anything that is properly a feeling. I then slide my hand over the velvet, not that I may perceive its smoothness, but that I may feel the agreeable emotion it occasions.

Sensation is, therefore, never to be taken as feeling, except in a blind and unconscious state. It is not an emotion, for that is awakened only in the agreeableness, or the contrary, of the thing perceived; it is not even a perception in touch, which we say *feels* thus, for that is a quality brought out in the consciousness, and for which the sensation was an antecedent condition. The sensation may be perfect, and a complete content of sense be thus given in the organ, but if the requisite intellectual agency in attention does not follow, there will be neither a perception nor an emotion in the consciousness. Sensation may be, with no conscious emotion following it.

The pure mind itself has no distinct organs that may receive any impressions given; but it may properly be said of mere mental agency, that the mind affects itself in all its varieties of action, and thus gives to itself a sensation which is a proper content for a perception. The mind, as such, is thus taken as an organ of sense, and any internal movement is an impression upon it, and thus inducing an affection in it; and such affections are each as much an occasion for the proper intellectual process to result in the perception of a thought, an emotion, or a volition, as an affection in a bodily organ is an occasion for perceiving a color, a sound, or a smell. The one mind is diffused through all the bodily organism, and becomes modified in the impressions upon bodily organs from the outer world; and such affections may be known as *external* or *organic* sensation: the same mind is also modified, in the impressions it makes upon itself in its own agency; and such affections may be known as *internal* or *inorganic* sensation. In each case, the modifications resulting from the impressions constitute a proper content, which may subsequently, be matured into complete perception.

II. CONSCIOUSNESS. This is the source of all conviction in experience, and, as general in the human race, has been put by us as the ultimate criterion in all cases of disputed facts, which may be used in an Empirical Psychology. We have been frequently referring to it in the previous chapters, and have rested on the common acceptation of what consciousness is, and the faith which all are constrained to put in its testimony, without any attempt to give an explanation of it. The place has now been reached for a distinct exposition and apprehension of consciousness, as one of the facts in a system of Empirical Psychology, inasmuch as it stands in the order of primitive facts proximately precedent to all perception. When any mental activity has been completed, consciousness must still intervene, or no apprehension of that activity can be effected.

Consciousness has been very differently apprehended by different writers, and certainly not seldom misapprehended. Some have considered it as scarcely to be distinguished from personal identity; others, as a separate faculty for knowing the action of all other mental powers; and others, again, as the complement and connection of all mental exercises, inasmuch as they are all held in one consciousness. Consciousness is doubtless ever one in the same person, (a few cases of morbid experience alone excepted,) otherwise some actions would be in one consciousness, and some in another, and the man's life could never be brought into one experience. But this does by no means confound consciousness in personal identity, for identity continues in and through a great number of states of unconsciousness. Nor may it be assumed as a distinct faculty for knowing the operations of other faculties, for when intellectually I know anything, this would oblige the consciousness to an act of knowing that I know, and which, as knowing act, would still need another to know it, and thus on endlessly without finding a first and conclusive knowing act. And merely to say, that it is a medium in which all other mental facts and states are connected, is still to explain nothing, and really to have said nothing to any purpose. These different, and in some cases at least, erroneous conceptions of consciousness, indicate that there is some radical difficulty in attaining the precise fact of consciousness. It secures that other facts shall appear, while itself does not appear.

If, instead of attempting to conceive consciousness as a distinct mental faculty, or in any way an agent putting forth specific exercises, we will consider it under the analogy of an inner illumination, we may both avoid many difficulties and gain some great advantages. When any organic impression is given and thus a content in sensation is attained, the self-active mind has at once an occasion for spontaneously going out to complete the perception. By an appropriate intellectual activity, hereafter to be described, the precise quality and its exact limits are constructed, and the object is thus made distinct and definite; and now, if all this be conceived as accomplished within the mind's own light, no farther agency will be needed. The distinguishing and defining of the content in sensation is all that is necessary to make it an object, and when it thus appears under this mental illumination, it is the same as saying that it appears in consciousness, or that the mind is conscious of it. The conception is not of a faculty, but of a light; not of an action, but of an illumination; not of a maker of phenomena, but of a revealer of them as already made by the appropriate intellectual operation; and as thus constructed in the illuminated mental sphere, they at once appear to the mind, and the fact of perception is consummated. The content in sensation, which has been distinguished and defined, appears under this illumination as the objective; and the agency, accomplishing this work, appears in the same light as the subjective; and thus both the object and subject, the not-self and self, are together given in the same revelation of consciousness. The reflection that the subjective agency is in the self, and that the objective content is from some other than self, is a direct discrimination of the self from the not-self—a finding of myself—an awakening in self-consciousness.

Whenever the mind loses this discrimination between the subjective and the objective, there is the loss of self-consciousness. The infant has the sensation and a growing perfection in the appropriate constructing agency; but for some length of time the infant is without self-consciousness, and acts only from instinct. The animal observes and attends, distinguishes and defines, sometimes more acutely and accurately than man; but the animal never completely separates itself from its objects, and thus never fully attains itself in clear self-consciousness. So in somnambulism, a man may execute many most surprising transactions; walk along a precipice, upon the roofs of houses, climb towers and steeples, and accurately guide and keep himself harmless in all these dangerous positions; because he distinguishes and defines his sensations exactly, while he never distinguishes himself from his objects, and is thus wholly lost to all self-consciousness. So under intense excitement, the man whose dwelling is on fire may act most energetically; but in this loss of self-possession, he may often dash the frailest articles of furniture together, and throw his crockery and mirrors from the chamber windows. Under violent passion also, the outrageous conduct of some men often show, that they have wholly lost themselves; and so also with the ravings and delirium of a burning fever.

Here too, lies the explanation of much of the wonders and modern miracles of animal magnetism. The mesmeric sleep, by whatever cause induced, unlike natural sleep, quickens and greatly intensifies the mental agency in distinguishing and limiting the sensations, but leaves wholly out the action of self-discrimination, and the slightest suggestions and influences control the subject, who is thus put completely within the power of the operator. In all these cases, there is simply the absence of self-consciousness—the person is beside himself. But in syncope, apoplexy, etc., there is not only the loss of self-discrimination, but also of all power of distinguishing and limiting the sensations; and when the lesion goes to the destruction of the power of sensation itself, it then becomes death. That there is sensation distinguished and defined, and also self-discrimination, is altogether the great fact that there is self-consciousness. In the one illumination of consciousness, the *object*, and that it is *my* object, are both given. The process of the thought, as it develops itself in reflection, to attain the truth in the valid being of the self and its objects is wholly for Rational Psychology; but so far as experience is our guide to facts, we have the process, as above, in that mental illumination which reveals the subjective and the objective together. Consciousness is therefore "the light of all our seeing."

The difficulty that has always been found in determining what consciousness is, at once hereby explains itself. It is sufficient to vouch for itself, *that* it is; but it is not competent to reveal within itself *what* it is. It is a light in which other things appear, but is too pure that it should itself be seen. It reveals all that can be brought within it, but it cannot be put in any position where it may represent itself. Without it, nothing can appear—it is thus primitively conditional for all perception—but while in it the mind sees all other things, there is no light higher than it, by which the mind can see the consciousness itself.

III. Mental states, as capacities for knowing, feeling, and willing. The self-active mind is perpetually energizing in varied specific exercises, which are each readily distinguished in consciousness. Some of these exercises are perceptions, reflections, recollections, comparisons, abstractions, etc., all of which are in some way subservient to the process of *knowing.* Others are sympathies, affections, emotions, passions, etc., all included in some department of *feeling.* Others, again are preferences, choices, purposes, volitions, etc., and all in some way concerned in *willing.* The one mind is the source of all these different exercises, and must put them forth at separate times and on different occasions, and must therefore in some way modify itself conformably to its diverse operations. As one agent, in the several ways of knowing, feeling, and willing, the one self-active mind must be in different states, in order to put forth the exercises which are peculiar to each kind of operation. It may here be assumed, that all single exercises of the human mind may be included in one or the other of these kinds of operation, and thus stand connected with either knowing, or feeling, or willing. Such assumption will be subsequently verified, but in taking it for the present, it will be competent to say, that inasmuch as the states of mind must vary as the kinds of general operation vary, so there must be the three general states of mind, as knowing, feeling, and willing.

In all human experience, there is often the consciousness that the mind is unprepared for certain exercises, to which at other times there is a readiness. At one time the man thinks with difficulty, and at another time with great facility. When absorbed in thought, there is a conscious unpreparedness in the mind, to open itself to the flow of emotion; and when overwhelmed with feeling, the mind is prepared for neither patient thought nor stedfast resolution; and thus generally, if the mind is prepared for one kind of operation, it is in that unprepared for another kind. A general state of mind is necessary, therefore, as preliminary and preparatory to all specific activity. The general state, in fact, becomes a capacity for the specific acts included within that kind of operation. We may say, in general, that the mind has the capacity for knowing, feeling, and willing; but a direct capacity to specific action, under either kind of operation, is not attained, except as the mind goes into its state appropriate for such action, and this direct production of the capacity is one of the primitive facts of mind. We may be conscious of many important facts connected with this direct capacity for specific action, and the clear apprehension of them will prepare us directly for the determination of the peculiar method necessary in attaining and classifying all the other facts of mind.

The mind, as self-active, produces itself into several different general states, which thus become each respectively a capacity for specific single exercises. It is here assumed that all single acts may originate in one or the other of these general states, and which states we will here denominate, from their different kinds of capacity, as—THE INTELLECTUAL STATE; THE EMOTIVE STATE; and THE WILLING STATE. These we will now farther investigate.

1. *These general states may be clearly discriminated in consciousness.*

When you take your seat before a public speaker and he rises to address you, there may be a very clear consciousness that your mind has gone out into a general state, before a single word has been uttered. There is, as yet, no specific exercise, but only a state of mind inducing a capacity for particular exercises. It is not attention, for there is no voice to which the attention may be applied; it is not perception, for there is no content in the sense to be apprehended; it is not thought, for there has been no thought communicated or awakened. It is simply a readiness to act, in any and all of these specific exercises, as the occasion shall offer; and is therefore, a state of mind capacitating for knowing, when the occasion for knowing shall have been given. It is, thus, an Intellectual State. So also, with an audience, before the curtain rises which covers some scenic representation; each mind has put itself in a state to know, when any thing shall be uncovered to its perception. And so, again, in the expectation of some musical performance; before the sounds have been given, and the opportunity afforded for attending to their inner meaning in the tune they will embody, the mind has already gone into an intellectual state in reference thereto. This may also be true in reference to any other sense; as the touch, taste or smell; and in reference to all mental action for knowing in any way; as remembering, thinking, reflecting, etc. The self-activity goes out into an intellectual state, as preparative for any specific exercises that may be concerned in knowing; and when the conditions are given, the specifice exercises for knowing are then produced, and the apprehension of the object or theme is consummated.

If now, the mind maintain itself wholly in the intellectual state, and exhaust all its activity in the intensity to know, there will be no preparation for emotion. But when, instead of abiding in the intellectual state, it opens itself for the coming up of the emotions which the discourse, the scene, or the tune, may be adapted to excite; there will in this be the consciousness of quite a different state, and that in it there is the capacity to quite a different set of exercises, from all that is concerned in knowing. Simply as having gone into the intellectual state, the mind was not thus prepared to feel; and if it should wholly absorb itself in intellectual action, it would have no capacity to feel, and no specific emotions would be exercised. The self-activity must produce itself into quite a different state, which we have termed the Emotive State, or its action would be a knowing without feeling. So also, in solitary thought and silent speculation. I may be intent merely to know; or I may pass out of the state adapted only to dry thought, and assume a state which is also in readiness to feel; and my intense speculation will then become a sweet meditation, in which the mind will not only be filled with thought, but will also overflow with emotion.

But we will carry out this discrimination still farther. You may imagine yourself to have been among the audience, which listened to the great Athenian Orator in one of his terrible Phillipics. In an intellectual state, you apprehended his exordium, so appropriate, so captivating; his narration of topics and arrangement of matter, so skilful, so logical; his delineation of acts and events, so graphic, so consecutive; and his whole argument, so comprehensive, so conclusive; that your mind was elevated and filled with the thought which revealed and proved, and made you to know so much. But you did not rest merely in knowing. You opened your mind to emotion, and felt the glow of patriotism, the deep sense of national honor, the shame of servitude, the disgrace of cowardice, and burning indignation against the tyrant. But neither did you rest in this state of deep emotion. In your self-activity, you roused every energy of your enkindled spirit, and held all ready for the most prompt and determined execution, while you shouted with the thousands of Athens—"Let us march against Philip." You found in yourself the capacity for a strong will, and the putting forth the most strenuous exertions. This last state of willing is clearly distinct in the consciousness from either of the former.

As concisely illustrative of these three distinct general states, I adduce the following examples from the sacred Scriptures. When Cornelius had sent for Peter by the direction of an angel, and had already received him into his house, he says: "Now, therefore, are we all here present before God, to hear all things that are commanded thee of God."—Acts x, 33. They were in the intellectual state. Again, the Psalmist in great distress, longs for the communion and manifested approbation of God, and waits for the emotions which his spiritual presence would induce, and he says, "My soul waiteth for the Lord, more than they that watch for the morning." —Ps. cxxx, 6. Here is as manifestly the emotive state. And finally, when Saul had been stricken to the earth by the brightness of a miraculous vision, and he found himself ready to undertake any duty divinely commanded, he cries, "Lord, what wilt thou have me to do?"—Acts, ix, 6. A clear case is given in this of the willing state.

2. *The occasions for going out in such general capacities.*

An original peculiarity of mind may be an occasion for these general mental states, in reference to particular ends of action. To some minds it is natively congenial to follow a particular calling, or to pursue a particular branch in literature, science, or art. The poet, mathematician, painter, or sculptor, seem often to have an innate propensity each to his special employment; and different trades and occupations often find such as have their natural adaptations to the particular pursuits. In all such cases, an occasion is given in the original bias of the mind for the self-activity to go readily out into a capacity both to know, to feel, and to will, in reference to the given end.

In the same way, the peculiar temperament, in the constitutional formation, may be an occasion for the self-active mind, to put itself in a readiness to know, feel and will in certain congenial directions. Prompting occasions also, are often given, from the thousand contingent circumstances in which the man may be placed, and from the casual incidents that fall around him, by which the mind is induced to put itself in a new attitude, and go out into a different general state from that previously occupied. Under any one of these conditions, a spontaneous movement puts the mind, at once, in the appropriate state for particular acts of knowing, feeling, or willing, in reference to a particular end.

Sometimes we are conscious of an effort of will to hold ourselves in readiness for specific acts toward specific objects, and such acts of the will become themselves an occasion for the self-activity to put itself into the wished for capacity. But in all such occasions it is important to note, that the state is not itself a volition; it is not the direct product of the will, but immediately produced by the self-activity on occasion of the will prompting to it. Just as an act of recollection may be prompted by an occasion of willing, while the remembering is not at all a volition, but the spontaneous product of the self-active mind in recalling its past perceptions. In all cases, the general state as capacity is attained, by the spontaneous movement of the self-active mind into it; and whether by occasion of native mental peculiarity, or of constitutional temperament, or casual circumstances, or an effort of will, the production is immediately from the sponta-

neous self-activity. Willing may give occasion for the movement, but no act of will can produce the state either to know, to feel, or to will. It may very often be wished, when the will cannot attain it, and thus volition is often not an adequate occasion for it. A ready state to know, or to feel, or to will, in a specific direction, is often as impossible to be reached by willing, as an act of clear recollection, or a state of sleep. Whatever the occasion given, the self-activity goes directly out in the production of the respective capacity, and spontaneously projects itself from one state into another. As the first act of knowing, in the infant mind, must have been spontaneous, with no occasion of a previous volition, so is every general state spontaneous, though often by occasion of volition.

3. *The order of connection in these general mental capacities.*

The self-active mind produces in itself these different capacities according to an invariable order, and while the law for such order cannot be brought into consciousness, the fact is manifestly given in common experience. This order, as given in fact, it is quite important fully to attain.

The intellectual state is immediately from the self-activity.—On occasion being given, the mind by its spontaneous activity, produces itself directly into an intellectual state, and stands prepared to act specifically in any exercise connected with knowing in that particular direction. This may as well be from a state to know in reference to a different object, as from a state of feeling,

or of willing. The mind, in a state to know all that a speaker may say, is not in that also in a state to know the music which an orchestra may be about to perform. The mind, in a state for the speaker, would be conscious of a manifest change, if the speaker should be suddenly removed and the orchestra at once presented. But in such case, and in all cases, the mind does not need to go into an emotive state, nor a willing state, in order that it may take an intellectual state. Whatever be its present state, it needs only the proper occasion, and it immediately produces itself into the required intellectual state.

The emotive state is attained only in connection with the intellectual state.—Emotion cannot be, except the object in which the emotion is to terminate be first given. But this object is given only as it is known; and it is known only in an intellectual state; and thus without a state to know, there cannot be a state to feel. If I am not ready to know any object, I cannot be in readiness for any emotion which is to terminate in that object. This is quite manifest in consciousness not only, but also appears in daily observation and experience. The mind, that reluctates any emotion, directly evades all occasion for bringing that object into consciousness; and the mind, that rejoices in any feeling, seeks also to keep the object within knowledge.

A most kind and benevolent provision in human nature is based wholly on this fact, and designed to obviate the evil consequences of any excessive and absorbing passion. When the object in which the passion terminates is vividly present in the mind, the emotion rises in its highest intensity, and thus becomes a violent paroxysm of passion, and then bursts from its own fullness, and flows off in its own peculiar channels. Deep grief vents itself in sobbing and tears, or, in its most passionate excitement, rends the garments, beats the breast and tears the hair; while joy overflows in laughter and singing, and when most excited, boisterously leaps and dances. In proportion to the intensity of the passion, is the violence of its explosion, and in this very outburst is the provision for its relief. The object is by this, for the moment, thrown out of the consciousness; the image which occasions the excitement fades away, or for the time is wholly vanished, and the emotion ebbs accordingly. Successive ebullitions of passion, may thus occur, and overflow again and again in reference to the same object; but this violent paroxysm is nature's kind interposition to snatch the object temporarily from the view, that its tides of feeling may not overwhelm the spirit. How salutary this is, may be estimated from the sad consequences of a passion which finds no such vent from nature, and leaves the fixed attention concentrated upon the object without cessation! The reason is overpowered, and often incurable madness succeeds.

The willing state is attained only in connection with both the intellectual and the emotive states.—A choice, or any act of the will, demands an object in which it may terminate, as truly as does an emotion. We can not choose except as there is something in the consciousness on which the choice may fix itself. There must thus be some object as known, and thus the necessity for an intellectual state. But the mere dry apprehension of an object is not a sufficient occasion for a choice. There is nothing which can properly be called a motive or reason. Some feeling must be awakened towards the object, either of desire or obligation, or the conditions for a volition are not given. We cannot choose, unless there be something congenial to be attained in the choice, and this can occur only in an emotive state. As well no object, as an object which awakens no feeling of interest, or of duty. The willing state, as capacity for putting forth any voluntary exercises, must thus be preceded by both an object known, and an object felt, and must thus be occasioned by both an intellectual and an emotive state. In these only is the condition of willing at all given.

4. *These general states of mind may be blended in the consciousness, but not confounded.*

The intellectual state may, under certain conditions, be taken by itself alone, but the emotive state cannot stand out separate from the intellectual state. So soon as an intellectual state should cease, the object of knowledge must fall away from the consciousness; and as this was the end in which the emotion terminated, with the loss of the object, the feeling must also become extinct. We are quite conscious, that only in the object known can any feeling be maintained; and thus, that except an intellectual state blend with the emotive, the condition for the latter cannot be given. The willing state, moreover, must stand blended with both the intellectual and emotive states, and cannot find its conditions for being taken, except as both the knowing and the feeling are at the same time in exercise. Only as the object is in consciousness, can there be any emotion; and only as some emotive exercise is put forth, can there be any occasion for willing, inasmuch as no volition can be, without some motive in the susceptibility; and thus a state of willing must blend with both a state of knowing and a state of feeling. The intellectual state may be in complete isolation; the emotive state cannot be, except as blended with the intellectual; and the willing state can not be, except as in combination with both the intellectual and the emotive states.

But, when thus blended, they are by no means confounded in the consciousness. We can readily discriminate the one from the others, even when they all stand in combination. When I choose one from two or more objects, I may be distinctly conscious of both knowing the object, and of feeling an interest in it, at the same time that my will goes out in an executive act to attain it. They are in exercise together; and the general states, which capacitate for their exercise, are also together; and I am conscious of their blended being, at the same time that I discriminate the one from the other. The blending is without confusion; as in the white light all the colors are given, but which are also readily discriminated through the prismatic medium. Knowing, feeling, and willing all coalesce in every volition, and yet are all distinguished, each from each, in the consciousness; and the general states, as capacities for each, alike coalesce, and are alike distinguished.

5. *These capacities may ordinarily be perpetuated by a stedfast purpose.*

As before shown, a native bias of mind and a constitutional temperament may stand as permanent occasions for a state of knowing, feeling, and willing, in that direction to which nature prompts. The native artist is ever prompt to know, feel, and will in reference to his favorite topics. The native poet, or mathematician, is permanently in readiness for all specific exercises, which relate to his congenial pursuit. But aside from all constitutional bias, an act of will may be an occasion for the self-active mind to produce within itself the required general capacity. Commonly, by a decided voluntary act, the mind can be put into either the intellectual, emotive, or willing state; and though the state is not itself willed, yet is it induced by occasion of willing. And as the state was induced by occasion of a voluntary act, so, ordinarily, may it be perpetuated, by making the voluntary action to become a stedfast purpose. This is qualified by saying, ordinarily; for there are sometimes exempt and extraordinary cases, when no volition can be made an occasion for either of the general states of mind now contemplated.

As an illustration, the presentation of a book may be supposed, and this may be an occasion for the mind, either spontaneously or through a volition, to go into a state to know the thoughts of the author as the reading of the book shall progress from page to page. This state may be perpetuated, to an indefinite extent, by fixing a stedfast purpose in reference to it: and while the attention might readily be diverted, and the intellectual state in reference to the book be transient, if all was left to the control of mere passing occasions, yet this settled purpose may hold the mind intent to know, until the reading of the book is finished. So, also, with the state to feel the emotions, which the meaning of the book may occasion; and voluntarily to put in practice, what the book may enjoin; a settled purpose may perpetuate all these states, and prevent the mind from passing off into other engagements. Thus, also, a man may fix on some pursuit for years, or for life; and in this settled purpose that fixes a perpetual calling, an occasion will be given for a perpetual state of readiness, to know, feel, and will, all that may at any time be disclosed, as bearing upon the success of that engagement.

Even against the prompting of occasional circumstances, or the native bias of constitutional temperament, a strong and decided purpose may give the condition in which the self-active mind shall go into a permanent state, to know, feel, and will, as would otherwise be wholly uncongenial. Thus, a man may discipline his own powers, and correct any constitutional biases, and educate himself to very different habits of thought, emotion and execution, from such as would have been prompted by circumstances or native inclinations. Thus, also, when any perpetuated states have been long retained, and habits of thought, emotion, and practice have been formed; a strong and resolute will may be an occasion for inducing general states of knowing, feeling, and willing in quite different directions; and thereby induce to the breaking up of old habits, and of forming others that shall be very different. No habit of thought, or feeling, or acting, is itself directly willed; the volition may become an occasion for the mind to pass into particular aptitudes for knowing or feeling, and the repetition of consequent successive exercises forms and confirms the habit.

6. *No general state will be permanent, except by a settled purpose.*

When constitutional biases become an occasion for specific habits of thought, feeling and willing, the constitutional inclination is soon also seen to have induced a corresponding determination of the will, and thus a moral no less than a constitutional disposition is settled. A change henceforth, if effected, must not only counteract constitutional temperament, but also deep seated purposes. "Old things must pass away, and all things become new." But where no particular bias is given from nature, and only passing circumstances prompt the mind to go into its general states, these will be especially fluctuating and unstable, if not held in one direction by occasion of a stedfast purpose. One state comes and goes, and others follow in fleeting succession, as summer shadows chase each other over the landscape, and the whole mental activity is in continual ebb and flow, with no steady current or perpetuated direction. Spontaneously will the self-active mind project itself from one state to another, as passing occasions are given, and never continue long in one stay.

Should any mind attempt to hold itself in suspense between two given ends of action, with no stedfast purpose in either direction, there will soon be a painful consciousness of the impracticability of maintaining such a position. The activity will soon have slipped away from all direction to either object, and the exercises of thought, and feeling, and willing, are soon going out on wholly different ends. But when, after due deliberation, a stedfast purpose is taken in reference to any object, this becomes at once an occasion for the mind to go into a permanent state in reference to that object, and to know, feel, and will, whatever the interests of that purpose may demand. It is not necessary that the purpose be a perpetual energizing of the will; the one fixed purpose has been the occasion for the self-activity to go into a permanent state; and, except such permanent purpose be taken, the mind will not hold in a perpetuated capacity for either knowledge, emotion, or volition. Nothing makes the man consistently stedfast, in either intellectual character, affection, or voluntary action, but the perpetual dominion of a deep and stedfast purpose. He is else "double-minded," and of course "unstable in all his ways."

In the foregoing General Facts we have one, permanent, self-active mind; and in the Primitive Facts, we have sensation, consciousness, and the self-active mind as competent to go spontaneously into the states which capacitate it specifically to know, to feel, and to will. The one mind is the actor in all; but it must pass into successive states, in order that it may produce within itself the capacity to particular exercises in either. We now affirm, that the self-active mind is competent to produce in itself general states or capacities for these three modes of activity, to know, to feel, and to will; these three, no more and no less. They all exist, as thus produced, in consciousness; and we are also quite conscious of our impotence to induce within us the capacities for any other varieties of mental activity. We can act in no other capacities than as intellectual, sentient, and voluntary beings. Aside from the primitive facts already attained, and which are precedent to and preparatory for these, all human mental agency is confined to knowing, feeling, and willing. We have in this the natural order for our psychological classification. Many have forced all mental facts within two divisions, substantially those of knowing and willing, though using different ways of expressing them; but the appeal is here confidently made to common consciousness, that the exercises in the emotive state are different in kind from the exercises of either knowing or willing, and that a sharp line of discrimination stands between these facts. As all emotion and sentiment differs from all knowledge and volition, so it differs from sensation, properly so called. Sensation precedes perception, and is a necessary condition for it; emotion succeeds the perception, and springs by direct occasion from it. We need to find a capacity for mental acts which is not at all employed in knowing or in willing, nor at all implied in organic sensation. A confounding of things which so much differ can only induce perplexity, absurdity, and error. The following is the true order of Mental Classification:—

The capacity for knowing, is—THE INTELLECT.
The capacity for feeling, is—THE SUSCEPTIBILITY.
The capacity for willing, is—THE WILL.

I. THE INTELLECT. . . .	1. The Sense. 2. The Understanding. 3. The Reason.
II. THE SUSCEPTIBILITY.	1. The Animal. 2. The Rational. 3. The Spiritual.
III. THE WILL.	1. Immanent Preferences. 2. Governing Purposes. 3. Desultory Volitions.

IV. THE COMPETENCY OF MAN, WITH SUCH CAPACITIES, TO ATTAIN THE END OF HIS BEING.

FIRST DIVISION.

THE INTELLECT.

THE Mind, as Intellect, is inclusive of the entire capacity for knowing, whether in direct perception, concluding in judgments, or comprehending in universal principles. All mental exercises subservient to any form of knowing, and which come clearly within consciousness, are facts belonging to the intellect. Conception, recollection, association, abstraction, comparison, etc., all come within this division, as being somehow concerned in the processes of knowing. The products of the intellect, when they are wholly subjective, and the creations of mind itself, are termed *Intellections;* and when they apply to an objective existence, they are termed *Cognitions.* Sometimes this distinction is made by calling the former *pure* cognitions, and the latter *empirical* cognitions. Sometimes, also, the cognitions are characterised from the different functions of knowing, as *sense*-cognition, *understanding*-cognition, or *reason*-cognition.

The mind, as intellectual capacity, has three distinct functions of operation, and from which we are to recog.

nize three different Faculties for knowing, each peculiar to itself in its forms of knowledge and the kind of cognitions attained. All confounding of one with others must necessarily induce obscurity into the system of psychology, and ultimately disclose itself in great error both philosophical and practical. This exact analysis will especially evince its necessity, in the coming Divisions of the Susceptibility and the Will, nor can either be correctly apprehended without it. These three different Faculties in the one capacity for knowing, are: 1. THE SENSE. 2. THE UNDERSTANDING. 3. THE REASON.

These will be examined in three different Chapters, and the particular facts under each attained, expounded, and assigned to their places in their proper order. So far as it may conduce to a more clear and full apprehension of the more important elements in some of these divisions, they will be investigated more formally under separate sections.

CHAPTER I.

THE SENSE.

THE primitive fact of Sensation has already been found, as a content in the vital organ, which an intellectual process is to bring to a complete perception. It has been common to apply the term Sense only to the capacity for taking this content in the sensation, leaving the intellectual process for a matured perception to come in under some other appellation. In this view, sense is no faculty for knowing, but only a receptivity for such content as may, subsequently, be brought into knowledge. But the whole intellectual process for producing the sensation given, into an object in perception, is so utterly distinct from all other forms of knowing, that it must needs have its separate consideration, and be assigned to its appropriate position, and must therefore have its distinctive name. And while the term sense may properly apply to the receptivity, yet by no means is the work of the sense completed in merely receiving the content, and only so when it has been completely envisaged in a distinct and definite phenomenon. We thus leave that part of the sense which is only capacity for receiving, to what has already been said in connection with the primitive fact of sensation; and here consider only the part, which pertains to the intellectual process of bringing out the sensation to a clear perception, and the peculiarities of the object so attained. The sense, thus, may embrace both sensation and perception—the receiving of the content and the completed representation of it—but while neither part should be held to exclude the other, the latter only can come within the consideration of the intellectual process as a knowing act.

The Sense, therefore, as in the division of the intellect, includes only the process of knowing, and the peculiarities of that which is so known; and is, thus, *the faculty for attaining cognitions through sensation.* This faculty for knowing in sense may be best studied by observing the distinction into *External Sense* and *Internal Sense.*

SECTION I. THE EXTERNAL SENSE. This applies to the faculty for perceiving through the media of bodily organs. These organs are the eye, ear, skin, nose and tongue, and which receive their content in sensation for objects in vision, hearing, touch, smell and taste. A sixth sense is sometimes made, by separating in touch the sensibility of the skin, and the resistence of muscular pressure. From the first is given the content which is perceived as heat and cold, titulation and irritation; from the last is attained the sensation which is perceived as hardness, roughness, weight, etc. Sufficient attention has already been given to sensation. In it we have a content that is, as yet, wholly undiscriminated and undefined. It is in the living organ only, and not yet in the consciousness as any known object. In order that it may be so known, an intellectual operation is necessary, by which this content in blind feeling shall be completely set in clear consciousness.

Two things are to be effected. The intellectual agency must first determine *what* the content is, as distinguished from all others that have or may be given; and secondly, this agency must determine its limits, in all the ways in which limitation can be referred to it, and in this *how much* the content is; the first operation may be known as *Observation*, and the second as *Attention*. We will give each of these more particularly.

Observation.—Sensation merely gives a content in the organ for a perception, but it does nothing towards making that content to appear in consciousness, as a distinct object. It is occasion for the self-active mind to pass into an intellectual state, and by a purely intellectual process to *distinguish* the particular sensation. This purely distinguishing act is what is meant by observation. It avails to give the content in sensation as a distinct object.

As thus brought into distinct appearance, it becomes properly a *phenomenon*, and what was before undistinguished content in sensation, now becomes a *quality*, discriminated from all others and known in its own peculiarity. The distinguishing of the sensation, as belonging to its appropriate organ, gives the quality as distinct in *kind;* viz. color, as sensation in the eye, distinct from sound, as sensation in the ear, or smell, as sensation in the nose, etc. The distinguishing of the content in the same organ, from all others that may be given in it, determines the quality in its distinct *variety;* viz. a red

color, as discriminated from any other, or the peculiar noise, or odor, as distinct from all other sounds or smells. The content is thus separated in its kind from all others, and also in its variety from all others, and made to stand out in consciousness in its own *individuality*, as having nothing farther to be separated from it, or discriminated in it, but which now appears in its own peculiar identity.

It is to be carefully noted that observation is exclusively a distinguishing act, and does nothing beyond a complete discrimination of the quality both in its kind and variety. When I have intellectually distinguished the sensation as a content in vision, and thus the quality of color in kind; and then have farther distinguished the particular color in the vision, and thus have found the peculiar variety, I have fulfilled the whole work of observation. The distinguishing may go on through all differences in variety, till the quality has nothing farther that can be discriminated as dividing it from others, and thus be completely and exactly individualized; and in this is exhausted the entire function of observation. It results in making the content to be a distinct object in the consciousness.

Attention.—When a sensation has been distinguished in kind and variety, by an observing act, there is given in this, a *distinct*, but not yet a *definite* object to the consciousness. We need, farther, a purely intellectual agency which shall completely define the quality within its own limits. When we have distinct *quality*, we need also to go farther to complete the perception, and attain the definite *quantity*. This is effected in attention. As observation was exclusively a distinguishing act, so attention is wholly a constructing act. Not a *holding to*, (*ad teneo*) but a *stretching to* (*ad tendo*) the limits of the object.

An attending agency, as a complete fact in the consciousness, may be best suggested to the apprehension in the following manner. If I would possess any pure diagram, in simple mental space, I must in my own intellectual agency construct it; it will not somehow come into the mind of itself. I can have no pure mathematical line, except as in my intellectual agency I assume some point and produce it through directly contiguous points, conjoining all into one form, and thus I draw the line. Thus of all pure figures, simple or complicated, circles, squares, triangles, and all sections of them, I can not subjectively possess them, except as I intellectually construct them. If now, you will carefully note in consciousness this constructing agency, which describes pure mathematical figure, you will in it attain the precise fact of an act of attention.

The distinct quality appears in consciousness from the act of observation, but as given in *space* it is as yet utterly formless. An intellectual agency must construct it, by describing its entire outline and apprehending its complete limits, and thus bringing its definite shape into the consciousness. Whether it be quality in vision or in touch, the attending agency must stretch itself all about it, or brood entirely over it, and thus take it in its exact limits and determine what space it fills. The quality, given in observation, is thus determined as to its quantity in space by attention.

So the distinct quality, as given in *time*, is by observation alone wholly without period. An intellectual agency must again construct it. Taking the distinct quality at the instant of its appearance, and conjoining the successive instants into one period up to the time of its disappearance, and thus stretching over the whole from beginning to concluding limit, the quantity of time that it has occupied is determined, and we have the quality now in its definite duration.

So, moreover, the distinct quality, as given in *degree*, is wholly measureless by the act of observation alone. An intellectual agency must begin at the point of an arising affection in the sense, and follow up, through all degrees of intensity in the sensation, to the point actually reached by the content in the organ, and thus by stretching over all degrees from zero to the given limit of affection, the full measure of the content in sensation is determined, and we have the quality in its definite amount.

No quality can have measure in any other directions than extension in space, duration in time, and intensity of degree; and when an act of attention has stretched over the limits filled by the distinct quality in all these several directions, it has determined it in all the forms which any quality can possess, and made it to be known definitely in all its measures of quantity.

The above operations of observing and attending are conditional for all knowledge in the sense. Without the first, the quality would not be distinct, without the last it would not be definite in form. I may know distinctly a distant color on a sign board to be black, and yet I may not be able to define the color and read the letters. I shall in such case have a distinct but not a definite knowledge. I may distinctly observe a white object at the bottom of a stream or a lake, and yet from the ripples on its surface may not by any power of attention be able accurately to define and exactly know its shape. So, again, there may be sensation with neither observation nor attention, and in this condition the sensation remains in unconsciousness. So, I am often unconscious of the book from which I am reading, of the chair on which I am sitting, and of the pavement over which I walk. The knowledge is as complete, as the distinguishing and defining are perfect. One operation cannot dispense with, nor compensate for, the other, but both must be fully accomplished.

All qualities may be distinguished; and all may be defined in the limits of time and degree; but only the qualities given in the vision and the touch can be fully defined in space. The content in the eye and the pressure of the fingers, can be constructed into complete shape in space, and these only. Sounds and smells can not be defined in shape, and only imperfectly in direction and distance, by the most careful attention; and tastes can be defined by no limits of extension in space. Such are the facts as given in experience, but it appertains to Rational Psychology to determine the principles why our experience must so be. The fact of sensation is given as primitive; the intellectual operations, distinguishing in observation and defining in attention, bring the content in sensation distinctly and definitely into consciousness. A complete object is thus before the mind, and we are said to *apprehend* it, in thus getting it within the mind's *grasp*, *out of* its former darkness. In its *appearance* in the light of consciousness, it is known as *phenomenon;* and inasmuch as it has been *taken through* the medium of sensible organs, it is termed a *perception*. As the impression on the organ has been made by an existence from without, the phenomenon is ascribed to outer nature as some quality of an external world, and perceived through an external sense. Thus may all the facts of external perception be gathered, as inclusive of all the phenomena of human experience by sensible organs.

The affection of the organ is from some external impulse, and no product of the mind, but inasmuch as the living mind is diffused through the entire organism, this affection becomes the occasion for an intellectual agency to distinguish and define it in the clear light of consciousness, and thus to know it as phenomenon. In this is readily determined what is objective and what subjective. Thus: I perceive heat. Is this heat in my mind, or in the object? That which has affected the organ, and become a content in sensation, is from the outer world, and that which has distinguished and defined it, is from an inner agency. The affection has been *given*, the peculiarity and the form have been *found*. That which has come in from without is to the mind wholly indistinct and indefinite, until in its own agency it has determined what, where, when, and how much it is.

It thus follows, that what has been given to the sense is not the thing itself. That outer thing has in some way affected the organ and induced sensation, and this sensation it is which the intellect distinguishes and defines. Not the thing itself is made object, but the color, sound, smell, etc., of the thing, appears in consciousness. The outer thing has so affected me, that I have come to know it in such a mode of its being, and apprehend, not it, but its qualities. The qualities are *real*, and not mere seeming phantasies, inasmuch as there has been a real impression and thus a real content in sensation; but they are only real *qualities* of things, and not the things themselves. I perceive a redness, a fragrance, a silky smoothness, through different kinds of sensation; but I do not by any sense perceive *the rose*, which is red, fragrant, smooth, etc. Moreover, these qualities, as gained by sense, are single and separate in the consciousness. They are constructed one by one, and perceived only as so many different phenomena, and cannot by any observation or attention be put together as the attributes of one substance. They are known in isolation, and not in their connection. And still farther, to the sense all things are in a perpetual flow. The phenomena are to it, only as they are in the consciousness; and in this, there is a continual arising and departing. One phenomenon is rapidly succeeded by another, and with continually varied sensations continually varied phenomena are perceived. And not merely do the phenomena pass rapidly on and off from the field of consciousness, but the same phenomenon to the sense is in continual succession.

The rays of light which give the phenomenon of color, and the undulations of air which occasion sound, are for no moment the same. The impressions on the organ are a series and not a constant, and thus the content in sensation is in no two instants unchanged. Like the river, its stream is perpetual, yet never the same. In the sense, all objects are coming and going, and the object itself is also never in one stay. Thus, the outer world comes into the consciousness only as to its properties, and we perceive the qualities of things only; and those, single, separate, and fleeting. Had we only the faculty of sense, in observation and attention, our experience could have no orderly connections, but would be only a medley of coming and vanishing appearances.

Section II. The Internal Sense.—The internal sense is a faculty for knowing the inner mental exercises. When considering the fact of sensation, we found the living mind itself an organ for receiving impressions from its own action, and thus taking a content in sensation with every affection which its own movement induced. The action in its different capacities of knowing, feeling, and willing gives the different *kinds* of content for thought, emotion, and volition; and, in each capacity, the *varieties* of content for peculiar thoughts, emotions, and volitions. The distinguishing and defining intellectual agency constructs these into complete phenomena as readily as the organic sensations. Inner exercises are hereby perceived as distinctly and definitely as outer qualities, and an emotion of joy or an act of choice is as clearly in consciousness, and as truly phenomenon, as a red color or a fragrant smell.

The difference in the forms, which can be given to inner and outer phenomena, is alone here remarkable. The affection induced in the mind by its own action does not have local position and topical expansion, as does the content of sensation in the eye, or the moving organ of touch, and thus no occasion is given for the intellectual agency in attention to stretch itself over any spacial limits, and determine any locality and shape to an inner phenomenon. Only duration of period, and amount of intensity, can be determined for any inner exercise, and thus no forms of space can have any relevancy to mental exercises. The conditions of space are wholly impertinent to all mental being and action. The members of the body, and the body itself, can give affection to its own organs, and thus its qualities can be constructed in space and known as having extension; and the mind may be conceived as somehow diffused through the body, and thus having locality; but this is *thought* only and not perceived, and thought even through the medium of a supposed container, without being able to think where in the body the mind is. The mind *appears* only in its acts, and to these no place, but only period can be given. A thought has a when, but not a where; a limit in time, but not a shape in space.

As in the outer, so also in the inner sense, the phenomena are given single and separate. The thought, the emotion and the volition are constructed in the consciousness one by one, and we thus perceive the exercises isolate one from the other. The act, and not the actor, appears; and no operation of construction, in attention, can connect the separate acts as together dependent upon one mind. Were there only the faculty of sense, we should know the mental phenomena only as successive appearances dancing in and out of the consciousness. These single exercises are also in continual flow. The acts not only pass away, to be followed by others, but the same exercise is a continually recurring energy, and no thought or emotion can stay in the consciousness for any two moments the same. The affection in the sensation is only a perpetual repetition.

In the sense, we thus know how the outer and the inner affects us. The sensations induced become, in consciousness, the qualities of an outer and the exercises of an inner world. They appear, and we know them as appearances, and apprehend them as the modes of a real existence; but we only perceive that which is attributed to things, and not by any means the things themselves.

All perception is an immediate beholding, inasmuch as the object is put face to face before the mind in the light of consciousness. Perception is thus *intuition*, in the sense of immediate view in consciousness. There is another meaning of intuition, which is a looking into things themselves, and is more properly *insight*, but which is for the reason and not the sense, and is distinguished as *rational* intuition. A sense intuition is an immediate beholding in consciousness. This is *empirical* intuition when the content in sensation is distinguished and defined, and thus a real phenomenon is given. It is the same, whether of outer or inner phenomenon: a perceived thought or emotion is a real phenomenon, immediately beheld in consciousness, as much as a perceived red color or a fragrant odor. It is a *pure* intuition, when the object in consciousness is wholly the production of the intellect, without any content in sensation. An intellectual operation, which shall be the same as an attending act, except as there is no content in sense to condition it, may construct any mathematical figures, or arithmetical numbers, and such pure forms in the consciousness are what is meant by pure intuition. All pure mathematic is thus a science of pure intuition, inasmuch as all its modified diagrams and complicated numbers are purely intellectual creations, with no content in sensation. The scheme, after which such pure diagrams must be made, is furnished by the reason, and thus no animal can be mathematician, but the construction itself is altogether a work in pure sense.

SECTION III. FANCY.—When the constructing agency, with no content in sensation, builds up for itself seeming mental pictures as the semblances of real phenomena, it is termed *Fancy*. The objects are mere phantasies as a seeming, and not veritable phenomena as an appearing; and, though the work of an image-making faculty, they are not properly termed products of the imagination. Imagination proper is the work of the pure understanding, as will be hereafter explained, but the fancy belongs wholly to the pure sense. Its semblances are grouped together from a capricious interest in the mere seeming, and not from any judgment or taste, and are thus wholly fantastic, with neither the principle of utility nor beauty. This faculty of the pure sense is lively in all the first wakings of the mind, and the earlier dawnings of self-consciousness. In a disturbed sleep, the fancy is ever busy, and the semblances come and depart in grotesque combinations and successions, or in more regulated order from previous habits of association, accordingly as the mind is more or less lost to all self-consciousness. There is also much day-dreaming, or castle-building in the air, which is but the empty reverie of an idle fancy. The half-stupor of an opiate obscures the self-discrimination and sets loose the fancy; and the horrible hauntings of *delirium tremens*, or *mania a' potu*, are the demons of fancy which torture the burning brain of the habitual inebriate. Children live in their fancies, and the savage mind is always fantastic. Their ornaments, amusements, music, and pictures, are destitute of all living art, and are only a gaudy display of that which is most ostentatious or striking to the senses. It is only after much cultivation, that the mind rises from the sense-play of the fancy, to the works of imagination and the creations of genius; and only the most cultivated can appreciate the highest products.

CHAPTER II.

THE UNDERSTANDING.

THE Understanding is that Intellectual Faculty by which the single and fleeting phenomena of sense are known as qualities inhering in permanent things, and all things as cohering to form the universe. In the sense, the operation of the intellectual agency is engaged in putting the content in sensation, within limits; in the understanding, this agency is employed in putting that which has been defined, into its grounds and sources. The first is a *conjoining* and the last a *connecting* operation. The sense-object is a mere aggregation; the understanding-object is an inherent coalition. In the sense, the object appears; in the understanding, it is thought. One is a perception; the other is a judgment.

We may best apprehend the peculiar work of the understanding, by looking through the whole connecting process. When distinct and definite phenomena are perceived in sense, they are not allowed to remain single and separate in the mind, just as the sense has taken them. A farther operation succeeds, and a ground is thought in which they inhere, and the single phenomena become thus known as the connected qualities of a common substance. The redness, the fragrance, the smoothness, etc., which have been separately attained by different senses, are successively thought into one thing, and the mind forms the several judgments that the *rose* is red, and is fragrant, and is smooth, etc. And so, also, with the distinct and definite inner phenomena. The thought, emotion, volition, etc., are successively connected in their common source as the exercises of one and the same agent; and thus the successive judgments are formed that the *mind* thinks, and feels, and wills. A common subject is thought for the qualities, and a common source for the changes, and they become thus connected as substance and qualities, cause and events. And still farther, the different substances are also thought as standing in communion together, and reciprocally influencing each other; and causes and events are thought as produced the one from the other, and thus in dependence; and in this way, the cohering things and the adhering changes are all connected together in one nature, and judged so to inhere with each other through space and time, that they all together make the universe.

The permanent substance, in which the qualities are thought to inhere, is no perception of the sense, and can be gained by no analysis or generalization of that which sense has perceived, but is itself wholly a new conception in the understanding. As distinct from *phenomenon*, it may be termed *notion*. The former is perceived in the sense, the latter is thought in the understanding. The notion is made to *stand under* the phenomena and connect them into itself, and the intellectual faculty which performs this connecting operation, is properly known as the *understanding*.

The genesis of the understanding-conception, as notion, may be apprehended as follows: Some external thing is supposed to have occasioned the impression made upon the organ, which induced a sensation; and then this sensation, and not the thing that made the impression, is taken up by an intellectual operation which distinguishes and defines it, and thereby makes it to appear complete in consciousness; and thus the phenomenon is solely the mode, in which the external thing has revealed itself in the sense. This external thing, thus making itself to be known in the sense only by its phenomenal qualities, is thought to be the ground of these qualities. Inasmuch as it cannot appear, it can be no phenomenon; but inasmuch as it is necessarily thought as the ground of the phenomenon, it is notion, and stands under the phenomenon. We thus call it *substance* (*sub stans*).

This substance, in the thought, is that which has separately given to the different organs their particular phenomena; and these are connected, in the judgment, as the several qualities all inhering in the substance. The substance cannot appear, and therefore the connecting operation cannot be in the light of consciousness, as was the constructing act of attention in the sense. The knowing of the understanding cannot therefore be intuitive. Each separate phenomenon is severally brought to the common substance and connected with all the others in it, and by this *discursus* of the thought through the common substance, the knowing of the qualities as inhering in it is *discursive*. The connection of quality and substance is not perceived, but is thought.

Again, when the qualities of the same substance alter in the sense—as when water congeals, or becomes vapor—it is thought, and not perceived, that another substance has been brought in combination with it, and so changed it as to modify its phenomena; and these new phenomena are thus known as *events*, which have come into the consciousness through the sense by this modifying *cause*. The substances do not at all appear, and therefore their modifying action cannot be perceived; but the understanding thinks this action to be the cause of the alterations of the phenomena, and brings these altered phenomena, as events, discursively to the cause and connects them in it, and thus judges them to be successive events depending upon their causes. The whole process is a thinking in judgments discursively, and not a perceiving of objects intuitively.

Lastly, when the qualities of different substances are altered reciprocally one with another—as when one body is put in motion and another body is retarded, by their contact—it is thought in the understanding that there has been an efficiency in each body, which has thus altered the phenomenon in each—on one side from rest to motion, and on the other from a given degree of motion to a slower. The substances are not themselves perceived, and therefore the action and reaction cannot be perceived; but the understanding discursively connects the begun motion and the retarded motion, in the *reciprocal efficiency* from the contact, and thinks the two events as co-etaneously occurring, and thereby judges these phenomena to cohere in the reciprocal causation.

In the use of these notions of substance, cause, and reciprocal efficiency, all separate qualities, and all events in sequence or communion, which are perceived by sense, are discursively connected into permanent things, and successive events, and cotemporaneous occurrences, according to their respective notional bonds, and are all thus bound together in a judgment which makes them to be one *Nature* of things (*a' nascor*); a growing together; a concretion; and in this an indissoluble and universal whole. What the same intellect has intuitively defined in the sense, it here discursively connects in the understanding, and thereby comes to know, in a judgment, the fleeting appearances as the altering qualities of permanent things, and these permanent things as constituting one universal nature. The knowing of the phenomena was a perceiving; and the knowing of the things, and their coalescing in one whole of nature, is a judging; and the difference of these two intellectual operations demands that they be referred to the distinct functions of two different faculties. It is the proper work of the understanding to connect the phenomena of the sense into one nature, as a universe.

It is, moreover, competent to the understanding to think in judgments, without any phenomena being given through the sense. The pure understanding can take its own empty forms, and use them as readily and as logically in all modes of connecting in judgments, as it can the actual phenomena which are given in the consciousness. This operation is in pure thought, and as thus excluding all content of sense is mere abstract thinking;

but its connected judgments from pure forms may be indefinitely comprehensive, and are as valid in their conclusions as when it is connecting appearing qualities into real things, and real things in a whole of nature. That the elements for abstract thinking may be given, there must be found several particular faculties for attaining and using them, and these faculties belong to the province of the understanding, and as mental facts for a system of psychology need to be attained at this very point of our progress. They will be given in separate sections, and the consideration of them particularly will, in the result, give a conclusive view of the whole logical process of abstract thinking. The examination of neither of them will need to be very extended.

Section I. Memory.—This is one of the most prominent, and in many respects one of the most important faculties connected with knowing. It follows perception, but is preliminary and auxiliary to all processes of thinking in judgments. When phenomena have been apprehended in clear consciousness, they do not altogether pass from the mind in vanishing from the light of consciousness, but leave what may be termed their semblance, or representative, behind them. The faculty of retaining these representatives of former perceptions is Memory; and the act of recalling them into consciousness is Recollection. The Memory differs from the Fancy in this—that the former retains only the representatives of perceptions; the latter constructs new forms, and modifies old recollections into new combinations. The Memory is *the faculty for retain-*

ing representatives of whatever has once been in the consciousness. Not the *phenomenon* perceived is retained, so that the recollection is but a repeated perception; but only the *representative* of the phenomenon is the object in memory. When I perceive the house, the horse, etc., a real content in sensation is given; but when I recall these up in memory, the sensation does not return, and only the resemblance of the once perceived house, or horse, comes into the consciousness.

All objects of consciousness are not recollected, inasmuch as the sufficient occasion for recalling their resemblance does not occur. But it may well be believed that every fact in consciousness has left its modification upon the mind, so that it cannot again be as if that fact had not occurred; and that an occasion of sufficient excitement might be given, by which its recollection would be secured. Remarkable instances sometimes occur, where, from some preternatural excitement, almost the whole transactions of a long life are vividly again spread out in the consciousness. Those facts that have been the most clear, and especially those that have been connected with the deepest feeling, and more especially those also that have called out the will and become matters of practical interest, will be the most readily recollected. An act of will may favor the act of recollection, by affording the most favorable occasions for it, but in all cases the recollecting act is itself spontaneous, and not a volition. Oftentimes the man is conscious, that no effort of will can secure the sufficient occasion for a specific recollection. Those facts, also, which at the time of occurrence

12

were more carefully noted, and such as have been orderly arranged in reference to their being retained, will be recalled with the greater facility. But artificial methods for helping the memory, by arbitrary associations and combinations, are of very questionable general utility.

Mere memory is not knowledge; it is not perception, nor thinking in judgments. It is the retention of so much of former things known, that they may again be called up and made materials for thought; and, through the proper processes of the intellect, elaborated into science. Without memory, the mind could neither attain its elements for logical or philosophical thinking, nor pass from particular conclusions to such as are more general. The thoughts, and the order of the thinking, would both be wanting. While mere memory is of little worth, however retentive, yet the strongest minds often falter, and even utterly fail, from the deficiencies of memory.

Section II. Conception.—When, in fancy, I have constructed any mental object, or group of objects, I have that in consciousness which may be called a *phantasm*. When, in attention, I construct a real sensation into a definite object, I have in consciousness a *phenomenon*. When I recall either of these in recollection, I have a remembrance of them in a *representative*. This representative from memory has been sometimes termed a conception, and which is nothing but a remembered perception; but a faculty for attaining conceptions is quite other than the faculty of memory.

When I have a remembered representative of an object formerly perceived, say of a house, it is the resemblance of that particular house. But I must soon have the resemblances of many particular houses, and of these the mind spontaneously makes a general scheme, which is not a resemblance of any particular house, but which includes that which is common to all houses. The general scheme embraces all of its class, while it is a resemblance in all respects to no one particular in the class. Thus, I perceive, or remember, a particular house; but I think that which is a general scheme for all houses. It is wholly an intellectual act, and belongs to the understanding, and needs only the occasion of some particulars in the memory, and its generalizing them will generate in one scheme all that can be like them. Such a generalized representative is properly termed a conception. A Conception is *that general representation which has in it all of its own class*. Thus, my conception of a triangle has within it all three-sided figures, and my conception of a quadruped has within it all four-footed animals. It can not be made to fit any particular; it *teems* with all particulars. Conceptions may be more or less generic, but must contain more than a merely remembered perception.

There is in this the whole matter of dispute between the Nominalist and the Realist of the old schoolmen; and in this also the occasion for its complete solution. The nominalist was right as against the realist, for in the generic name (quadruped) there is supposed no real animal; but the realist was also right as against the nominalist, for there is more in the generic than a mere name, even the scheme for all of that family. The proper word for all such generic representation, is that of conception, and gives the truth on both sides; excluding the real particular, and including the scheme for all particulars.

Sometimes the word conception is applied to generalizations, other than such as have their particulars in the phenomena of sense. We may think substances and causes, but cannot perceive them in consciousness; they come within the understanding, but not in the sense. They may, however, be generalized, and are thus conceptions; but they need their discriminating mark. They are *thought-conceptions*, or *understanding-conceptions:* while the former are *phenomenal* or *sense-conceptions.* We may also have conceptions of the ideal in the reason, as well as of the notional in the understanding, and such are discriminated as *reason-conceptions.* Not the substance but the thought of the substance, and not the absolute but the idea of the absolute, come within the consciousness; and as thus remembered thoughts and ideas, they may be generalized into conceptions.

Any conceptions, thus formed in a generalizing act of the understanding, are the materials for forming new judgments, and may be used by various methods of connecting in thinking, to carry the mind onwards in science to the most comprehensive conclusions.

SECTION III. ASSOCIATION.—The representatives of former objects of consciousness, when they have fallen, as it were, into the memory, do not lie in this common mental receptacle separately. They are as clusters on the vine, attached one to another by some law of connection peculiar to the case, and which has its general determination for all minds, and its particular modifications in some minds. When one is called up in recollection, it does not therefore come up singly, but brings the whole cluster along with it. This action of the mind, to attach its representatives in the memory one to another, is called association, and may include a number of different modes in which such attachments are formed. In many cases, the phenomena were together in consciousness, attached both in place and time, and their representatives have thus gone into the memory, already associated. In other cases, there is that in the one, which fits it as an occasion for the mind spontaneously to call up the other, though they may have had no previous relation in the consciousness. The likeness of one thing to another, or even the contrast of one thing with another, in quality or form, may very readily induce the calling up of one in the presence of the other. This is sometimes termed *suggestion*, but which only differs in the method and not in the kind of attachment. In other cases, again, the mind can voluntarily make itself to put its conceptions together, and associate its remembered perceptions and thoughts at its own pleasure, and thus secure an arbitrary attachment, where neither from the original reception, nor from any inherent occasion, was there any relation between them. Association differs from philosophical and logical thinking in judgments, inasmuch as in all regular thinking the conceptions become subject and predicate, and have their necessary copula as a discursive conclusion; but in association, no formal judgments are made, and no conceptions predicated one of the other, but one simply brings the other up into consciousness with itself. If we call these remembered perceptions, whether generalized into conceptions or not, by the common name of thought; Association will then be defined, *the operation of bringing up one thought into consciousness by occasion of another.*

This operation of association goes on spontaneously and perpetually. One thought introduces its fellow, and passes off from the field of consciousness, and this again introduces its successor, and thus a constant march is going on across this field, through all our waking and dreaming hours. Some minds associate by slighter, or more distant relations than others; and some thoughts introduce their successors much more rapidly than others; and thus the trains of spontaneous thought will be greatly modified in different men, even under very similar circumstances. From such different trains of thought, general habits and manners must differ among men, and the particular air, address, and characteristic demeanor, must be very much determined from the peculiarity of the mental associations. Specially must this modify the conversation, for the man's words must be an expression of his thoughts. Attachments, formed through slight, unusual and unexpected relations of thought, may make one man's conversation lively, striking, original; or, in its peculiar way, another man's, humorous, witty, figurative. The will may have much to do in regulating and controlling the association of thought, and an earnest and protracted effort may cultivate and discipline this faculty in various directions. A man may make himself a rhymer, a punster, a dealer in charades and anagrams, by certain habits of associating thoughts with words; or observing, inventive, practically effective, by certain associations of thoughts with things. An orderly and methodical train of thought may also be cultivated, by keeping the operation of this faculty under the regulations of time, place, and circumstances, so that the thought may be appropriate to the occasion.

The power of recollection is very much dependent upon the laws of association. The fact we want may lie quite submerged and lost in the memory, but if we can lay hold of some associated thought and bring that up into consciousness, the lost thought is thus found, attached to and brought up with its fellow. Our processes of generalizing must also use the faculty of association, as a direct auxiliary. We associate objects by their perceived relations, and thus readily generalize the individuals into the class, order, species, and genus, to which they belong in the conception. And all communication of thought, from man to man, must very carefully regard the principle of association. All illustration of meaning is by the introduction of such comparisons, analogies and figures of rhetoric, as the laws of association determine will bring up, and bring out, in the consciousness, the intended thought the most completely.

SECTION IV. ABSTRACTION.—The mind has the faculty to take out one, or any given number, from the cluster of its conceptions, or trains of thought, and make these the direct objects of its attention, and withdraw its attention from all other passing thoughts. It can also take any one conception, and separate any one part of it from others, and give to that part only its attention. The same is true of a real content in sensation; the mind can fix its attention on any part of it, separate from all the rest, and thus make its perception of that part more distinct and definite. Of all figures, the mind may take the triangle; from all kinds of triangles, the isoceles; and from this, any part of the same, as a side, an angle, the area, etc. From any general conception, it may also fix on a particular, and thus have both a distinct and a definite individual thought in the consciousness. All this comes under the operation of abstraction. Abstraction *is the taking of one from many, or a part from a whole, and fixing it particularly in the consciousness.* It is in fact, the taking of a generalization to pieces, or the detaching from an association.

Abstraction is the chief operation in all analysis. It separates the many into individuals, the compounded into simples, and the total into its parts. No mind can know clearly and accurately without exercising vigorously this power of abstraction. Thoughts must be considered singly; things must be examined in detail; the mind must be able to detach its attention from all others, and hold itself to the particular point, patiently and protractedly, or its knowledge will ever be confused and obscure.

SECTION V. REFLECTION.—When the mind *turns back* upon its passing train of conceptions, and takes up any one for more deliberate examination, it is termed an act of *reflection*. The onward spontaneous flow of thought would continue uninterrupted, in the order determined by the laws of association, did there not occur occasions for arresting the march and holding some one passing thought to a more particular and extended operation of the mind upon it. It may be for analysis, for determining its philosophical or logical connections, or for using it to illustrate some other conception by comparison or contrast; but for whatever end it may be, such a return upon the track of passing thought is an exercise of the faculty of reflection. The occasion for it may be given in many things of which at the time we took no notice, and thus many a time the mind is found earnestly at work in reflective thought, when the occasion for it cannot be recalled. At other times it is occasioned by a deliberate purpose, and the man determinedly puts his mind back upon some portion of his former experience, and is thus said to intently reflect upon it.

The habit of reflection is always with difficulty attained. All things conspire to induce the onward flow of associated thought, and any occasion which interrupts the current is felt as an obstacle intruding itself into the placid stream, and violently disturbing its wonted serenity. Severe mental discipline is always demanded for the attainment of the power of patient and protracted reflection, and yet such a control of the train of thought is a necessary condition to all clear and accurate knowledge.

Not a single conception the mind may have, can be said to be accurately and adequately known, except as it has been made the subject of steady and repeated reflection. A rapid journey through a country affords opportunity for only hasty glances; it is only by a return and more careful observation, that we know its objects accurately, and retain the knowledge permanently.

SECTION VI. JUDGMENT.—Conceptions stand singly in the mind, or attached to each other only by the laws of association, except as they are made subject to reflection. But in reflection, we not only attain the conception more completely; the mind also determines its various peculiarities. There is the general conception, and also the several characteristics which qualify it. The original conception is called the *subject*, and that which qualifies it, the *predicate*, and that which connects the two, after its particular form, the *copula;* and thus we say, the house is white; is of brick; is two stories high, etc. The conception is a thought in the understanding, and the quality is discursively predicated of it, and the intellectual process of forming such connections is *a thinking in judgments.* A Judgment *is a determined connection of two conceptions as subject and predicate.* More than two conceptions may be so thought in connection, and it will form a *compound* judgment. Affirmations in the sense differ wholly from judgments in the understanding. We sometimes speak of mathematical thinking, and of mathematical judgments, but whatever the sameness of the phraseology, we must carefully distinguish the difference of the thing. The conceptions in the sense are always definite constructions in consciousness, and we immediately behold the relation. When I say the color is a square figure; the sound is at a distance; or the radii of the same circle are equal; I can *intuitively* apprehend, in an immediate construction, the relation of these predicates to their subjects, and I do not at all *think* them. But my conception of house, as subject of the predicates above, cannot be constructed; it must be notion, and not phenomenon; thought, and not perceived: and thus the connection of its predicates can be *discursive* only, not *intuitive*. We have here to do with judgments in the understanding, not affirmations in the sense.

Thinking in judgments is of *two kinds*, and of *three varieties*. The kinds differ in the manner of attaining the predicates; the varieties differ in the forms of the copula. The *kinds* of judgment are:—

1. *Analytical judgments*.—The manner of attaining the predicates is, here, by an analysis. The conception, as subject, is taken, and an analysis made of it into its several parts, and these are connected as predicates of the subject, and thus form the particular judgments respecting it. The general conception of body may be taken as an example, and from a mere mental analysis, I can find in the conception of body, extension, figure, impenetrability, divisibility, etc., and can say, all bodies are extended, have shape, are impenetrable, are divisible, etc., and thus predicate of body all its primary qualities. Or the conception may be of something that experience

has given to us with all its ascertained characteristics. Thus of the conception of man, as experience has revealed him, we can by an analysis say of all men, that they are intelligent; rational; responsible; mortal, as to the body; and immortal as to the soul, etc. The analysis may thus take out all that has been put into the conception, and predicate each analytical conception of the original subject. All such judgments are analytical.

An analytical judgment does not at all enlarge the field of knowledge, for all the predicates, ultimately made, were already given in the original conception. I have made my knowledge more distinct, more detailed, but not more extensive by my multiplied judgments. The method of analytical judgments is especially demanded for all conceptions that are obscure, perplexed, confused, or complicated. The analysis, carefully made, lays open the whole conception, and the consecutive judgments thus formed determine at length all the characteristics of the subject.

2. *Synthetical judgments.*—When we attain some new conception, and can predicate that of some other conception already possessed, we add so much to our knowledge of that conception, and the judgment is thus much extended beyond any former judgment of that subject. All such are synthetical judgments. The new conception to be predicated of the former one may be attained in various ways, and the judgment formed will be as valid as has been made the possession of the new fact. Thus, to all that I may get from an analysis of body in its primary qualities, and to all that former

experience has attained in the conception of some peculiar body, as gold, and which may be analytically predicated of it, I may enlarge my experiments and find what before had not been observed. To the yellowness, incorruptibility, malleability, etc., of gold, I may attain and add the surprising new fact that it is soluble in *aqua regia*, and I shall then predicate this new fact of all gold. Or from the patient induction of Newton, in attaining the new fact of the law of gravity, we may take another example of a synthetic judgment in henceforth affirming, that all matter gravitates towards all other matter, directly as its quantity, and inversely as the square of the distance. So also, in the conception of all phenomena of sense. I may some way attain the thought of a permanent substance, and can then predicate this new thought of the phenomenal, and say, all phenomena must have their permanent substance; or farther, I may attain the conception of causality, and then say, all events must have their cause, etc.

The validity of the experimental judgment is tested in the validity of the new fact discovered, but the validity of the notional judgment in the predicating of substance and cause for all phenomenal facts, cannot be tested by any experience. The substance and cause do not come up into consciousness in any experience, and can only be thought and not perceived. Such synthetical judgments are perpetually made, and we rest all our natural science upon their validity, but we cannot make these judgments to be science, except through Rational Psychology. All natural philosophy, and all inductive science, rest only on assumption, until, in Rational Psychology, we have laid the basis for demonstrating the validity of the law of substance and cause. But all synthetical judgments add thus new predicates, and augment the knowledge as much, and as validly, as the newly attained conception reaches. Synthetical judgments are the only ones that can be employed in invention and discovery. All progress in knowledge must be through their intervention.

The *varieties* of judgments, and which depend upon the forms of copulation, are as follows:—

1. *Categorical judgments.*—These directly affirm or deny the connection of subject and predicate. The former is an *Affirmative* categorical judgment, as—the sun shines; the rose is red, etc. The latter is a *Negative* categorical judgment, as—the sun has not set; the man is not dead, etc.

2. *Hypothetical judgments.*—These present the copula under a condition or limitation, as—if the sun shine, it will be warm: so far as reason goes, responsibility follows, etc.

3. *Disjunctive judgments.*—These subject the copula to one or more alternatives, as—either the fire, or the sun, warms me; either the world is eternal, or it has originated in chance, or God made it.

There are other modifications of judgments given in logical formulæ, and which distinctions may all have their use for various purposes there occurring; but the above is here sufficient, for the general fact of judgments in the understanding. The process of thinking in reflection is to determine these connections of conceptions, and to find how one may be predicated of the other.

SECTION VII. SYLLOGISTIC CONCLUSION.—To any comprehensive judgment may be applied the principle, that what has been found true of the whole must also be true of all the parts. In this, an occasion is at once given for arranging conceptions in the order of the syllogism, and attaining to particular judgments. The first, or comprehensive judgment, is termed the *major premiss;* the second, or induced judgment, is termed the *minor premiss;* and the third, or deduced judgment, is termed *the conclusion.* As an example we have—

Major premiss—Heat expands all metals.
Minor premiss—Iron is a metal.
Conclusion—Heat expands iron.

The form of the major and minor premiss may be of either the Categorical, Hypothetical, or Disjunctive judgments, and the syllogism will vary accordingly. The one already given is in a categorical form, and a hypothetical is as follows:—

If man is immortal; and
If a Hottentot be a man; then
The Hottentot is immortal.

Or disjunctively—

Man is bound in fate, or he is free.
Man is not bound in fate.
Therefore man is free.

All comprehensive judgments may thus take on the form of the syllogism, and though no augmentation of knowledge can be attained by it, since the major premiss already contains all that can be distributed in the conclusion, yet may the validity of particular judgments be thus determined. The conclusion is made distinct from all that is comprehended in the major premiss, by reason of the interposition of the judgment in the middle term, or minor premiss.

The content of the judgment may be altogether abstracted, and the empty form of it maintained in names that signify nothing, and yet the conclusion is as validly determined in the syllogism, as when the conceptions had been themselves supplied—

Thus—A is modified by X.
But B, is contained in A.
Therefore B, is modified by X.

It is to be distinctly noticed that all syllogisms must be founded on some comprehensive judgment, and the validity of the conclusion can rise no higher than the validity of the judgment in the major premiss. But to establish its validity, we need to attain it as a conclusion from some more comprehensive judgment in a higher syllogism. An endless series of syllogisms may thus arise, and must even be demanded for the absolute validity of any conclusion. The logical understanding can arise to absolute truth only by an infinity of syllogisms. With all the precision of the most exact logic, the understanding must hold on in its endless march, and can never hang its last syllogism on the confirmed hook of an absolute premiss. It must at last convict itself of the sophistry of a *petitio principii*. Its stately march from syllogism to pro-syllogism may be called *reasoning*, but until it knows how to employ reason in attaining universal and necessary principles, the reasoning has no root in reason, and is mere logical deduction from assumed premisses.

SECTION VIII. INDUCTION.—The *deductive* syllogism, just above given, is properly analytic, and proceeds from the whole to its parts. It is the true and proper form of logical syllogism. But there is a directly reversed form which may be used, and which can never come within the deductive process. This is the process of *inductive* reasoning, and is wholly synthetical, proceeding from the parts to the whole. Its validity depends upon the principle, that what is true of all the parts is true of the whole.

The form of the inductive reasoning is a perfectly inverted syllogism, having the major premiss of a deductive syllogism as its conclusion. As a *deductive* syllogism we say—

Major premiss—B is the same as A.
Minor premiss—x, y, z, are the whole of B.
Conclusion—x, y, z, are all the parts of A.

But as an *inductive* form, we say—

First term—x, y, z, are the parts which make A.
Middle term—But x, y, z, are the whole of B.
Conclusion—B is equal to A.

As a logical formula, the inductive is as valid as the deductive, and wherever it may be strictly applied, the inductive will give a valid judgment, in its conclusion, for the major premiss of a deductive syllogism. It might thus appear, that a pro-syllogism absolutely valid would in this way be attained for our analytic logic, and relieve from the necessity of perpetually going back without finding an absolutely valid major premiss. Get such major premiss from an inductive process. But, precisely in this is the impracticability of relief from an inductive logic. The empty logical form is perfectly valid, but in practical application the logical form cannot be followed. The end sought is, to reach an absolutely universal and necessary judgment; and, as this can never be attained by climbing the endless ladder of an analytic logic, it is now sought to effect it, by the interposition of a synthetic judgment in inductive reasoning. The valid form demands *all* the parts of the universal, and this is of impracticable attainment; and thus all its conclusions, practically, are wholly illogical. The inductive syllogism practically would be—for an instance—

First premiss—Heat expands z, y, x, w, etc.

Middle term—z, y, x, w, etc., are all the parts of universal things.

Conclusion—Heat expands all things.

Were the whole alphabet included in the induction, without an etc., the logical form would be filled, and the concluding judgment valid; but so long as it is impracticable to include the universal in our middle term, we can not make the valid universal conclusion. No inductive process can thus reach to absolute truth, nor find the necessary and universal judgment, on which to hang the chain of deductive conclusions, in an analytic logical process. The logical understanding is thus doomed to an endless tread-mill process, and can find no landing stair above, and no stepping off from the stairs beneath. No swing from deduction to induction relieves the ceaseless tread, for the induction of universals is yet endless.

All inductive logic, therefore, rests as completely upon assumption, as does the deductive, and the whole validity of the judgment is, that in making the broader induction there is an increase of probabilities. But even this is in the exclusion of the higher faculty of reason. To the logical understanding, the probabilities of uniformity in nature are the result solely of a subjective habit. The understanding knows what *has* been experienced, but has no ground to determine what *must* be, and thus no right to conclude what its future experience shall be, except only that long habit in finding things thus induces the credulous expectation that they will continue thus. The inferring of a law of nature, from any past uniformity, is evidently rising to a supernatural that controls nature, and is quite above the province of a logical understanding, to which the ongoings of experience can be nothing but a series of sequences; the antecedent and the consequent having no conceived necessity of connection. Did not induction assume more than the logical understanding can reach, its widest generalizations would never amount to other than a mere habitual expectation for the future, and which, in the last analysis, would be solely this—that we have become so accustomed to a certain uniformity, it would now be uncomfortable to us that it should be interrupted.

A *true* induction uses the higher faculty, and fixes its hold upon the reason. It cognizes that nature has laws, and its whole questioning of nature is to the end of finding them. Hence it never goes forth to any promiscuous collection of facts, but always with hypothesis in hand, fitting this on to every fact it examines, and only trying this upon such facts as the very hypothesis itself demands should exactly fit into its archetypal conditions. Did not reason *a' priori* determine that nature has laws, and thus prompt to the adoption of some hypothesis what the law in a given class of facts is, the logical understanding would never set out on its errand of induction, and strive to gather so large a share of the parts as might give plausibility to the inference what, in fact, is the law for the whole. In the absence of complete universality in the induction, mere logical processes are worthless sophistries. Tried by the logical formula, they amount solely to the following:—

First term—x, constitutes A.

Middle term—1, 2, 3, 4, constitute an indefinite portion of x.

Conclusion—1, 2, 3, 4, constitute A.

The syllogistic conclusion, therefore, whether deductive or inductive, can never give absolute judgments. The deductive can never say the major premiss is proved; the inductive can never say the universal has been reached.

SECTION IX. IMAGINATION.—There is often no other signification given to the term imagination, than that which the word itself implies—the faculty for making images. But this is not an adequate conception of the imagination in its strict meaning, unless we retain the image-making within the domain of the understanding. The purely sense constructions are properly images, so far as outline and shape can be an image; but such image-making is properly fancy, and not imagination. A product of the true imagination must be vivified with thought. It must be an image which has a concrete being, and has grown into completeness in the conception that active forces operate all through it. It is no empty form, nor a mere dead form; but stands forth with its own inherent efficiency, competent to exist and to act as a power amid the sphere of substantial things. If it use pure forms, as in geometry, they are put together in view of an end, and have thus the connection of thought through all their construction and arrangement. If it use the conceptions of sensible phenomena, it puts them together for some end of utility, or beauty, or science; and the whole grouping is no fantastic arrangement, but made consistent through an intelligent design. Its products can always be expounded by some law of order, and all the parts are made to subserve the general bearing of the whole intention. The image is in this way a complete, self-consistent production, competent to evince both what it is, and why it is, and why thus and not otherwise.

When the connecting of the image into one whole is an original invention, and the product of spontaneous thinking, the faculty is known as the *productive* imagination; when it is fashioned after some former model, or made the likeness of some already existing thing, it is called the *re-productive* imagination. The distinction between fancy and imagination is as broad as between the sense and the understanding. Fancy is the work of a *conjoining* operation, and imagination of a *connecting* operation; while one merely appears, the other embodies thought. A fanciful dress merely strikes the sense; imagination puts thought into it, and makes it to express some conformity to character and circumstance. Fancy may be pleased with a mere jingle of sharp sounds; imagination will be interestingly intent to what is going on in the sounds, and making out the meaning of the tune they embody.

CHAPTER III.

THE REASON.

THE faculties for knowing in the sense and the understanding might be fully given, and be in perfect exercise, but neither one nor both of them could give the capacity for studying themselves, and coming to a knowledge of the laws and principles of their own working. The intellect in the sense would perpetually employ itself in the operations of distinguishing the qualities, and defining their quantities, and its life would be wholly absorbed within its own perceptions. With the higher faculty of an understanding superinduced, the intellect would farther employ itself in connecting these perceptions into judgments, and think the fleeting phenomena to be the qualities of substances and the effects of causes, and thus wholly absorb itself in perceiving phenomena and judging them to belong to one nature of things. Or, the understanding might shut itself in upon itself, and exhaust all its operation in the logical processes of abstract thinking, and live on wholly absorbed in deducing formal conclusions from empty conceptions.

With solely such faculties the mind would have no interest in examining how it perceived, and how it thought in judgments; for it would be faculty for perceiving and judging only, and not at all faculty for comprehending its own operations. So the animal perceives and judges;

apprehends the fleeting phenomena, and puts them together as real things; and even passes on in the logical understanding, and deduces general rules from the remembrances of past experience, and thereby learns utilities and attains to dictates of prudence; but the whole animal life is here circumscribed, and within this sphere is exhausted all that can be called brute-knowledge. There is no faculty for *looking around* and *looking through* these processes of knowing; and as thus without *comprehension* and *insight*, the brute has no impulse to study its own mental operations, nor to attain any science of its own facts of knowing, or of the objects given in its knowledge. So man would intuitively behold the objects of sense, and discursively think the objects of an understanding, and with these faculties only would know the appearances and connections of nature; but there could be no oversight nor insight of either himself or of nature, and therefore no interest nor capacity for philosophizing in reference to either.

But man is not thus restricted in faculty. He has the capacity to attain principles which were prior to any faculty of the sense or of the understanding, and without which neither a faculty of sense nor of understanding could have had its being; principles strictly *a' priori* conditional for both faculties; and in the light of these principles he has an insight into both sense and understanding, and can carry his mind's eye all around, and all through, the processes of both perceiving and judging, and thereby make his knowledge to include the processes of intelligence itself. He can philosophize about both the knowing, and the things known, and in this way his knowing becomes truly *science*. This higher capacity is THE REASON. It differs in kind from either the sense or the understanding, and is no merely higher degree of knowing through some improvement of the same faculty, but is wholly another kind of knowing, and demanding for itself the recognition of an entirely distinct intellectual faculty. That agency which *limits* cannot thereby *connect*, nor can either of these in the same function *comprehend*.

The determination of the process by which both the sense and the understanding, and indeed all intelligence, are apprehended, belongs exclusively to Rational Psychology. The *principles* conditional for all knowledge can not be given in any experience, and cannot therefore properly belong to Empirical Psychology; but the *operations* of reason in the use of such principles come within the consciousness, and so far the facts of the reason are the proper elements of an empirical science. The operations of the reason affect the mind, and induce an inward sensation, which gives a content for the inner sense, as truly as any exercise of either the faculty of the sense or of the understanding; and this content in the inner sense, from the exercise of reason, may be distinguished and defined and thus brought clearly into the light of consciousness, as readily as any other inner sensation. The reason must thus attain its necessary and universal *principles* by its own insight, and not by experience, and all such attainment and investigation of principles belong wholly to a transcendental science; but as attained and applied, the *results* and *convictions* induced become matters of fact, and our knowledge by the reason, of that which was conditional for experience, is in this knowledge, as a result, made to be a fact of experience.

That the results of the operation of reason come, thus, within consciousness, will secure a modification of all our experience. Our reason will affect our experience in every faculty. Neither sense nor understanding, as faculties of knowing, nor the capacity for feeling, nor that of willing, can be the same in the presence as in the absence of a rational constitution. The higher light of reason will reveal its results, and as these become facts in experience, they will at once modify all other facts in the consciousness. The human mind, as rational, must know, feel, and will, quite differently from brute mind, even where they participate in the same common faculties. That which is animal can be distinguished in the consciousness from that which is rational; and the modifications, which the presence of the rational makes in the animal experience, may also be distinctly apprehended; and it is this fact of the universal modification of the experience by the reason, which makes it so important to discriminate the reason from all other mental faculties. A true psychology cannot otherwise be attained, for some of its most important facts cannot otherwise be apprehended. It will sufficiently appear hereafter, how extensively the rational endowment modifies human feeling and will; it needs here to be made apparent how the reason affects the sense and the understanding. It will also be necessary, so far as the facts appear in consciousness, to determine its operation in its own field, and thus attain its original and specific peculiarities. This may be clearly, and at the same time concisely affected.

SECTION I. THE REASON MODIFIES THE SENSE AND THE UNDERSTANDING.—In the sense we perceive, and from our endowment of reason our *perceptions* are greatly modified. In the inner sense there is the perception of mental phenomena, and all these are limited in their periods. In the external sense, we perceive outer objects, and these are limited in their places and periods. Were there nothing but sense, we should construct only as the sensations were given, and as conditioned by the sensations, and should thus have defined places and periods precisely where and when we should have definite phenomena. Our spaces would be as the places of the phenomena, and our times would be as the periods of the phenomena. When the object of perception was gone, its space and its time would have gone with it; and the next phenomenon would be a new construction in a new place and period, and thus in a new space and time, and which would also be as evanescent as the perception of the object. It would be space and time just so far as the construction defined them, and only within these limits could anything of space and time be known. Both space and time would be lost from the consciousness, when the phenomenon had passed out of the consciousness. Space would be, to mere sense, like space in a mirror, wholly indeterminate and uncognizable except as the phenomena were given in it; and time would be like time in a dream, all gone so soon as the objects in the dream were gone from the consciousness. Space and time cannot themselves become phenomena, and be perceived, and the places and periods are constructed only in the defining of the sensations given, and thus the mere sense can give no more of space and time than the places and periods of its perceived objects. With only sense as faculty of knowledge, the recognition of space as one whole of space, and all places as parts of this one space immoveable within it—and so, the recognition of time as one whole of all time, and the periods as parts of this one time each fixed in its own order of occurrence—would be impossible. To the mere animal, the conception of pure space and pure time separately from all objects perceived, must be an utter impracticability.

But the insight of reason determines at once the universal necessity, that the space and the time must first have been, or the objects perceived could not have been, for there would have been neither place nor period for them. The sense attains its space and time in attaining its places and periods, and these are attained only in the apprehension of the objects; but the reason determines its space and time for itself quite irrespective of the objects, for it *a' priori* sees that the objects perceived could not have been, but on the condition that their places in space and their periods in time had first been. The sense-space-and-time is through experience; the reason-space-and-time is independent of all experience, for it must first have been, as condition that any experience can be. In the sense, space and time are the contingent and transient places and periods of passing phenomena; but in the reason, space and time are the necessary and immutable, the universal and eternal conditions of all place and period for any phenomenon. The insight of reason penetrates the very act of perception, and determines what it is, and what is conditional that it could have been, and thus comprehends both perception and the phenomena given in it; and thereby determines for every object a whole of space, of which the place it occupies is an immoveable part, and also a whole of time, of which the period it occupies is an unalterable portion. No mere abstracting of phenomena can give a whole of space and of time; for the phenomena have given each its own place and period only, and the place and period as wholly conditioned by the phenomenon; and should the phenomenon be abstracted, its place and period would fall away from the sense with it, and leave nothing of either space or time for the consciousness. By the light of reason upon all the operations of our senses, our perceptions of objects come to be in place and period not only, but in a place which is a determined portion of one whole space, and in a period which is a determined portion of one whole time. We perceive objects, and know them to have a determinate place in the one space, and a determinate period in the one time. So different is perception to a mind with reason from a mind without it!

And so also, in the understanding we think, and from our endowment of reason our *judgments* become greatly modified. The mere action of the understanding would think the phenomena perceived in one place and period to be connected in one common ground, and thus make them to be the qualities of a common substance, and would know the aggregate qualities and substance as one thing. And so, moreover, it would think any alteration of these phenomena, as originating in some change in the substance induced by the working of some efficiency upon it, and trace all observed alterations in the same thing up to the source of some efficiency working upon the substance, and would thus know the changes as dependent upon their cause. As experience goes on, it would perpetuate this thinking in judgments, and connect all phenomena into things, and all changes into their causes, and thus perpetuate a determined order of experience as the series of events pass onward through the consciousness. But such connections of phenomena and events would be effected no farther than the phenomena and their changes occurred in the perceptions of sense. All the material thus afforded in perception would be worked up into things, and causal series, by the understanding; but the connecting operation would be effected only as the occasion was afforded in the objects perceived. The remembrances of the past would induce its expectations of the future, and an animal sagacity might arise that would observe prudential considerations in adapting itself to the anticipated occurrences. But the present connections and the anticipated occurrences would all stand in the occasions furnished by the experience of the senses. The judgment would find all its data from the perceptions actually occurring, and would thus be exclusively a thinking and judging according to sense. Those phenomena, which came together in one place and period would be thought as connected in one thing, and those events, which came together in one order of succession, would be thought as connected in a series of causes and effects; but no judgment of a substance or a cause would arise as conditioning the phenomena and the events, and only as suggested or implied in the phenomena and events themselves. All is posterior to the perception, occasioned by it, and conditioned upon it, and taken as a conclusion from it. The whole thinking and judging is prompted from the perceiving, and has no impulse nor guide beyond the facts as exactly given in the sense itself. So the connections are, but nothing determines why they so are.

But in the possession of reason, the human mind has this judgment in experience, not only, but a judgment over experience, determining how this must be. By its own insight into sensation as a fact, it determines for it that it must be a product, and that antecedently to an impression upon the organ of sense something already is, or that impression could not be. It determines that the mode in which this something exists must condition what the affection, and thus what the content in sense shall be; and consequently, that all changes in the organic affection, and thereby all alteration of the phenomena perceived, must have had their previous changes in that substantial something which produced the organic impression. It thus determines that a substance is conditional for all phenomena, and that a cause, inducing some change in the substance, is conditional for all alteration in the phenomena; and hereby comprehends, universally, phenomena in their substances, and changes in their causes. The reason truly penetrates the understanding itself, and determines what is conditional for all thinking in judgments. It concludes not merely, as in the understanding simply, that the manner of the appearance indicates a common ground for the phenomena, and also a common source for the events; but more than this, that the phenomena could not have been, had not their substance previously existed, and the changes in those phenomena could not have been had not their cause previously existed. In the light of the reason the judgment is modified from this—that these qualities belong to a substance; and these new events depend upon a cause—and becomes the necessary and universal judgment which no experience can give—that all quality must have a substance; and all events must have their cause. It is not the judgment, solely in experience, that the perceived qualities determine for the percipient what the thing is, and that the perceived events determine for the percipient what the cause is; but that this substantial thing has permanently existed and determined what its qualities shall be, and the successive causes have previously energized and determined what the events shall be. The substance has perdured from the beginning, and all its altered qualities have inhered in it; and the causes have operated in an unbroken series, and all the changed events have adhered to them. All phenomena are thus comprehended, through all time, in their permanent substances and successive causes.

SECTION II. THE INSIGHT OF REASON FINDS A SUPERNATURAL IN NATURE, AND COMPREHENDS NATURE BY THIS SUPERNATURAL.—Substances are modified by contact or combination with each other, and this occasions corresponding modifications of impression upon the organs of sense; and, thus, in the ongoing modifications of substances, old phenomena are continually passing away and new phenomena perpetually coming in to the human experience. The present perceived phenomena find the conditions of their being in the proximate preceding changes of the substances, and the phenomena preceding these changes had their conditions in the next antecedent changes, and thus backward in all the indefinite series of change. This linked succession in its adhesions is Nature, and involves a perpetual progress of conditioning and conditioned, as nature goes onward, and a perpetual regress of conditioned and conditioning, as nature is explored backward. The one substance, which now appears in the grape, may successively appear in the phenomena of the expressed juice, the fermented wine, the acetous fermented vinegar, etc.; and in the same way, with all the changing substances and their events in nature. The onward changes must be thought as a conditioned and determined order of progress. The onward march can never cease, nor vary its order or direction, for the present is conditioned by the past, and conditions all the future. No attempt to follow back the order can ever reach to an unconditioned, for the very law of thought, in an understanding, is the connecting through some notional efficiency, and the highest point attained must still be as it is, because it is so conditioned by something going before it.

The most subtle and profound German thinking has found no way to leap these barriers. Its, so called, absolute thought is still strictly conditioned thought. The Hegelian process of development is by perpetual duplications and identifications of the thought—going out from absolute being, through origination, into determined existence, and thence into being *pro se*, etc., etc.—but is still as thoroughly determined through all the process by antecedent conditions as the materialism of the French Encyclopedists. The ideal Spirit, as original in this process of development, is utterly misnamed the Absolute, for he is bound ever more to continual repetitions of himself in the living act of progress. The *free* thought, as it is termed, is free only in this, that it makes its own limits and annuls them, and in this free process of making and annulling its own limitation, it holds on in its progress of development by a necessary law. Just as the vital spirit in the germ, by its living act, goes out into the bud and limits itself by it, and then annuls the bud, and its limitation in it, by positing the bud in the permanent blade, and thus the tree grows as the bud is perpetually both produced and also left stated in the stock; even so does the world-spirit develop itself, and in its eternal living action, limiting and annulling the limitation of itself, nature grows, and the universe is in constant becoming and remaining. There is no absolute, for the only supernatural is the intrinsic spiritual life of nature herself. So true is it, that the most athletic logical thought, in chase of the unconditioned being, leaves even his conception altogether unapproachable. In its highest ascent, its movement is still discursive, and it is forced to connect the present, by some medium, with the past, and its highest conception of an originating act is precisely the same as that of every subsequent progressing act—a so called absolute spirit, existing only in the perpetual activity of a negation and affirmation of itself. Is man's highest faculty of knowing, that of the logical understanding? then is the conclusion of Sir William Hamilton impregnable—"the human mind can never know the unconditioned." We cannot look beyond the prison-walls of nature. An absolute being is inconceivable. If we assume to worship in any other than nature's temple, we must "worship we know not what," and inscribe our altars "to the unknown God."

But it is itself a perpetual demonstration against this conclusion, that the human mind never gave its submissive assent to it. However entangled and fettered by its logic, it has ever fought up against the delusion, and resisted that sophistry which would hold it down by a perpetual affirmation that its first must still be conditioned to a higher. All the grave injunctions to humility, and distrust of human faculties, are here impertinently applied. It is no impulse from pride, and conceit of false philosophy, which so untiringly resists all attempts to make the mind ignore the being of its God. To reason's eye, "his eternal power and Godhead" are "clearly seen in the things that are made." With no attempt to comprehend the Absolute himself, the human mind does comprehend universal nature in the Absolute, and stays its own conscious dependence upon him. The reason, by its insight into nature, determines for nature an absolute Author and Finisher. There is no attempt to attain the Absolute from the conditioned processes of logical thought; but, inasmuch as human reason knows itself, and in this, knows also what is due to itself, and is thus a law to itself; so it knows that the Absolute Spirit must have within himself his own rule, and stand forever *absolved* from all rule and authority imposed upon himself by another. In this is the complete idea of a personal, absolute Jehovah, competent to originate action in himself, without its being caused in him by a higher efficiency. The existence of such a being, the human reason is constrained to see in his works, and to know him as creator of nature, and the governor and user of nature at his own pleasure. When the logical understanding would run up the endless series of conditioned connections, the reason cuts short the vain chase, and interposes the clear conception of the self-sufficient originator of being, and in him finds a beginning, and in him also a sovereign guidance to a foreseen termination; and thus encompasses and comprehends the processes of nature, in an absolute Being who has begun and will also make an end. What, to the mere understanding, must be an endless series, with no possibility to reach a first nor to forecast an ultimate, has thus, in the comprehending reason, become a work and a providence; the creature of an independent and self-existent creator; and in this absolute creator the human mind finds its God, and owns its rightful allegiance.

SECTION III. THE REASON ATTAINS ITS OWN IDEALS OF ABSOLUTE PERFECTION.—When any phenomenon is apprehended in the sense, there may be made an abstraction of all that was a content in sensation, and there will thus remain in the consciousness only the pure form which the attending operation had constructed. This pure form is limit and outline only, and has in it no contained quality. The fancy, also, may construct any such pure forms originally from itself, without any previous content in sensation, and may so modify the outline and shading in space as to represent any figure in nature, or to give new figures of its own construction which have no patterns in nature. The mind may thus amuse itself in a perpetual sense-play of abstractions or fanciful productions; taking the forms off from nature, imitating the forms in nature, or constructing wholly new forms of its own. Such are the forms, when given in colors, that interest children, savages, and all uncultivated minds. Such, also, are mainly the forms, a little more chastened by the judgment, which appear in calico-prints, curtains, carpets, etc. Such a mere sense-play interests only as successful imitation, or as presenting some striking novelty. At the highest, it is only a chastened fancy and has within it no meaning, inasmuch as there is nothing of the insight of reason, and thus nothing properly rational.

But our inward emotions give themselves out in certain forms, and passions express themselves in peculiarly delineated features, or in specially modulated tones. The insight of reason directly detects the feeling in the form, and finds the hidden meaning uttering itself through the arranged measure. It is thenceforth no mere fancy-sketch and sense-play, but living sentiment; the dead form is now quickened by the presence of an inner spirit. The image, the picture, the tune, are all inspired; and in this insight of reason we immediately commune with a beating heart and a glowing soul, under that which the sense has presented to us as empty form. The sense can construct the measures and outlines; the understanding can arrange these constructions, according to experimental convenience and utility in attaining its ends; but the reason, only, reads the living sentiment embodied in the form, and discloses the hidden meaning of each peculiarity of modulated tone and delineated figure. This utterance of human sentiment in sensible forms gives *beauty;* and when the disclosed sentiment is that of a superhuman spirit, and we stand awe-struck in the presence of an angel or a divinity, the beauty rises proportionally and elevates itself to *the sublime.*

And now, the reason, in its insight, reads the hidden sentiment expressed in all the forms of art and nature, not only; but in its own creative power, it originates the pure forms which enshrine the particular sentiment the most perfectly, and in these attains a beauty or a sublimity which is wholly its own, and can reveal itself to no other eye. This pure form, created by its own genius, which fullest and highest enshrines the intended sentiment, is the *absolute* beauty; the beauty, to that creating reason, which is unsubjected to, and wholly absolved from, the determining measures of any applied standard; and which, as the *beau ideal*, will itself measure and criticise every other form it may find in art or nature. We may say that the artist "studies nature;" or, even that he "copies nature;" but we do not mean correctly by this, that he goes hunting experimentally through nature till he finds the right particular pattern, which he takes off, and henceforth makes to be his guage and measuring rod for all other forms of beauty. He could not so study nature and select his copy, were it not true that he already had his own archetype, which told him how to study and where to copy nature. The nature he studies and copies is that which is *nascent* in the sphere of reason, and by which he can determine when nature itself is natural, and of all her beauties can say which is most conformed to the higher archetypal nature. This is ΤΟ ΚΑΛΟΝ, THE BEAUTIFUL: comprehending within it all that is beauty.

So also, in all arrangements and combinations after the guiding direction of a principle that puts every element in organic unity with the whole, and thereby makes it an organized system, reason has its insight that immediately catches the hidden truth, and philosophically reads and expounds the whole combination. There is an *idea* which runs all through it, and determines every part of it, and in the accordance of such idea in the mind with such an *in*forming law in the system, there is *truth;* and such truth, so rationally apprehended, is science. But, as in beauty, so here in truth, the reason can carry forward some necessary principle in the building up of a system, which shall the most completely enshrine its truth, and make it to subsist in itself impervious to any other eye; and by this its own systematic idea, it will measure and criticise all the organic combinations in nature, or in other men's published philosophies. Neither nature nor published sciences will be of any significancy, nor possess any philosophy, till the insight of reason shall find within them a law corresponding to her own pure idea. Her own ideal embodiment of truth is comprehensive of all utterances that can be given to it, in nature or in philosophy. Here is for the reason ΤΟ ΑΛΗΘΕΣ, THE TRUE: the absolute measure of all science.

And so, finally, the insight of reason into its own being gives, at once, the apprehension of its own prerogatives, and its legitimate right to control and subject nature and sense to its own end, and hold every interest subordinate to the spirit's own excellency. That which, to its own eye, will most fully secure and express its own worthiness, must be its absolute rule, and will contain an ultimate right which is comprehensive of all right that it can recognize. The absolute Reason demanding, in his own right, the subjection of all nature not only, but of all finite reason to his own end, will give an exemplification of the highest possible claim of authority and sovereignty; and the finite rational personality will, from an insight into the attributes which are essential to this absolute Jehovah, see that his own worthiness is most exalted in giving full effect to these claims of the Deity, and bowing before him in profoundest adoration. In such subjection and adoration is the highest claim satisfied, and this inherent excellency of the Absolute Spirit is comprehensive of all moral dignity. He is ΤΟ ΑΓΑΘΟΝ, THE GOOD: and all finite goodness fades in his presence.

Thus it is that reason is the measure of all things, and in its own distinctive function is comprehending faculty for all things. Its absolute ideals stand out unmeasured and unsubjected, and bring all else within their measure and authority. Sense cognizes the phenomenal, the understanding cognizes the substantial, and the reason cognizes the absolute.

SECTION IV. REASON INSPIRES BOTH FANCY AND IMAGINATION, AND THUS IS GENIUS.—The mere fancy is solely a sense-play, and has no meaning; the imagination embodies thought in all its productions, and has a meaning for the judgment, and an adaptation to some end. The naked imagination is, however, wholly from the understanding, and while it embodies thought, calculation, adaptation, and thus applies to use and convenience, it has no sentiment; no warm glow of feeling. It is the faculty for planning, inventing, adapting means to ends, and arranging in view of results. When the activity accomplishes this with the facts of nature in hand, it is judgment; when it uses past experience, and goes with some remembered pattern out to nature to find and arrange its materials, it is the reproductive imagination; and when it invents wholly new combinations of forces and influences, it is the productive imagination. But when the reason comes to this work, it infuses a sentiment into the fancy, and puts a living soul into every combination of the mere imagination. It inspires the whole image, whether from the fancy or the imagination, with living feeling and overflowing emotion. Its combinations are not merely contrivances, embodying thought and plan, but they all express an inner life, and have a true biography, and are thus properly ideal creations. The characters and the plot may have an infinite diversity, but the inner life, which the insight of reason sees to be the nature for such a creation, runs through and actuates the whole. The creation has thus its own inner spirit, and the outer life conforming to it is true to its own nature. It may be such a creation as the empirical nature never knew, but if there is the free utterance of its own spirit, it will not be unnatural. Whether Milton's Satan, or Goethe's Mephistopheles, or Shakespeare's Caliban; its world is its own, and its entire action in it is true to its ensouled sentiment. Fancy or imagination, thus endowed with the higher power of reason, and competent to breathe an inner living soul into its otherwise dead products, becomes genius, and is the prerogative of man only as he is rational spirit.

The animal may both fancy and imagine, but no brute was ever a genius. The brute may perceive more acutely, and judge according to sense as accurately, if not as extensively, as man; and thus the pure constructions of fancy, and the arrangements of the imagination may be effected by brute mind; but man only has reason superinduced upon the sense and the understanding, and thus man as rational, and not as animal, can give forth the creations and inspiration of genius. In the gift of reason, the human is a being different in *kind* from the brute, and this difference is made to pervade his entire mental organism. He is thereby elevated to the sphere of the moral and the personal, the spiritual and immortal; becomes competent to know himself, and to comprehend nature in its Author and Governor; may commune in the region of art and poetry, and be both philosopher and religious worshipper.

SECOND DIVISION.

THE SUSCEPTIBILITY.

The human mind may be said to have a susceptibility to every varied form of feeling, that may come into consciousness. It is susceptible of joy, wonder, hope, the emotions of beauty, the obligations of morality and religion, the affections of sympathy and love, etc., etc., and thus, taken in detail, man has many susceptibilities. But the term is here applied in the most comprehensive acceptation, inclusive of the entire sentient or emotive capacity of the soul. Sensibility might be used as expressive of the same thing, but it has been more familiarly applied to the capacity for organic sensation: and sensitivity, and emotivity, have also been used as the scientific terms for the capacity of feeling; but they are less familiar, and in literal meaning less expressive of the capacity intended. All feeling must be taken under the condition of some antecedent impression or affection of the mind; and if antecedent to consciousness, as in organic sensation, the affection on the organ is the immediate occasion; or if subsequent to conscious perception, as in all emotions, the object apprehended is the immediate occasion; and thus, in all cases, feeling is a *susception*; (*sub capiens*,) and the capacity to thus take under an antecedent affection is properly a *Susceptibility*.

This capacity opens before us one of the most interesting fields in psychology for our investigation, in which lie all the joys and sorrows incident to humanity, and where must be found all our subjective motives to voluntary action. Its careful consideration is the more important, since most writers on mental science have omitted altogether to give it a classification as a distinct capacity, and have confounded its facts with those of the will. Others recognize it as distinct from both the intellect and the will, and yet in no case, so far as I know, has it received a very full, nor, according to my view, an accurate analysis. How very important such analysis is, in avoiding much confusion and error relative to responsible action, will become quite manifest in our subsequent investigation. The intention is to give such an examination and analysis, as will enable us to classify accurately the leading distinctions of feeling, and more especially as they stand related to the will, and look toward moral responsibilities; although a detailed examination and arrangement of every particular feeling will not be necessary, nor in the present work attempted.

The leading distinctions of feeling are numerous, and it is of importance that we discriminate them, for many purposes, though for the great end most in view here—in their bearing upon voluntary agency—such particular discrimination is of less consequence. A concise explanation and consequent definition, of these distinctions in feeling, will here be sufficient; while we shall afterwards take up the grand generic distinctions that more immediately look towards moral responsibility, in separate Chapters.

When any impression is made upon any portion of the bodily organism, that is in communication with the brain as the grand sensorium, we have a *sensation*. The same also is true, when any inner agency of the mind affects itself, and thus induces an *internal* sensation. All this has been sufficiently considered under the head of Primitive Facts, and we need only refer to what has already there been attained. The sensation is antecedent to consciousness, and conditional to the perception of any phenomenon. We take, thus, sensation, in the absence of all distinct and definite consciousness, and we can only say of it, that it is mere *blind feeling*. No object is thereby given, and no separation in consciousness of the mind from its objects, and thus, as yet, no self-consciousness is attained. Still, this blind feeling is not indifference to some end. There is an intrinsic congeniality to certain results, which can only be known as a natural sympathy, or spontaneous attraction to a particular end, and thus in its blindness, the feeling has its impulses in very determinate directions. It is feeling in a living agent, and prompts the agency, in the direction thus inherently congenial with itself. The impulses of such blind feeling are known as *Instinct*.

This is the same, from the lowest to the highest orders of sentient beings, who ever act in the absence of self-consciousness. The earth-worm, or the muscle, may have its simple and imperfect organization; and thus upwards, through all ranks of animals, to the most complicated and completed organizations of man; the sensation in each will be as manifold as the occasions for impressions upon living organs; but in all cases, it will be such, and so much, blind feeling, going out towards its congenial ends, and thus, action only under the impulses of instinct. There is no light of consciousness, or of reason to guide; but the whole is controlled by that original creative act, which determined the congenialities of the feeling to its objects. Brute nature, unendowed with reason, but yet fitted with its adaptations by the Absolute Reason, is everywhere instinctively acting out its most rational issues. Thus "the stork in the heaven knoweth her appointed times; and the turtle, and the crane, and the swallow, observe the time of their coming."—Jer. viii, 7. Thus the ant lays up its winter store; and the bee constructs its surprising mathematical cells; and in many ways, the instinct of man attains its salutary ends, where all his high endowment of reason would fail.

When feeling is no longer blind, but has come out in consciousness, so that it may properly be known as a self-feeling, it at once loses the directing determination of the natural sympathy, or congenial attractiveness to its end, and is thus instinctive impulse no longer. The agent feels in the light, and no more waits on the instinctive prompting, but seeks the guidance of conscious perceptions. Not feeling blindly impelled, but feeling waiting to be consciously led to its end, and thus an appetency to its object. In such a position, sensation has risen from an instinct to an *appetite*. The feeling is living and active as before, and tends towards its congenial end; but it has raised itself above, and thus lost, its instinctive determining, and waits on perception in experience to guide it. Thus the blind feeling of want in the infant, that instinctively reaches the breast, becomes conscious hunger in the man, and looks around for an object to satisfy it.

When the feeling, as appetite, has gratified itself in an appropriate object, and that object has thereby become known as competent to impart this gratification, and thus there is no longer an appetency for something that may gratify, but the object that gratifies is itself known; the sensation has risen from a mere appetite, and become a *desire*. Hunger craves without a known object, but as an appetite it seeks for such object; desire also craves, but it is for a specific, known object, and as having already its understood capacity to gratify the feeling.

In all desire, there is a craving; a longing that would attract the object to itself, and as it were fill up a void in us by it; but when the feeling would go over to the object, and permanently ally itself with it, it has lost all its characteristic of a craving, and as it were an effort at absorbing it, and thus is no longer a desire, but an *inclination*. A desire craves, and at once expires in exhausting the object; an inclination bends towards, and permanently fixes itself upon the object.

There is that in the constitution, or that which has been subsequently acquired, which determines the direction of the inclinations, and without which, and against which, it would be impracticable that the particular inclinations should be experienced. This constitutional or acquired impetus to a given inclination is a *propensity*. We shall subsequently better see how propensities are to be controlled, and how inclinations that are determined from them are nevertheless responsible; but at present the sole object is, to define the different leading divisions of feeling, and thus discriminate them in our consciousness, and not to look at them in their different aspects toward moral accountability.

When the mental activity is passing on in even flow, whether thinking, feeling or willing, there may suddenly on occasion arise a perturbation of feeling, a ruffling and disturbing of the placid tranquil experience, and which, for the time, to a degree confuses and bewilders; arresting all onward movement to an object, and holding the susceptibility in a state of agitation, without any prompting of inclination or direct craving of desire; and such a state of feeling is properly termed *emotion*. The feeling in desire and inclination has its distinct object, not only, but also a distinct action towards it; the feeling in emotion has also its object, but it is as if in commotion before it. In wonder, I stand before the object astonished; in awe, I stand confounded; in joy, I stand transported; in fear, I stand transfixed; in all, I stand before the object with feelings so confused and disturbed, that there is no direct current of feeling towards any end. That normal state of the susceptibility which predisposes it to emotion, is *excitability;* and this may be a general sensibility,

16

that awakes in agitation with every changing wind that passes over the mental surface; or it may be a tendency to agitation from certain sources only, and thus a predisposition to particular characteristic emotions.

When the onward movement of desire, or inclination, towards its object is suddenly invaded, and the whole mind put in confusion, and yet the emotion, instead of arresting the current, goes on with it, and makes it to be a perpetually perturbed and agitated flow of feeling; the desire or inclination being so strong, that the emotion does not suspend nor change its direction; it is then *passion*. The distinction between emotion and passion, is, that simple emotion is agitated feeling with no current, while passion has the strong current of desire still rushing onward to its object, though so agitated as to pursue it blindly and furiously. And still farther, the distinction between inclination and passion is, that simple inclination is an even flow, while passion is that flow disturbed by a strong emotion. A sudden danger to a child may so arrest the current of natural affection, that the parent stands transfixed in an emotion of fear; or it may be that natural affection rushes on in spite of all disturbance, and strives to rescue in a frenzy of passion. Othello's love for Desdemona is not arrested by Iago's representations of unfaithfulness, but only terribly agitated, and pushes on in a frenzy of jealous passion. No increase of emotion or of inclination can make passion, but strong emotion and inclination must be blended, to induce passion.

When the susceptibility is quickened by the presence of a rule of right, given in the insight of reason, there is at once the constraint of an imperative awakened; the conviction of duty arises, and the feeling is that of *obligation.* In desire, the feeling goes out in craving for its object; in inclination, it goes out to rest upon its object; in obligation, the object comes to it, and throws its imperative bonds upon it. The forecasting of a time of trial, and arraignment before some judicial tribunal, awakens the peculiar feeling of *responsibility;* and the inward consciousness of having resisted the current of obligation, is accompanied with the feeling of *guilt;* and the apprehension of exposure, and subjection to sovereign displeasure, induces the feeling of *remorse.*

When the inclination goes out to its object, under the determination of a permanent propensity, it is *affection.* If this permanent propensity is constitutional, whether it be temperament of body or original conformation of mind, it is *natural* affection; if the propensity is in a state of will as reigning disposition, it is *moral* affection. All affections are feelings, but the prepense direction to them may come from physical constitution, or from ethical disposition.

This may be sufficient for the discrimination of the leading acts of the susceptibility, without here attempting to find every specific feeling that may come into human experience, and classifying them all under some of the above definitions; yea, it may be that there are other generic forms of the activity of our sentient nature, and thus that farther discriminations might be necessary, before we should make our analysis complete in this direction; but the above is sufficiently comprehensive for all necessary direction and illustration, while the designed order of classification in our psychology will now proceed, under quite other divisions of the feelings. Without particular regard to the above discriminations, any farther than the obvious propriety of applying terms according to distinctly apprehended meanings, the susceptibility will be analyzed, according to the permanent capacities in human nature, in which it has its distinctive exercises. Man participates in both an animal and a rational nature, and thus his susceptibility to feeling will be modified accordingly. As rational, he is also free spirit, and his feelings must be modified by the disposition given to the free spirit. There will thus be occasion for the three Divisions of the *Animal*, the *Rational*, and the *Spiritual* Susceptibility, which will each be investigated under its distinctive Chapter.

CHAPTER I.

THE ANIMAL SUSCEPTIBILITY.

All our emotive capacity waits upon our intellectual capacity. Only as the intellect is aroused and goes out into specific acts of knowing, can our emotive nature be excited and go out in specific acts of feeling. Antecedently to all self-consciousness, the knowing and the feeling are confusedly blended together, and the mind has in this state no capacity to any distinct emotion. The one mind becomes capacity for feeling, by producing itself into an emotive state. It is thus a susceptibility; a capacity for taking feeling, under the condition of a preceding impression made upon it.

Inasmuch as man has an extended intellectual capacity, so his capacity for feeling may be extended, and all varieties of knowing must give their modifications of feeling. While, therefore, the human intellect operates in higher and wider spheres than the animal, and thus has a susceptibility proportionally elevated; there is also a sphere of knowing common to both man and brute, and, in this particular, a sphere of feeling that is to each the same. Whatever may be the greater clearness and completeness of knowledge in the same field, this will not modify the feeling to make it different in *kind*, but only varying in degree. In the man, it will still be animal feeling, and so far as the feeling waits upon the knowledge given in sense, this will bring no prerogative to the human susceptibility. Here is, thus, the lowest form in which the human susceptibility develops itself in specific feelings, and yet a form completely and permanently distinct from that which originates in man's higher rational being. The importance of this division in our classification is in the fact, that there is this inherent and lasting distinction in human feeling, separating the sensual or animal feelings from all others in our experience. The Animal Susceptibility is *the capacity for feeling which has its source in our animal constitution.*

The exercise of this susceptibility must be in such feelings only as terminate in the sense, or which may come under the judgments of the understanding relatively to objects of sense, and can never transcend the limits of the natural world. Were the capacity for feeling restricted to this form, we could never rise into the region of art, philosophy, ethics or religion; and all the elevating and ennobling emotions, which dignify man as a being of taste, morals, or piety, would be wholly excluded. Confined to the sphere of the animal constitution, all the feelings are impulsive and transitory, coming and departing with the impressions made upon our constitutional organization. They are thus desultory and involuntary, and can be restrained only by reciprocal counteraction; the agent controlled only by setting one opposing feeling over against another, and strong desire repressed only by strong fear. In all the working of this susceptibility, man is only animal, though from the completeness of constitutional organization, an animal of the highest grade.

The feelings of the animal susceptibility may be arranged under the following sections :—

SECTION I. THE INSTINCTS.—The lowest form of mental excitement is found in organic sensation, and which is induced by some impression made upon the organ. It must precede, and is conditional for, an awakening in self-consciousness. In mere organic sensation, the intellectual and the sentient are both present, for the impression gives its affection to the mind itself through the sensorium; but they are present as wholly indiscriminate, and therefore neither as distinct knowledge nor distinct feeling. We recognize the whole, not in consciousness but only in speculation, and can apprehend the sensations only as mental facts of knowing and feeling, in their confused and chaotic being. The intellectual agency as distinguishing and defining, must move over this chaos, before it can be brought out in clear form.

But precisely in this state of undiscriminated mental feeling, there is an inherent impulse to action in a determinate direction. The feeling has its own congeniality to certain ends and objects, and thus spontaneously goes out under the determination of this attractiveness to its object. The sense guides itself, by its innate adaptedness to certain ends, and thus acts directly towards its congenial objects, before the mind can discriminate these objects in consciousness, and guide itself to them in its own light. The reptile turning under the tread; the young of animals or man clinging to the breast; the adult just rousing from a sleep or a swoon; are all illustrations of the impulsive nature of instinctive feeling. It has many degrees of obscurity from its darkest strugglings up to its half-conscious agency; but whether in man or animal, it is everywhere, so far as it is instinctive feeling, the constituted congeniality and adaptedness of the sensation to its given result, and thus an impulsive working to its end in the absence of self-consciousness.

Among the examples of instinctive feelings may be given, the impetus to the preservation of life; the shrinking from pain and death; the sudden closing of the eye, lifting of the hand, or dodging away of the body, when any danger threatens; and, in fact, the whole action of infancy, the tossings in a troubled sleep, the delirium of a fever, the movements of the somnambulist, and the marvelous exhibitions of mesmerism; all are the promptings of blind sensation, in the absence of self-consciousness, and are determined in their intensity and direction, solely from the impulse of an intrinsic congeniality in the sensation to the end induced. What is meant by the instinct is, not the affection in the organ, but that congeniality or attractiveness in the sensation towards the end, which at once gives the impulse in that direction. Hunger in the infant and the adult may be the same sensation; but in the infant, there is an instinctive prompting to the object of gratification, which is wholly lost in the direction that the light of consciousness gives to the adult. The migrating bird not only feels the air in which it moves, but this sensation has its attractiveness towards the warm gales of the south, when the rigors of winter are approaching.

SECTION II. THE APPETITES.—When any constitutional sensation is awakened, and the instinctive impulse which determines it towards its end is lost in the rising light of self-consciousness, there is still the feeling seeking its end, though waiting for the perception in consciousness to guide it. In all such cases of seeking its appropriate object of gratification, the feeling is properly termed an *appetite.* It is often expressed as a *longing* after its end, and this is only descriptive of the feeling, as if in its seeking it elongated itself in the direction towards its object.

There are some sensations which seem eminently to have this appetency to a particular end, and which are thus more emphatically termed appetites, as hunger and thirst. In a peculiar state of the great organ of digestion, when the stomach is empty of food, and the gastric juice, with the movement of its own surfaces, acts directly upon its own substance, there is induced a peculiar sensation common to all animal being, and which at once seeks for some congenial object to relieve it. This is known as hunger, when the stomach is empty of food; or as thirst, when destitute of drink; and these seekings or longings in hunger and thirst are eminently appetites. But all other constitutional sensations, which go forth in longing for some congenial end, are equally appetites, and belong here to this division of the animal susceptibility. The sensation of fatigue, which longs for rest; of protracted wakefulness, which longs for sleep; the longing for health in sickness, and for buoyant spirits in nervous dejection; the going forth of animal inclination between the sexes; and the longing for a shade from the heat, and for a covering from the cold; they are all sensations seeking for gratification, and are as truly appetites, as the seeking in the sensations of hunger and thirst. To these should also be added the longings which go out for gratification in the sensations of all other organs. The eye and the ear, the smell, taste and touch, give sensations that long for gratification as truly as the uneasiness of an empty stomach, and as thus truly appetitive, the seeking feeling should, in each case, be known as an appetite.

When the experience has tried the particular object that gratifies the longing for relief, and thus the sensation now goes out specifically for a particular object of known gratification, the appetite is then lost in a desire, and the general seeking or longing for relief becomes the direct craving for a distinct gratification. This may also be so agitated by the sudden presentation of the object, that the desire or inclination goes out furious and frenzied in enjoyment; and in this hurried rush of feeling, the desire becomes a passion. The appetites may thus readily be raised to desires, and these excited into passions; but through all these forms of seeking their objects, they are still animal feeling only, and exist in brute and man of the same kind, however they may be modified in forms or degrees. It should also be noted, that the appetites are nearly allied to the instincts, differing from them only in rising to the light of self-consciousness, and thus liable to sink back again to a mere instinctive impulse, when an absorption in the pleasure of gratification so far obscures the discriminations of self-consciousness. An animal and a man may be so intent in gratifying appetite, and absorbed in the pleasure, as to lose all consciousness of what is about them, and what they are; and thus absorbed, their gratification is as instinctive as that of the infant at the breast.

The opposite feelings to appetite, as loathing or satiety, need not be particularly considered, inasmuch as they follow the same laws, and are subject to the same determinations, except as throughout they are the converse of the former.

Section III. Natural Affections.—There is a love which is solely pathological, originating in constitutional nature, and determined in its action and direction by an innate propensity. Such an inclination differs wholly from that spiritual affection which appropriates its object freely, and strikes its root deeply in the moral disposition. Of this last we shall speak fully, under another division of the susceptibility; but of the former only are we now concerned to attain an adequate conception.

There is in the parent a deep propensity to an anxious and watchful solicitude for the welfare of the child. This is strongest in the breast of the mother, and though the most tender and wakeful towards the child in infancy, yet is it perpetuated through all stages of experience until death. A benevolent provision is in this made for the care and nurture of the child in its helplessness, far more effective than any governmental regulations could secure. The strength and tenderness of maternal love may be regulated and elevated by moral and religious considerations, and thus come to partake of the characteristics of a virtue, but in so far as any such considerations mingle, they are wholly foreign to the maternal inclination as here contemplated. The whole feeling is that of nature, and to be destitute of it, in the case of any mother, is to be simply unnatural. The inclination of the father towards his child, finds its origin, also, in a natural propensity, but its strength and constancy depends mainly upon the action of connubial love. If the mother be not herself loved, the love of the father to his children will be easily overborne by opposing considerations. In lawful and affectionate wedlock, the natural regard for the offspring is secured perpetual and active in both the parents. It is useless to enquire for any parental instinct, by which natural affection might be directed to a child not otherwise known; for one condition of natural parental affection is, that the child be not only the parent's own, but known to be so. That the mother deems the child to be her own, is a necessary, and the sufficient condition, that her love should go out towards it.

This love is strongest in the parents; reciprocated in the children towards the parents; mutually directed towards each as brothers and sisters; and extended to all the kindred, in modified degrees, according to nearness of relationship and circumstances of communion. Nature itself prompts to communion, as occasion may offer, through all the family circle, but if circumstances prevent all intercourse, the ties of natural affection become thereby much weakened. In the mere animal, the maternal solicitude appears, occasionally connected with that of the male where they procreate in pairs, but continued only during the helplessness and dependence of the young, and lost when they are competent to provide for themselves. It is because man can trace the lines of kindred descent, and diffuse his communion through all the circle, that he comes to perpetuate and extend his family affections beyond those of the mere animal. The occasion for their exercise and cultivation is thus given in man's higher endowments, but the source of natural affection, in man, as in brutes, is solely in constitutional pathology. It is nearly allied to the appetites. The feeling has its intrinsic congeniality with its object, and adaptation to its end, and thus seeks its object as an appetite; but it differs both from an appetite and a desire, in that it seeks its object for the object's sake, and not that it may absorb it into its own interests. It is not merely an inclination, as tending towards, that it may connect itself with, the object; but it inclines toward the object, solely that it may subserve *its* welfare. It is thus an affection; but as merely pathological, and finding its whole propensity in constitutional nature, it is *natural* affection only.

SECTION IV. SELF-INTERESTED FEELING.—An appetite seeks its end in gratification, and a desire craves its object that it may fill itself with it; but in distinct self-consciousness, I may come to appreciate any object solely in the use I may make of it for my happiness. I contemplate myself as a creature of appetites and desires, and the objects which my appetites seek and my desires crave I contemplate, simply as ministering to my happiness in gratifying these appetites and desires; and with the objects turned towards me in such an aspect, a large variety of feelings may be induced, all of which will agree in this, that they wholly terminate in my own interest. It is not a mere seeking that terminates in its object, nor a craving whose only end is to be filled by the object; but a self, that can estimate both appetites and desires with all their objects, as they bear upon its own enjoyment. All the feelings here contemplated will not go out direct towards any object, but will all be reflex upon the self, and terminate solely in self-interest. They will be impossible to him who could not contemplate himself aside from his desires, and estimate his very desires and their objects as the means of so much self-enjoyment.

Thus I shall have the feeling of joy, in the possession of such desires and their objects, as bearing upon my happiness and not for the object's sake. In the loss of such objects I shall feel grief, not on their account, but my own. The feelings here will be mainly emotions, excited in reference to my own immediate interests in the objects. Joy in the prospect of possessing, and grief in the danger of losing; hope and fear; pride and shame; tranquility and anxiety; animation and despondency; patience and perplexity; all may be awakened, as I am made to view objects in their varied relations to my own interest.

Here also come in all the feelings connected with *the acquisition and possession of property.* All objects that minister to my wants touch, at once, the feeling of self-interest, and excite the propensity to get and retain for future use. As it is my enjoyment which is to be secured, so the objects must be in my possession, and my right to them capable of being defended against the claims of any others. An immoderate anxiety in securing such possessions is the feeling of covetousness, and an immoderate eagerness to hoard them is the feeling of avarice. If this goes so far as to deny itself the enjoyment of the use, and makes mere accumulation the end, the feeling then becomes the *passion* of avarice, inasmuch as the inclination to hoard is disturbed, and perverted from its end. When money, or that which may be exchanged for the objects that may minister to our enjoyment, is accumulated, we have the secondary or *derived* feelings, which regard the possessions not in themselves, but in their relative bearing upon such as we may want and may by their means attain. There may also be a complete passing over of the feeling to the simple object of exchange, and in the perturbation of the passion, that thing be hoarded for itself. So the miser *transfers* his feeling from the objects of gratification the money might get, to the money itself, and refuses all use not only, but all accumulation of anything but hard specie.

Here, also, are found the feelings which originate in a *generalization of consequences.* Experience abundantly teaches both man and animals, that certain present gratifications of appetite are followed by greater coming evil. They learn by experience to avoid certain practices, that would in themselves be agreeable; since from the past, they know how to anticipate the future consequences. Such a generalization of experience, and deducing prudential considerations therefrom, very much modifies the feelings. Present desire is suppressed, and a provident foresight awakens new inclinations. The feelings of self-interest are addressed from a new quarter, and the judgment of an understanding according to sense is made a strong means for exciting the susceptibility. The man may take into his estimate a far broader field of experience, and deduce a much wider series of consequential results, than the animal; but the intellectual operation is the same in kind, and the prudential feeling is of the same order in both. It is solely animal feeling, awakened by calculations from animal experience, and prompts to action in the end of self-interest only. Mere prudential claims never reach those emotions, which are stirred by the authority of a moral imperative. There may be the gladness of success, or the regret of failure; the gratulation of prudent management, or the self-reproach of improvidence; but there can never be the moral emotions of an excusing or an accusing conscience.

From considerations of self-interest there also arise the many painful and *dissocial* feelings, which are directed against whatever is supposed to interfere with self-enjoyment. Envy and jealousy, hatred and malice, anger and revenge, are all aroused amid the collisions of opposing interests. These may all become moral vices from their connection with an evil will, but the animal nature alone has within it the spring to all such naturally selfish emotions.

SECTION V. DISINTERESTED FEELINGS.—There is in human nature a strong propensity to society. A rational and spiritual susceptibility elevates to social communion in much higher spheres, qualifying for scientific, moral, and religious intercourse; but the yearnings of the animal nature itself are for company and fellowship with those of its kind. Brutes are more or less gregarious, and even the animals that live mostly in solitude, seem to be forced to this isolation, from the scarcity of their prey or the necessity of their hiding places. This social propensity stands connected with many feelings which find their end in the welfare of others, and that have no reflex action and termination in self. Inasmuch as they refer to the interests of others, and are exclusive of self-interest, they may be termed the *disinterested* feelings. The self is gratified in their exercise, inasmuch as it is so constituted that it enjoys the play of these emotions for others; but the end of the feeling is in others, not in self, and it thus comes in as one of its own enjoyments, that it should feel for its fellows.

Here are found all the natural sympathies of our nature. Other men have all the varied feelings which belong to our own experience, and the witness of these feelings in others naturally enkindles a kindred feeling in ourselves. Except as the selfish feelings have been allowed to predominate, and thus to repress our disinterested emotions, we shall naturally rejoice with the joyous, and weep with the weeping. According to the varied experience of our fellow-men, our own emotions will be excited; and we shall feel pity or fellow-pleasure, condolence or congratulation, just as we see others to be affected. Such animal sympathies extend to all sentient being, and the happiness or suffering of the brute creation strongly affects the susceptibility of man. Even animals themselves deeply participate in these sympathies, and are moved by the glad sounds or the cries of other animals. There is often a quick sensibility in very immoral men, and the natural sympathies of some good men are slow to be aroused; and thus quite aside from all moral disposition, the natural feelings of men may render some far more amiable than others, just as some animals may enlist our sympathies much more strongly than others.

The disinterested feelings may be modified by a *calculation of general consequences*, in the same way as before of the self-interested feelings. Experience may teach as plainly what is best for others, as what is most prudent for myself; and this general consideration of consequences will at once awaken its peculiar feelings, in reference to others on whom the consequences are to come. All the feelings of kindness, or natural benevolence and philanthropy, are here exhibited. They prompt to the denial of self-gratification for the happiness of others; or rather, these disinterested feelings make the man the most happy, when he is making others happy. The whole is pathological only, and is kind, just as the animal is sometimes kind to his fellow brute; and in this working of natural sympathy, many acts of self-denial are put forth, and human distress relieved, where the moral susceptibility has not been at all moved, and the charitable deed has had in it nothing of ethical virtue. Even animals sometimes deny themselves for their kind, and thus manifest this natural kindness of feeling; and in man, the disinterested feelings may be more comprehensive, and his calculation of consequences for other's benefit far more extended, and thus his plans of benevolence may reach much farther than any provisions the animal may make; but in one case as in the other, the whole may be the impulse of animal susceptibility only. In such cases, nature, not moral character, must have all the credit of the kindness.

CHAPTER II.

THE RATIONAL SUSCEPTIBILITY.

In the rational, we rise to a sphere of feeling altogether above anything reached in the animal susceptibility, and in which man as rational only, and not at all as animal, participates. We have already found the reason to be organ for apprehending absolute truth; and faculty for comprehending in necessary principles and universal laws; and such higher capacity of knowledge is occasion for a higher sphere of feeling, and which will be as different in kind from all exercise of the animal susceptibility, as the cognitions of the reason differ from the perceptions of the sense and the judgments of the understanding. The feelings of the rational susceptibility are as truly grounded in constitutional nature as those of the animal, and are therefore still removed from all moral accountability in their origin, inasmuch as they are necessitated in the nature which is given to man; but these are found in man as he is constituted rational, while the former belong to him as he is constituted animal being. All the rational feelings accord in this, that they are awakened by some insight of the reason, and never from any perceptions of the sense, nor any judgments of the understanding according to sense; and hence they must be known, as originating in an entirely distinct sphere of our generic susceptibility, which must be carefully and accurately discriminated. But though they are all of this one higher order of feeling, yet will they be found to differ in other things, each from each, according to the different directions of the insight of reason; and therefore presenting, of the same order, still many varieties. These varieties will be clearly distinguished, and the general investigation will fully determine the line of separation between them and all feelings of the animal being.

We may give all these varieties under the following sections:—

Section I. The Æsthetic Emotions.—The field of the Fine Arts separates itself from all else, in virtue of the artistic products which have their significancy only to the insight of reason, and this field, on that account, admits of only such emotions as the rational insight into these artistic products occasions. They awaken no feelings of appetite, nor the cravings of desire, but these products of art attain their whole end, in the contemplation of that which the insight of reason finds within them, and which is always some sentiment of a living being. All that belongs to this field of the fine arts is therefore properly termed *æsthetic*. (Αἰσθητικὸς, *conversant with sentiment, sentimental.*) The whole feeling may be included in what is termed *the love of the beautiful.*

These æsthetic feelings may be brought up and discriminated in consciousness, as facts to be recognized in empirical psychology, by the following considerations.

The feelings of living beings can be represented to others, in certain shapes to the eye and certain tones to the ear. It is not of any importance what the content of color that fills the shape, nor what the content of sound that fills the tone; the feeling is expressed in the pure shape or the pure tone, without any regard to the matter which fills either of them. Shape is given limit in extent, and tone is given limit in intensity; and as thus limited, we may apply to both shape and tone a common term expressive of the limitation, and call it *form*. The living feeling will thus always be expressed in some pure form.

Now the animal eye and ear can perceive definite figure and definite sound, and thus apprehend the phenomena of nature when the content for them is given in sensation; but it is to the mind's eye and ear only that pure form, without all content, can be given; and when the pure form is thus apprehended, it is not any sense, but the insight of reason only, that can recognize the living sentiment which may there be expressed. The feeling embodied in the form can be perceived by no mere animal; it is object only to the organ of reason. Such rational apprehension of living feeling, in any forms, will also awaken its own peculiar feeling in the bosom of the observer; and as the insight was all of reason, so the susceptibility awakened is wholly rational, and completely distinct from the animal susceptibility.

And now, this rational insight may attain the expressed sentiment, and awaken the consequent feeling, from the thousand scenes and sounds of nature, or from painting,

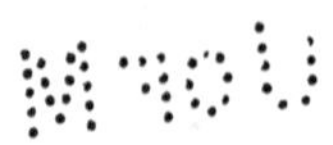

statuary, and music; the contemplative mind at once interprets them all, and thus truly communes with both nature and art. To the sentient spirit, visions and voices are on every side, and it catches each peculiar sentiment of the sunset, the moonlight, or the tempest; the field, the grove, or the deep forest, as readily as those inscribed by the pencil and chisel in the galleries of art: it reads the meaning of the sounds in the breeze, the stream, or on the ocean shore, as distinctly as that which is expressed in the measured numbers of poetry and song. It is as if the cold marble had its beating heart, which was sending its warm pulses of feeling through all the statue; as if nature herself had a living soul, which was looking out through all her features, and expressing before us all its deep emotions; and so soon as the piercing insight catches the living sentiment, our own souls respond in sympathy, and we feel at once the spirit within us, to be kindred to that which is glowing without us, and in a thousand ways addressing itself to us.

This affection is faintly induced in us by the presentation of some mere sense-beauty, and the reason is applied to partially illuminate the fancy, when flowers are made to have a meaning, and the trees to speak, and birds and beasts communicate in language, and thus sentiment comes out in fable: but far more adequately and completely, when all sense and fancy are discarded, and an inspired imagination awakes to catch nature's true expression, and with no phantasm, no fable, but in strictest reality, the rapt vision of the seer detects the genuine living sentiment that verily is there. This it is

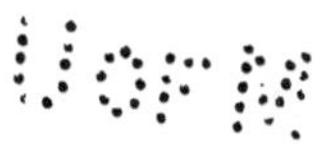

which fills all nature with beauty, when we read her expressions of sentiment, either as joyous or sad, and find them such as our human hearts can reciprocate, and with which our mortal feelings can blend in sympathy; but at once all nature rises to grandeur and sublimity, when we catch the sentiment of the supernatural, and read any where the uttered feelings of an approving or an offended God.

So a creative genius may originate some new ideal of beauty or of sublimity, expressing the given sentiment more perfectly than nature anywhere presents it, and may labor to put his ideal into some form on the canvas, or on the marble, or in the epic verse, or in the notes of music; and just so far as our insight can penetrate his inspiration, and sieze the very sentiment which he has embodied in his artistic product, will our feelings be kindled in sympathy, and our souls glow with his enthusiasm. Reason only can speak to Reason. This only can embody the sentiment, and this only read it as thus expressed; and thus the rational soul, and not the animal, can be touched with beauty, and roused by sublimity, and be conscious that it stands face to face with another living spirit, communing directly and intensely in one common sentiment.

Section II. Scientific Emotions.—All true science is a comprehension of its subject in its ultimate principle and necessary law. Rightly to philosophize is to take some necessary truth, and bind up all the appertaining facts in systematic unity by it. If the necessary

and universal law for the facts cannot be yet attained, the facts cannot yet be subjected to science; and the whole subject waits for its philosopher, as the movements of the solar system long waited for Newton. No science can be made of mere facts; they are but its elements, and must be held in combination by some principle which conditions the facts to be, and to be just as they are. If mere omnipotence make facts to be, but follows no *a' priori* law beforehand determining how the facts must be, the whole is a mere arbitrary jumble of existences, as destitute of all possibility of science to the maker as to any outside observer. All induction of facts is with the assumption that such a conditioning law exists, and in the direct interest of finding it; if it be assumed as a deduction from a long list of consenting experiments, the general law thus assumed gives merely *inductive* science; if the law itself be seen in the pure insight of reason as *a' priori* necessary for the facts, and thus conditioning the facts, and therefore that so sure as the *a' priori* principle is, so sure the facts themselves must be, then is the science itself absolute in its absolute principle, and is an *a' priori*, or *transcendental* science. Philosophy is thus a seeking for truth, and can never rest satisfied until it is found in its own absolute being. The principle by which she binds up all her facts in order, and in the light of which she expounds them all, must be seen by her in its own necessity and universality, and that the whole process of the philosophizing ultimately strikes its root in the reason, or she cannot yet be satisfied with her work, nor feel justified as having yet accomplished her mission.

Now the feeling, which gives its impulse to all such activity, is *the love of truth;* and all attainment of truth awakens its own peculiar emotions in the mind; and thus, all scientific feeling must necessarily originate in a rational, and can never be educed from any animal susceptibility. The Absolute Reason has put his own necessary and universal laws in all nature: nothing exists as an arbitrary or anomalous fact, but all is as the *a' priori* principle in the creating of nature conditioned that it must be: and thus the power, which gave birth to nature, was determined in its action by absolute truth, and is therefore absolute wisdom; and all sympathy with the truth of nature, and all impulse to the study of nature, and all the emotion excited by the successive degrees of insight into nature—reading her deep secrets and detecting those inner laws which have bound her from the beginning, and which are themselves the accordant counterpart of those eternal archetypes that were in the creating mind before the world was—all these elevating and ennobling feelings are among the prerogatives of our rational being over our animal nature, and belong to man and are found in man, because the reason in his own soul can stand over against the reason hid in nature, and look its truth directly in the face, and know it, and love it, and commune with it, as both having the same conscious divine origin. The same organ that reads the sentiment in nature, detects also the inner laws of nature; in one is seen beauty, and in the other truth; and all the emotions of each are in the one rational susceptibility, differing only as the direction of the insight varies.

SECTION III. ETHICAL EMOTIONS.—The reason has an insight into itself, and knows itself, not relatively only as distinct from animal being, but directly and particularly in its own prerogatives and capabilities. The spirit itself knoweth the things of the spirit; its own spirituality, and in this its intrinsic dignity and excellency. In thus knowing itself, it knows what is due to itself; what it has an absolute right to claim from others, and what is the inherent behest of its own being that it should do for itself. Reason is thus ever *autonomic;* carrying its own law within itself, and, from what it knows itself to be, reading its own law upon itself, and binding itself at all times to act worthy of itself. That it should in any way deny itself, and act for some end that was other than its own worthiness, would be to degrade and debase its own being, and thus to make reason no longer reasonable. This gives an ultimate right quite other than the useful and the prudent. By generalizing what *is*, we learn what is useful and thus what is prudent for ourselves, and what is useful and thus what is kind or benevolent for others; but we cannot thus determine that which *is*, and from the generalization of which we get the prudent and the benevolent, to be right, and cannot thus say that either prudence or benevolence is a virtue. If nature is not as it should be, then its working is to be resisted, and as far as possible counteracted, both for ourselves and others, no matter what injury nature thus working wrongly may do to us or others for it; i. e. no matter, as nature wrongly is, how imprudent or unkind our resistance of it may be. But by the direct insight of reason into itself, and seeing what is due to its own excellency, we find at once the law written on the heart, and by which we can judge of all experience in nature whether it be such as it should be, and thus whether prudence to ourselves or benevolence to others, in following out the generalizations of nature, are virtues or not. The ultimate rule is determined, not by the enquiry, what may the endless ongoings of nature do for me? but, what does the worthiness of my own rational being demand of me?

Such rational insight awakens its peculiar feelings, and in which no animal perceptions nor judgments according to sense can possibly enable us to sympathize. We may have all the feelings which prudence or kindness involves, through the excitement of our animal susceptibility—for the rules of prudence and kindness may be determined by just such intellectual operations as the animal can perform—but we can never have the feelings which the ultimate right occasions, except as in our rational being we have the insight to find the absolute rights of reason itself, and therein see what its own excellency demands. All the former are solely economic emotions, and are of the animal nature; the latter only are ethic emotions, and are of the rational susceptibility.

These feelings come mainly under the working of natural conscience, and as they are of so much moment in all that regards our moral and accountable being, it is important that they receive a more extended examination. We thus distinguish the source of all our ethical feelings as originating in one particular susceptibility which is known as—

THE CONSCIENCE.

The distinguishing prerogative of the reason to know itself, and thus in all cases of self-reference what is due to itself, is not a mere dry intellectual apprehension, but is accompanied with a feeling of constraint or obligement that is known as *duty*. The knowledge of what is due, and the feeling of constraint to secure that what is due shall be rendered, is duty; and both are properly included in the term conscience. Not mere self-knowledge, but this knowledge accompanied with its imperative, is τὸ συνειδός, the CON*scientia*, which we have now to consider. There is the intellectual act—which has by some been solely taken as conscience—and the awakened feeling of obligation—which has by such been called the *moral sense*—both combined in the completed work of self-knowledge, and each would be inefficacious to fix the sentiment of duty without the other; and yet, as the *feeling* is the most prominent in the consciousness under the pressure of duty, it is mainly of the susceptibility that conscience is predicated in common use. In this sense we so consider it here, and define Conscience as *the susceptibility which is reached by the insight that determines a rule of right.*

The conscience, as a susceptibility, will be farther explained under the following divisions:—

1. *Different applications of the rule will modify the feeling of conscience.*—The rule may be viewed in reference *to what is to be done.* When the claim of duty is felt *antecedently* to the act, there is always a distinguishable feeling of conscience in regard to the rule. It may

be a claim viewed as resting upon *another*, and the feeling awakened is one of conscience. Thus Paul speaks of the conviction one may have of what another ought, or ought not, to do, and calls it "conscience." "Conscience, I say, not thine own, but of the other."—1 Cor. x, 29. This might be fully expressed by one man saying to another—'I am persuaded in my conscience that such is your duty.' It may be a claim viewed as resting upon *myself*. So again, Paul speaks of his prejudiced apprehension of duty as conscience, when he says, "I verily thought with myself that I ought to do many things contrary to the name of Jesus of Nazareth,"—Acts, xxvi, 9; for he subsequently says of it, "Men, Brethren, I have lived in all good conscience before God unto this day."—Acts, xxiii, 1. This might be directly expressed by the man in saying, 'I feel bound in conscience thus to do.'

Or, the rule may be viewed in reference *to what has been done*. When an imperative is felt to have been applicable, but the action under it *has already occurred*, there is also a very distinguishable feeling of conscience, accordingly as with or against the imperative. It may be in reference to what *another* has done. Thus Paul and his fellow-laborers did what others thought they ought; and this conviction of others is termed "conscience,"—"by manifestation of the truth, commending ourselves to every man's conscience in the sight of God."—2 Cor. iv, 2. This may be plainly stated by one man to another in saying, 'I conscientiously commend, or I conscientiously condemn, your conduct.' It may be in reference to what *I myself* have done. Thus the Scriptures speak of "a good conscience,"—1 Peter, iii, 16, and of "an evil conscience."—Heb. x, 22. When I view my conduct as conformed to the rule, I shall feel self-approbation; and when as contrary to the rule, I shall feel self-condemnation; and I can directly say, 'I have an approving conscience;' or, 'I have a guilty conscience.'

These varied feelings of conscience are all from an apprehension of the rule of right in some aspect, and can be awakened only in such an apprehension. I may see that I have been imprudent or unkind, and feel regret or ashamed; but only as I see that I have violated an imperative of duty, shall I feel guilt, or remorse. Such feelings may sometimes be termed *moral* feelings, but this is only because they have their connection with moral and responsible action, and not that the workings of conscience are themselves participants in moral character. The action of conscience is necessitated, and as truly in constitutional being as an appetite, and cannot be determined voluntarily. Whether good or wicked beings, all must approve of the right and feel obligation, when it is apprehended; and all must feel complacency or remorse, as they see they have kept or violated it.

Wilful and persevering violence to conscience may make it callous to all feeling, and for such desperate perverseness the man must stand responsible. Such are spoken of as "past feeling,"—Eph. iv, 19; and as "having their conscience seared with a hot iron."—1 Tim. iv, 2. But this effect upon the conscience, and all the feelings any way induced in it, are of nature and not of the will; and are not thus moral, in the sense of direct responsibility.

2. *The operation of conscience is ever in accordance with the apprehension of the rule.*—All awakened susceptibility is as the apprehension of its appropriate object. As the painting is apprehended to be beautiful, or the philosophy to be true, such must be the feeling awakened thereby, and no change of the feeling can be made but by a change in the apprehension of the object; and thus also with the conscience. It can be aroused to feeling by nothing but an apprehension of a rule of right, and the feelings will follow the apprehension whether it be correct or erroneous. No conscience can feel obligation to what is apprehended to be wrong, nor other then obligation to what is apprehended to be right: and in the same way after the act; no conscience can feel remorse for apprehended well-doing, nor other than remorse for apprehended evil-doing. The conscience, as a susceptibility, can never act deceitfully. As the light reaches it, such must be its consequent feeling, and thus be ever true to the intellectual apprehension.

A good man is not to be disturbed by the suspicion, that perhaps the feelings of his conscience may have been delusive; nor the pangs of a bad man relieved by any persuasion, that perhaps his remorse is from a false conscience. When conscience approves, the act in that point is virtuous; and when it condemns, the act in the point of condemnation is vicious. No matter if the rule was really a nullity, and conferred no obligation from itself; nor, even if its claims were really the very opposite to what was apprehended; the action having been as the rule was apprehended to be, the conscience must accuse or excuse accordingly, and the man in that act must have been vicious or virtuous accordingly. The point of responsibility is not in reference to the feeling of the conscience; that must be true to the apprehended application of the rule. Hence Paul decided, that though meat offered to an idol, and afterward sold in the market, had no defilement, because "an idol was nothing," yet if any one who thought differently ate of it, to him it was sin. "He that doubteth is damned if he eat, for whatsoever is not of faith" (belief that it is right) "is sin." —Rom. xiv, 23. The feeling of the conscience never deceives.

3. *The rule may be apprehended partially or erroneously.*—The simple rule of right is in the same ground ever the same thing, and thus, knowing nothing of mutability in itself, can never give forth conflicting claims. But finite reason is not always veracious. The medium through which the rule is brought within the apprehension may give a perverted insight, and thus contradictory obligations may be felt, in reference to the same matter, by two different persons or by the same person at different times. Conscience may bind in one case, and loose in another. This perverting medium is made an occasion for conflicting convictions of duty. The conscience, as susceptibility, is true in its feelings to the apprehension, but the apprehension is perverted. So in the case of Paul, above; he "verily thought that he ought to do

many things contrary to the name of Jesus of Nazareth," while Stephen would lay down his life, and Paul himself afterwards, in the conviction that no action might be contrary to the will of the Lord Jesus Christ. The rule was not double, in this case, and duty in conflict with itself. The reason's eye, in Paul, was made to look through the perverting medium of pharisaicaleducation and prejudice. His apprehension of the rule was erroneous, and the feelings of the conscience went out accordingly. And perversions as effectual may originate in various sources.

Partial and obscure light may prevent a clear apprehension, and thus one man have far more adequate views of duty than another—as, a heathen cannot know all the duties of a Christian. A bias of self-interest may induce an obstinate perversion—as, the maker or vender of ardent spirits may determine to look at his business through the general custom; or, the license of the civil law; or, the assumption that another would do worse than himself in his place. A long habit may preclude all examination—as, for a long time, good men pursued the slave-trade. Violent passion may ruffle the mind, and so disturb it as to distort the truth; and even a fit of anger may be induced, for the very purpose of excluding truth from the conscience. The point for all responsibility, and all correction of conscience, is in the insight of the reason; not at all in the feeling, which must be as the apprehension. If a false view was unavoidable to the man, he is not responsible for it; if it could have been avoided, in that, and to just the extent of the neglect, is his guilt.

Honesty and care in attaining the rule are incumbent upon all, and the sin in a perverted apprehension may be very great.

4. *The conscience must be the controlling susceptibility.*—The animal susceptibility may prompt to action through appetite and desire, and the rational susceptibility may also give the impulse to action through the love of beauty, or the love of philosophic truth, and these may sometimes be in harmony with the impulse of duty; but whenever they may come in collision with the feeling of obligation, that must control and restrain them all. Truth and beauty are higher than sensual gratification, but duty is higher than philosophy and art, and thus virtue is above all. In all collision of motive, the appeal to conscience must be supreme. This is abundantly manifest. To violate conscience, for anything, subjects the man to conscious baseness; and the loss of self-respect is the necessary loss of his manliness, and the highest evil that can be incurred. No added pleasure to any susceptibility could be sweet, when conscience reproached and accused. Not only *is* conscience found to be the susceptibility that has this highest prerogative; it manifestly *ought* to be so. If we could conceive of a being so made, that appetite might domineer over conscience, and conscience quietly yield as if appetite had the right to be supreme; it would at once reflect a reproach upon the maker of such a being, and the insight of reason would infallibly announce that he had been made wrongly. A perversion of conscience is therefore man's utter ruin; and, of all incorrigible delinquents of the claims of duty,

we may say emphatically, good were it for such that they had never been born.

Where the conscience fully controls, the agent is virtuous; and the weaker capacity is as truly righteous, in such a case, as the stronger. But while moral character will thus be as the control of conscience, the moral worth of the agent must also include the capacity. Adam, in innocence, was as truly virtuous as Gabriel; but the angel, having the higher capacity and thus the greater strength of faculty in righteousness, is of more moral worth than the man. The true dignity must be the compound of character and capacity. And as much as conscience must condemn for all known violation of duty, as truly as it must approve for all fidelity to right, so it must follow that every moral being carries the elements of his own retribution within him. The material for his own hell or heaven is laid up in every man's conscience.

SECTION IV. THEISTIC EMOTIONS.—The animal eye can perceive the phenomena of nature, but as there is no insight of reason, it cannot apprehend a God in nature. Inasmuch as to animal being there can be no theistic perceptions, so to it there can be no theistic emotions. But in the things that are made, the rational mind of man sees the eternal power and Godhead of the Maker. Nature is comprehended in a personal Deity, who originates it from himself, and consummates it according to his eternal plan. Such recognition of a God, at once occasions its own peculiar emotions. Feelings are awakened that could arise from no other object in the insight.

Man, from his conscious weakness and helplessness, is obliged to feel his need of such a full source of supply, and his utter dependence upon it. In God alone he lives and moves and has his being, and is utterly empty without this unbounded fullness.

Without including here other feelings than such as are necessarily awakened by the apprehension of a present God, it is manifest that such a rational insight must lay its foundation in the mind for its peculiar rational susceptibility. Not only can no perceptions of the sense enkindle these emotions, but they differ also wholly from such as are awakened by the apprehension of beauty, or truth, or ethical right. They make the man, in his very constitution, a *religious* being. He must feel awe and reverence, and entire dependence, in the presence of Jehovah. The very source of all beauty and truth and right is here, and thus the Absolute Good is known, and in this is an occasion for faith and love and worship, when the willing spirit shall joyfully yield itself in full devotion. Such homage of the spirit will open a new susceptibility, hereafter to be considered as the spiritual; but the capacity for this is our rational being as it gives the insight to a God, and such apprehension of the Deity necessitates, in wicked as in holy men, the peculiarly constitutional emotions we here term theistic. Without the insight of reason, as revealing God in nature, this susceptibility could not be, and with such an insight and revealing, this distinctive susceptibility must be. Man can no more divest himself of his religious nature and responsibility, then he can of his ethical being and obligation.

Now, in all the above sources of feeling, Æsthetic, Scientific, Ethic, and Theistic, we have a wide sphere of susceptibility altogether removed from, and elevated above, the animal. And it is necessary to observe, in conclusion, only this, that the impulse to action in all the rational susceptibility is wholly and consciously different from that of the animal susceptibility. The animal nature craves, and makes the man uneasy and unhappy in his want, and forces his activity for a supply. He must *work* to relieve his want; he must get happiness only through *toil*. But the rational nature knows no uneasy cravings, and demands no toilsome work. It seeks not to devour its object, but simply to contemplate it; not to use it to the end of filling "an aching void," but to keep it as having perpetually a serene complacency in it. The action that goes out towards it, is ever cheerful and glad, and is thus known as the *play-impulse*. The soul goes out after beauty and truth as a delight, and seeks virtue and the worship of God as a blessed activity. The Beautiful and the True, the Right and the Good, are taken themselves as ends, and contemplated in their own dignity, and giving full complacency in their own excellency, and are not to be degraded as means of gratifying any appetite, nor held as mere utilities for satisfying wants. Our activity is spontaneous and joyous as it terminates in either of them, and is never to become the forced and irksome toil of trying to make them subservient to us. The artist does not wish another to bring out his own ideal forms of beauty for him, nor the philosopher wish another to make up his science to his hand.

We do not choose that some others should practice virtue nor offer worship for us, and then give us the profits in some rewarding gratification; if we cannot have the serene complacency in our own practical virtue and piety, there is no reward for us. One may hire another to do his work, but no one will thank another to do his playing. The animal susceptibility may get its gratification by any barter, and buy in happiness at any market; but the rational susceptibility has its end only in the contemplation of that which is made to conform to its own perfect ideals. There may be the love of the beautiful, of the true, of the right, or of the good; but in all these cases, the love must be solely for the object's sake, and not that the object can be sold out in exchange for what may gratify some clamorous appetite.

CHAPTER III.

THE SPIRITUAL SUSCEPTIBILITY.

THIS sphere of the susceptibility is quite as important and as strongly marked as either of the others, and in order to a true psychology, it is also as necessary that it be carefully discriminated from both the animal and the rational, as that they should be accurately distinguished from each other.

Both the animal and the rational susceptibility are *constitutionally* in human nature. In so far forth as man is animal, he has constitutionally the capacity to all animal feeling; and in so much as he is endowed with reason, he has in this higher constitution the capacity to all the feelings of the rational being. These compose the entire sphere of constitutional susceptibility, inasmuch as the animal and the rational exhaust all the distinctive kinds of sentient life in which the human nature was created. Within this constitutional sphere of feeling, appetites and desires, impulses and obligations, may continually be going forth, and in them the race of mankind, as constitutionally endowed, will all participate. In these activities of sentient being, man can only differ in degree and not in kind, inasmuch as all participate in the same original constitution. The feelings are necessitated in nature when the occasions for them are given, and as the tiger must have his appetite for flesh, and the ox his appetite for grass, so the man must have his whole sphere of constitutional susceptibility necessitated in its own nature. The feelings can change, on the given occasion, only through a change of the physical constitution.

But in the spiritual susceptibility, we come to a sphere of feeling in all these respects widely different. The rational nature of man is so superinduced upon the animal nature, that while each preserves its own functions and faculties, they yet together make but one being, and the man both as animal and rational is a unit in his own identity. To have solely the animal nature is still to be a thing, but to have the endowment of rationality is to be elevated from thing to person. With this comes self-law, conscience, responsibility, and proper immortality. In this personality is perpetual spiritual activity, and as this goes out in its direction towards its objects, and stands permanently disposed in the direction to distinct ends, it gives to itself a proper spiritual *disposition.* The disposition is as abiding as the given direction, and responsible when found to be for or against a known rule. This going forth of the personal spiritual activity, which is properly its disposition, determines *character;* and so far as the disposing of the activity comes under the approbation or condemnation of conscience, the disposition has a *moral* character. And here, we are to fix our attention upon this *spiritual disposition*, and we shall find it to be an independent source of feeling, and thus occasion for a distinct sphere of susceptibility, which has not yet been at all recognized. Altogether aside from the activities of the animal and the rational susceptibilities, peculiar feelings will originate in the spiritual disposition; and while all of constitutional being remains the same, a change of this spiritual disposition will at once induce a change of feelings, which can only follow their appropriate modification of disposition. In this we shall find a clear consciousness that the spiritual susceptibility has its source in the personal disposition, and that it is utterly exclusive of all that belongs to constitutional nature, whether of the animal or of the rational. It will be necessary to determine respectively, the process in which this spiritual susceptibility is induced; the leading distinctions which it may embrace; and also the point at which responsibility attaches itself to this susceptibility.

SECTION I. THE PROCESS IN WHICH THIS SPIRITUAL SUSCEPTIBILITY IS INDUCED.—In the former cases of susceptibility we have found them already potentially in the constitutional being. All that was necessary tc awaken the actual feeling was the presentation of the proper occasion to constitutional nature. No process was requisite in order to the attainment of the susceptibility, but the hand that made us had already put it within us. Not so in this case. Mere constitutional being will not originate it, but the constitutional faculties must have their direction; the personal activity must have disposed itself toward some end; a disposition, determinative of the state in which the spiritual personality is, must have been effected; and though we determine nothing here of the time or the conditions of this process, yet the fact, that such a personal spiritual disposing must occur, may be made clear in the consciousness, since, without the disposition, we are conscious that the connected feeling cannot be. Animal and rational nature may have their complete constitution, but only as the person has a spiritual disposition, can he be susceptible to the peculiar feelings here in view. We have, thus, to notice the process by which a particular disposition determines a susceptibility to its own peculiar feelings.

We may *first* take an illustration, from a case where a disposition is *deliberately formed.* A young man may have just concluded his college course, by which he has become intellectually fitted to enter upon any course of direct professional study. The question presses for a decision, 'What distinct profession shall I pursue?' He may, perhaps, readily dismiss all others, but is quite indeterminate in reference to the profession of Law or of Divinity. He will study for the Bar or the Pulpit, but which he should take he cannot at once decide. He deliberates; estimates his own qualifications and circumstances; calculates carefully all the consequences that may be apprehended; and ultimately disposes the whole mind in a direction to one pursuit. We now suppose it to have been, judiciously and conscientiously, the Gospel Ministry; and with the mind so made up, there is no need of a perpetual energizing to keep it in that direction: it has already gone into a fixed state, and become a specific bent or permanent disposition. And here, the point to be noticed is, that this disposition to the Ministry has induced a susceptibility to feelings and emotions, which could not have been in his experience, had his mind been disposed on the profession of Law. Every day will come up feelings and sympathies, that originate wholly in a susceptibility determined in this disposition of his mind. His constitutional susceptibilities have not at all changed, for constitutional nature has not at all been modified; but the mind has become disposed in a new direction, and bent to a new and permanent end; and at once, in this permanent disposition, there is a new susceptibility to feeling, and which susceptibility could in no other way have been induced. The same may be said of any other determined pursuit. The Physician, the Farmer, the Sailor, the Soldier, etc.: all have their classes of sympathies and emotions peculiar to each other, and which can not be exchanged the one for the other, but in the corresponding change of disposition. The constitution remaining wholly unchanged, these feelings become possible, in the securing of the appropriate disposition for them.

Still more prominent is the peculiarity of some feelings, where the disposition has *not been so deliberately formed.* Wealth, or fame, or pleasure, may be proposed as ends to be attained; but the strong bent of the mind, in its particular direction to either, may have been effected gradually, insidiously, and almost imperceptibly to the man himself. The disposition may have had its beginning and growth so unnoticed, that it may emphatically be said of the man, "ye know not what manner of spirit ye are of." But the disposition, whether avaricious, ambitious, or voluptuous, has in it its own specific susceptibility. The avaricious man has feelings which neither the ambitious nor voluptuous man, as such, can have. A miser's feelings are not possible but in a miser's disposition. Physical organization and constitutional temperament may be of any modification; but the avaricious sentiment cannot be, without the spiritual disposition bent on hoarding money. Change that disposition and you change all these peculiar feelings, without at all changing the constitutional nature, or the constitutional susceptibilities.

So, in a more eminent degree, and without here attending at all to the subjective manner in which the disposition is secured, let the whole bent of the mind be directed to *the rule of right* as its end, exclusive of any gratification that can come in conflict with it, and this is the disposition of the righteous man; and in this disposition solely is the susceptibility of the good man. No matter what his constitutional nature and its susceptibilities, he cannot feel as the good man does, nor sympathize at all in any sentiment he has, except as he has first attained the good man's spiritual disposition. The susceptibility to virtuous feeling is no where else but in the virtuous disposition.

Constitutional nature as it is, the susceptibility to constitutional feeling, whether animal or rational, is already in it; and the occasion needs only to be presented, and the feeling necessarily follows. But no modification of constitutional nature can give the spiritual susceptibility. That must be induced in quite another process. The spirit itself must dispose its activity to some determinate end, and thus have its perpetual bent in one direction and on one object, and in that disposition will ever be a susceptibility peculiar to itself; capacitating the man to feel after its peculiar manner, and needing nothing but the appropriate occasion, and with this the specific feeling spontaneously awakes in exercise. With such a constitution, under given occasions the constitutional feeling must be; and with such a disposition, under given occasions the spiritual feeling also must be. The process to the spiritual feeling is not at all any appeal to constitutional susceptibility, but the securing of the spiritual disposition, and an appeal to the susceptibility that is in it.

SECTION II. SOME OF THE PROMINENT DISTINCTIONS IN SPIRITUAL SENTIMENT.—When, as above given, there is the making up of the mind in reference to a particular occupation or pursuit in life, such a disposing of the spiritual activity will in itself give the susceptibility to the particular feelings and sympathies which belong to that employment, and which constitutes *the tie of a class*, by virtue of whose connecting bonds all the members are held together in kindred sentiment. This is a most widely operative principle in human society, and is at the basis of the multiplied castes, associations and parties, into which mankind arrange themselves, and constitutes that *esprit du corps* which is so pervasive and effective in all party movements. So soon as the disposing of the spirit in the direction to the party-end occurs, the susceptibility to its peculiar sentiment is possessed, and the tie of the class attaches. There may mingle the influences and interests of many constitutional gratifications, but quite independently of all natural appetite or constitutional desire, the spiritual sentiment is the common bond of attachment among the members. Varied as this may be in the multiplied associations of life, it forms a distinct class of spiritual feeling; and whether for good or bad ends, and for the attaching of good or bad men together, it is everywhere the same principle of a kindred sentiment among those of a kindred pursuit, and is variously named as sectarian feeling; party spirit; denominational sentiment; class sympathy, etc. This tie of a class, though so pervading and effective through all communities, is still among the least prominent, and less generally noticed sentiments of the spiritual susceptibility.

Among individuals there may be kindred interests, pursuits, and constitutional temperaments; and these may render two, or any number of them, mutually congenial to each other, and the intercourse of such may be intimate and highly agreeable. But, as yet there is no spiritual sentiment, and thus no living bond of affection between them. The changes of business and pursuit, of interests and habits, may throw out some and introduce others, or even wholly remove the man to other congenial social circles, and he feels little loss and finds for it ready compensation. But when there has been a decided commitment of soul, and a reciprocal flowing out of the spirit each to each, there is in this a union of dispositions; and at once a cordiality of feeling springs up, much deeper and sweeter than all the congenialities of common interest or similiar temperament. The sentiment of *friendship* is experienced, and like David and Jonathan, the soul of one is knit to the soul of the other. When this mutual commitment of soul is between two persons of different sexes, and to the end of exclusive connection and cohabitation for life, the sentiment is that of *connubial love;* and becomes the tenderest and deepest of all human attachments. It is the blending of personalities, and the source of all the connections of consanguinity. Neither the feelings of Friendship, nor of Connubial Love can be, without the actual commitment of the spirit to the object, and thus the attainment of a permanent disposition, in which alone is the susceptibility to the cordial sentiment.

So, when a man commits his spirit to the highest advancement of the liberties and civilization of his country, he has the disposition of a patriot; and in this, the susceptibility to every *patriotic sentiment.* No matter how strong the feelings of self-interest, nor even how controlling the sentiment of party; there is nothing of patriotism, until there is the disposing of the spiritual activity to the end of his country's highest freedom, and in this patriotic disposition is the susceptibility to every patriotic feeling.

The above are all instances of spiritual sentiment, which cannot be said to be themselves *radically distinctive* of personal moral character. The disposition, out of which the susceptibility to the spiritual feeling springs, is not sufficiently deep and controlling to settle the question of moral character. Strong friendship, deep connubial love, and strenuous patriotism may be, where there is no radical universal commitment to eternal righteousness. They are affections; sentiments; and which may be termed amiable; but they are not properly virtues, except as contained in a more radical spiritual disposition. Passing all these, and other similar spiritual sentiments, as though originating in a disposition, yet not so deep as to be called virtuous; we turn to such as come completely within the sphere of moral goodness, and stamp the character as truly righteous. These will be of distinctive elevation, according to the elevation of the disposition.

The purely ethical sentiments.—When the man has a spirit devoted to the ultimate rule of right, and which excludes every end that collides with its own highest excellency and worthiness; such disposing of the spiritual activity, in a permanent state, is a spiritual disposition, and in the comprehensiveness of its end, subordinating all that can conflict with it resolutely to it, it is a virtuous disposition; a flowing out towards right for its excellency's sake. In the very fact of attaining such a disposition there is the securing of a susceptibility to feel all the sentiments which a good man ever experiences. Except in the virtuous disposition, the susceptibility to virtuous sentiment cannot be; and thus, until the man's spirit is disposed towards the right, exclusively, comprehensively, and permanently, he cannot by any possibility share in the good man's feelings. He can have no susceptibility to truly virtuous sentiments. In the disposition is the spiritual susceptibility to all the complacency, joy, and blessedness, of the truly moral man. As yet, the disposition knows no higher end than the ultimate ethical right, and the exclusion of all gratifications that may conflict with the spiritual excellency; and, thus, the sentiments can rise no higher than the purely ethical.

The religious sentiments.—When a man recognizes the being of a personal Deity; absolute in his own perfections; maker of himself and all things, and perpetual benefactor; and also recognizes his own dependence and accountability; there comes an occasion for the disposing of the spiritual activity to quite another and more exalted end, than when simply contemplating the excellency of his own spiritual being. The devotion of all I am, and all I have, to this Absolute Lord, is my duty and his due. And now, such a disposition, actually attained, at once induces a susceptibility to higher sentiments than the purely ethical. The feelings of religious confidence, divine gratitude and love, adoring praise and worship immediately break forth, and I have all the glad experience of the truly religious man. These feelings could not be, until first the disposition were attained, but this disposition is found in no constitutional temperament, and only in the supreme bent and inclination of the soul towards God.

The truly christian sentiments.—When the man as a conscious sinner, helpless and hopeless in his condemnation, recognizes the crucified and ascended Redeemer; and knows that all his own morality and all his religion is induced by his gracious interposition, and that through repentance and faith, pardon and justification with God may be applied for his sake, and this consistently with every claim of God and his whole government; there is, then, an occasion for a disposition of spirit more than merely religious. And when a disposition, directly going out and fixing upon this crucified Savior, as the only source of help and hope, is truly possessed; it has in it a susceptibility to feelings, which no merely religious devotion to God in the man's own name can ever attain. The love that has much forgiven; the gratitude for grace imparted; the confiding constancy, which owes all and commits all to this only Savior; all these christian sentiments now come out, and the spirit glows with emotions to which angels must themselves be strangers. Till this disposing of the soul on Christ, this susceptibility to christian feeling and sentiment was impossible. The source of the feeling is no where else but in the christian disposition.

One condition is common to all forms of the susceptibility, animal, rational and spiritual, namely, that there must be the apprehension of the object to which the feeling is directed; and as that object is congenial or otherwise, so the feeling will be for or against it. The difference between both the animal and the rational as constitutional, and the spiritual as responsible, is not in their conditions of the apprehension of their respective objects, which all must have, but in the different sources of their origin. The constitutional is in nature, and can be changed only in changing nature; but the spiritual, as responsible, is in the spiritual disposition, and may be changed in a change of disposition. So, in the christian feelings, which all have Jesus Christ as their object; as the disposition towards him is, such will be the susceptibility; and when Jesus Christ as object is presented and intellectually apprehended, the feelings must come forth accordingly. Where the disposition is towards Christ, the feeling will be christian, and where it is against Christ, the feeling will be unchristian. The disposition must be towards Christ, or christian emotions cannot be experienced.

Christian Love is widely distinct from any constitutional feeling. We may speak of a love of fruit, or a love of beauty—one of the animal, and the other of the rational susceptibility—but these are both determined in our constitutional structure. A love of the Lord Jesus Christ is possible, only as the spiritual disposition has gone out towards him. So long as the spirit is disposed on some other object, the feeling of christian love cannot be; there is no susceptibility to it. The religious claims, induced in the apprehension of the truth regarding Christ, are unwelcome, and their pressure becomes irksome, and hence the feelings of aversion and hatred are the necessary result of pressing christian truth upon an unchristian disposition. *Evangelical Repentance* has the same law in the mind for its exercise. As a feeling, it is godly sorrow for sin. That spirit, which is fully disposed towards Jesus Christ, cannot look upon sins, at any time committed, without feelings of penitential grief; while another spirit is fully set against Christ, and the dishonor which sin occasions to Christ is no occasion of sorrow to such a soul, nor can any view of sin against Christ bring out from such a disposition, any other feeling than hardened impenitence. The disposition must change, or there is no susceptibility to godly sorrow. *Evangelical Faith,* in so far forth as it is a joyful confidence in Christ as a Savior, is a feeling, and springs from a spiritual susceptibility in a christian disposition, like christian love and repentance. Of all proposed methods of salvation, the spirit has gone out to Christ in his appointed way, and with such a disposition a new feeling of confiding security and sweet reliance is at once called into exercise. But let the disposition go out after any other Savior, and this feeling of confiding christian repose cannot be in exercise.

So of all christian sentiment; there must first be the christian disposition, or there can be no susceptibility to the feeling. The modifications of no constitutional susceptibility can secure them. They are spiritual, and distinct from all other spiritual emotions, in that they originate in a susceptibility which must stand only in a christian disposition.

SECTION III. THE POINT AT WHICH RESPONSIBILITY ATTACHES TO THE SPIRITUAL SENTIMENTS.—It is quite necessary to note, that neither the spiritual susceptibility itself, nor any of its exercises, are the products of the will. They are never volitions, and cannot be directly willed into being. They are as necessary, in their conditions, as those that belong to constitutional nature. The disposition being given, the susceptibility is determined in it; and then, to this susceptibility, the occasions being supplied, the specific feelings are necessitated. How then may I be commanded to sorrow for sin? to rejoice in the Lord? or to feel the complacency of the virtuous man?

Were these sentiments the product of constitutional nature, we could have no responsibility for them. All men participate in the constitutional feelings, in virtue of their common humanity. Difference of degree will make no difference in kind, and what the susceptibility is has been determined in the constitution given by the Creator. This can be changed only by a physical power which changes the constitution. That the lion should eat straw like the ox, would demand that the physical structure should be wholly changed. That known transgression should escape remorse, would demand that the man lose his rational nature. The constitutional feelings are without the sphere of responsibility.

But in one radical point, the spiritual susceptibility completely differs. Constitutional nature continuing unchanged, the spiritual susceptibility changes in the change of disposition. The susceptibility must be as the spiritual disposition is, and hence, so far as man is responsible for his disposition, he is consequentially responsible for the susceptibility and its feelings which are determined in it. In this disposing of the spiritual activity, there may be various ends to which it is directed, that shall be altogether too limited to determine therefrom any moral character. A good man and a bad man may both be disposed to the same employment for life, and have all the kindred feelings which come in under the tie of a class, and such disposition determines nothing in respect to their radical character. The disposition is not yet brought under the determination of a rule of right. But let it be known, that this disposition towards the calling for life is involved in a broader disposition towards the right; the authority of God; or the will of Jesus Christ as a Savior; and such broader disposition will have its radical character, giving also its own character to the subordinate disposition of the mind towards its objects of pursuit. Thus always shall we be able to determine any lower disposing of the spiritual activity upon its end, by the character of the broader; and that disposition, which is inclusive of the universal right as end, must give its radical character to the man and all his minor dispositions of spirit. A disposition towards God, in Christ Jesus, to the exclusion of all that can stand in opposition, must be radically a holy disposition; and a disposition towards anything else as end, to the exclusion of God in Christ, must be a sinful disposition radically.

As then radical moral character is as the generic disposition of the man, so the radical spiritual susceptibility, which is in this disposition, will have its character accordingly; and all its sentiments, as in actual exercise, will participate in the same. So far thus, as the man is responsible for his radical character, is he responsible for his spiritual susceptibility and all its sentiments and emotions. This spiritual susceptibility is his *heart*, in a moral and scriptural meaning; and all its exercises of feeling are the different specific *moral affections*, as distinct from all feelings of constitutional susceptibility. The consideration of the question of *freedom*, in the radical disposition, can only be given in the investigation of the Will.

THIRD DIVISION.

THE WILL.

This division of the mental capacity has been very differently viewed by psychological writers, and its various facts contradictorily apprehended and expounded, and in consequence it has been a field of most strenuous controversy. Vital points in morality and theology are determined, by what is deemed to be fact in regard to some of the peculiar characteristics of the human will, and more especially in reference to the question of its freedom; and inasmuch as all dogmas concerning divine sovereignty and human responsibility must be modified by the views taken of voluntary agency, it is not surprising that different assumed positions should be both attacked and defended with great zeal and determined perseverance.

Questions of fact, in reference to the will, can only be settled on the field of psychological investigation, since both morality and theology assume their facts of human responsibility, and do not at all attempt to expound them. Consciousness is the only criterion, and in any points of disputed fact the decisions of universal consciousness, or common sense, must be the conclusive umpire. It is as competent to make the valid appeal to consciousness, for the facts of the will, as for those of the intellect and the susceptibility; since, although the ultimate principles in each are beyond consciousness, yet the facts of the insight of reason and the convictions it gives are within the consciousness for the will, as truly as for the intellect or the susceptibility. Other considerations which are also facts of consciousness, may be adduced as confirmative and explicative of the facts of the will, but direct consciousness is the ultimate appeal in all cases of impracticable reconciliation of opposite opinions. Caution, candor and comprehensiveness are all that is necessary in making the final appeal; and after such a process of trial, each one of us may as authoritatively announce his conclusion, as any renowned champion on either side of the question.

The mind, as capacity for willing, puts forth exercises different in kind, from those which proceed from it in its capacities of knowing or of feeling. All varied cognitions and emotions may be distinguished from volitions, and it is concerning the capacity for the latter that we now directly enquire. The exercises of the capacity for willing may be distinguished by various names, and though generally comprehended in the term volitions, yet may the willing be variously, disposition, purpose, choice, preference, etc., according to its peculiar characteristics. Other points of conscious distinction from all exercises of knowing and feeling will readily present themselves in the exercises of willing, but the grand matter for enquiry is about their difference from the others in the point of their necessity. In all the exercises of the intellect and the susceptibility, one fact has been invariable through all the examination, that, in the specific conditions, the exercise was wholly unavoidable. In such a condition, the intellect found no alternative to the knowing, and none to the knowledge just as it then was in the experience. The perception could only be of the red color, when there was a redness; and the judgment could only be of an affirmative predicate, when there was the including subject. And so also of the susceptibility; under the particular condition there was no alternative to the particular feeling, inasmuch as such conditions were a sufficient occasion to no other exercise of the susceptibility than the actual one. They have been thus wholly in necessity, inasmuch as under the given conditions no other way lay open. The great enquiry is, does this necessity extend itself over the capacity for willing? Are its exercises, in their conditions, without an alternative? If, as a matter of consciousness, they have their alternatives, how are the different ways open? and how is the certainty determinable, in the given conditions, which way shall be taken?

These questions involve the determination of the inherent constitution of a capacity for willing; and that activity, which can go out to its object with still an open alternative, must possess a constitutional being different from an activity that goes out to its object with no alternative. Unless the distinct conception of two such different activities be first clearly apprehended, all questions of fact in relation to the exercises of the will must be premature, inasmuch as with no such stand-point of observation, or only looking at the exercises from one only, the satisfactory determination of all question of necessity and liberty in the facts must be impossible. An intelligible definition of a capacity for willing cannot be given, until first there has been attained the conception of an activity that, in going out to one end, had, at the point of going forth, an open way to a different end. If there is no such conception possible, then is no conception of liberty possible, that is not in its expression only another name for necessity. And if such assumed conception is only a disguised and surreptitious introduction of some connection of nature's causes and effects, then must the exposure of the delusion throw that conception back among necessitated physical agents, no matter how loud the pretension may have been of having explained the question of human freedom by it. We cannot, thus, in the investigations of the will, at once define what we mean by it, and then put its manifest subdivisions into as many Chapters — as we have done in the consideration of both the intellect and the susceptibility — but we must first, with much care, explain what a necessary conception of will is, in its own constitutional being. This will best be done, by presenting a number of distinguished differing conceptions, and which are either some form of the working of mere natural cause and effect, without any alternative, sometimes openly so avowed, and at other times mistakenly deemed to rise above the necessities of nature; or, an insufficient, because incomplete, assumption of the distinctions of spiritual activity above nature; neither of which can give a conception of the will that shall accord with the convictions of consciousness. Such conceptions need not be referred to any authors, since oftentimes the real author has not been the most prominent expounder.

CHAPTER I.

A COMPLETE CONCEPTION OF THE CAPACITY FOR WILLING.

THE mind, as a self-acting existence, has been already considered. On occasion of the presence of an appropriate object, it is capacity for an energizing, or going forth, towards this object. But this simple capacity for a *nisus*, or energizing towards a presented object, is no distinguishing mark of any particular capacity of the mental activity, but is common to them all. The intellect and the susceptibility, in all their different faculties and functions of agency, are as much capacity for going out in activity towards their objects as the will, and such energizing cannot therefore be discriminative of the will. We have already distinguished in consciousness the different forms of energizing in knowing and in feeling, and have thus discriminated the susceptibility from the intellect; and here, we must distinguish in consciousness the different form of energizing in the willing from that presented in the feeling, and thus consciously discriminate the susceptibility from the will. In all the activity of the constitutional feelings, there is nothing of liberty, but a consciousness, in the conditions, that the feelings are determined from the nature of the case, and are thus in that case unavoidable. Nor is there any other distinction, here, in the spiritual susceptibility, than that perhaps we may find the disposition, in which the susceptibility is, to be avoidable, and thus mediately the susceptibility be the subject of change; but always on condition of the given disposition, the feeling is unavoidable. The point of this unavoidability will give opportunity for discriminating between feelings and volitions, and it is in this direction that we need to look in attaining the conception of what is properly a capacity for willing, in distinction from a capacity for craving, or for feeling obliged. In other words, it is a consciousness of freedom, in some sense, that discriminates a capacity for willing from a capacity for feeling.

With the attention fixed on this point, we shall make the surest progress to a complete conception of the will, by first noticing some of the prominent conceptions that have been formed, and distinctly marking their incompleteness or their error, in not conforming to this consciousness of avoidability in all proper acts of will. We need only to state the conceptions in the most concise manner that perspicuity will admit.

Section I. Different conceptions of the capacity for willing.—We will give these, in the order in which the conception seems most to strive that it may rise above the necessitated connections of cause and effect in nature. We do not say that the order will give a constantly nearer approach to truth, but that the authors of the successive conceptions seem, in this proportion, to have apprehended what the true conception demanded.

The will is simply capacity for preference.—Preferring to do, or not to do, is an act of the will, and thus to have the capacity for preferring is to have a will. This is determined from some uneasiness in the mind, which is to be relieved by the doing, or the not doing. This uneasiness of mind, craving for relief, is desire; and the greater the uneasiness, the stronger is the desire; the highest degree of which must determine the direction of the preference, or will. The question of freedom has no reference to this capacity for preference, or will; but solely to the power *to do*, as we prefer, or will. To prefer is from one power; to do, as we prefer, is from another power; the first is that of will, and the last only admits the question of liberty. To enquire whether the will is free, is thus wholly irrelevant, and merely the absurdity of seeking if one power is not another power. Liberty belongs to the power doing, not to the power willing. The agent, as willing, has no freedom; but only in doing as he wills. Whether he shall choose is determined from the uneasiness of desire; but whether he shall do as he chooses depends upon his ability, and in this is the sole question of his liberty. All must will as the stronger desire; the ability or not, to put in execution the preference, is the determination of the free-agency.

Here then is, expressly, a conception of will unavoidable in its action; and only the fact of executing the choice, in overt action, is avoidable. But nothing more need be noticed to show its conflict with human consciousness, than that the man feels responsible for his choices;

his inward preferences; and not merely for their outward execution. He is conscious of some alternative in the willing, and not merely in the doing as he may will.

The will is power to choose what is agreeable to the moral taste, or heart.—The moral taste, or heart, is connate or concreated. It is as truly in the constitutional being as his sensuous taste, or his natural susceptibility. It may be created agreeably to righteousness, and there is the power to choose the right; or it may be born agreeably to sinfulness, and there is no power to choose other than the sinful. The taste, or the heart, is thus of nature, and though called *moral*, yet is not so because avoidable, but only because it is at the fountain of all moral character. It is no part of the capacity for willing, but the will is the executive capacity for carrying out its impulses. This prompts agreeably to its own nature, and then the executive agency, which is the will, is free to go out in the execution or attainment of the congenial end. The will can go out in execution, but can have no reflex action upon the taste, or heart, itself. This is beyond the reach of the voluntary agent, and any change must be wrought by the hand that originally made it; the voluntary action is solely in going out in execution, and not at all in going back to the modification, of the moral taste. The will is thus free, only in the sense of unhindered. There is no avoidability in its action, for this action is determined in the natural moral taste; but it goes out freely, that is, unobstructedly from anything in the heart, upon the congenial objects of the moral taste. The exercise of the will is not at all the agreeable prompting of the taste, but the going out in gratifying such natural prompting.

This conception of the will recognizes rightly, the necessity for some permanent source of moral activity, which shall give its own character to the man and all his action. But it quite erroneously puts this in constitutional nature, and denies that it is any part of the voluntary capacity, or that it has any avoidability in reference to the agent himself. The man's moral taste is as truly in his constitution as his sensuous taste, and his aversion to God is just as physically unavoidable as his aversion to wormwood; and each are alike back of all action of the will, which is determined by them. But our consciousness testifies that we are responsible for the heart; and also for the executive acts which go out in gratification of its desires; and that this heart must itself be somehow within the voluntariness of our being, and not wholly beyond the capacity for willing. It must itself be *a disposition;* an inclination and bent of our spiritual activity; and not a component element in our constitution. To satisfy our consciousness, we must recognize, in some way, an avoidability in both the characteristics of the moral taste and in the executive acts for gratification, but this conception allows no alternative to the man in either of them.

A power of arbitrary self-determination.—The capacity for willing is a power absolute in its own arbitrament, and can both act, and direct its acts, in its own naked self-determination. No matter what the motives on each side, or if all be on one side; the mind is competent to suspend itself in *equilibrio*, and act either for or against the motives from its mere determination to do so. It wills solely because it will, and no other reason is needed than that it determines itself to do so. This conception may not have been original with any person, but was that to which Edwards forced his opponents, by logical consistency from their method of statement.

It involves two absurdities: viz. one, that the will is blind, and chooses for no reasons, and is thus a choice without any interest in choosing, and which is really the same thing as a choice without choosing; and another, that all volition is itself the product of a determination, and therefore that the determination to will is itself a willing, and needing a previous determination for itself, and that again another for it, and thus on endlessly with no first act of will. The real conception was doubtless that of power to originate and direct action; but from its incompleteness and obscurity in not apprehending that there could be no origination of choices without conditions, their expression of it was made to involve the foregoing absurdities. There was manifestly the conviction that the human will had more in it than the unavoidable successions of natural cause and effect, but the conception and expression were imperfect and logically indefensible.

Will is the power to choose happiness.—Happiness is the only good, and benevolent action the highest good, because productive of the highest happiness. In order to an act of will, there must be some object appealing to a susceptibility as an occasion for gratification, and the end of willing is such gratification or happiness. There is, essentially in mind, a generic susceptibility which craves all attainable happiness, and in all comparative happiness desires the greatest, and which may be known as self-love. The estimate of what the greatest happiness is, which the mind makes in the light of self-love, determines the choice. This estimate may be erroneous, but in simple certainty the will follows it. The will may affect the estimate in subordinate, but not in predominant ends. The honest enquiry for the greatest happiness on the whole gives occasion for an unbiassed judgment, and such decision may be termed *the estimate of reason;* but a sudden or violent impulse of appetite may pervert the judgment, and such perverted decision may be known as *the estimate of passion.*

From the constitution of the human mind, there is thus ever an occasion for bringing before it the end of reason and the end of passion, and thus ever the conditions for a choice, which shall gain or defeat the end of the man's being in highest happiness. In suspending all former purpose, and holding all present passion in abeyance, and carefully weighing all consequences, a rational estimate may be made, and the predominant purpose taken accordingly; but when passion is permitted to operate, the estimate is perverted, and the will wrongly directed. On this estimate of the understanding all radical character depends, inasmuch as there is the certainty that the choice will follow the estimate of the highest good. When making the passionate estimate, there is simple capacity to the opposite choice, but not the condition for it from the neglect to deliberate. A rational estimate will always determine the highest happiness to lie in the course of benevolent action, and the governing purpose following accordingly, the man is radically righteous in character; but the passionate estimate leads to the purpose of present selfish gratification, and the character is radically sinful.

This conception clearly apprehends the necessity of given conditions in order to choice, and thus wholly excludes a merely arbitrary will; and also assumes that there must be power to the opposite; but it has its incompleteness and thus its error. The most serious evil is felt on its ethical side, as it makes virtue to stand in simple prudence. I find myself, and nature about me, to be such, that I shall make myself the most happy in striving to make others happy; and from purely prudential reasons I do this, and am therein virtuous!

But its psychological defect is also obvious to close inspection, and originates in this want of all truly ethical end, and thereby really excludes all alternative and avoidability in the act. The happiness of benevolent action is in the gratification of a constitutional susceptibility, and the craving for it is as purely pathological as in the case of any other appetite. Man finds himself so made that he is happy in making others happy, just as he is happy in taking food when hungry, or rest when weary. To withhold the kind action, when self-love prompts, would be a self-denying sacrifice; since the strongest want can be satisfied by nothing but beneficence. There is no insight of reason which sees what is due to the spirit, and which thus in its own right makes a demand; but a logical deduction from consequences determining greatest happiness, and thereby waking self-love to feel a want. The "estimate of reason" is a reasoning from sense, and no intuition of reason itself which sees the law written within; and nothing of this meets the testimony of consciousness. A man may be kind from mere constitutional good nature, or from the calculation of greatest happiness in the long run, but he will also be conscious of a higher claim to kindness in the worthiness of his own character from it, and that to be unkind will debase his spirit, no matter how much happiness may be paid to him for being so. Not any reward in happiness, even for eternity, can equal the claim of the man's conscience for benevolent action, but that the man himself may *be* just what reason sees he *ought* to be, let the happiness for it be as it may.

And farther, such a conception of the will gives no alternative, and thus no avoidability in the acting. It is not a will in liberty, but solely the *brutum arbitrium* of the animal. Gratified constitutional susceptibility is ever one thing, as motive to will, however distinct the particular appetitive cravings may be. It is still highest happiness, whether attained from one generic susceptibility or from an aggregate of many, and nothing but a question of *degrees* in happiness can come within the estimate, with no regard to *kind*. Benevolent action is better than anything else, solely because it gives *more* happiness. There is no real alternative between five degrees and ten degrees of the same thing, and no condition for any choice between them. The happiness from following the rational estimate differs in nothing from the happiness in following the passionate estimate, so far as it is to influence the will, except that it is greater, and to this a less degree offers no condition for choice. The very reason for taking at all is the reason for taking the highest, and with such an estimate there is no alternative. The taking of the highest is not choice, but an act in that condition inevitable. An animal might as well leave its food, half satisfied, for no other reason than that it is half its want, as the man take half the degree of offered happiness only, when the whole is the sole reason why he should not.

The will is pure spontaneity.—The vital principle in the germinating seed goes out in its development to maturity. There is an inner law, which determines its whole order and form of development; but to this, and all the process of its growth, the plant is insensible. The animal not only grows, under its modified law of order and form, like the plant, but it also goes out to the attainment of its objects under the control of its appetites. It has sensation, but no self-consciousness in which the law of its growth and the determining principle of appetite is apprehended. Man grows, and feels appetitive cravings, not only, but his spirit is a spontaneous activity going out freely in an order and direction of which itself is conscious. It has conditions and laws of agency, but these are no restraint upon it and only principles within it, according to which it acts in its own gladness spontaneously. It is joyous in its self-consciousness, in its law of action, and in its activity; and thus the whole of spiritual life is a cheerful play, with no toil, no drudgery, no bondage. It shakes off all outward incumbrances, and rises above the sphere of all nature's annoyances, and lives in its own sphere, tranquil and delighted. The spirit is thus contemplated in its own pure activity, and such conception of spontaneous action is that of the will.

This conception sees the necessity of rising above the fixed order of connection in natural cause and effect, and predicating a proper will only of the spiritual existence; but its law is inherent in its own constitution, and determines all its activity as really as the physical laws in nature determine its ongoing. The only difference is that the spirit knows itself and its laws, and acts on with no reluctance. Its action in thought has the same spontaneity as in will; for thought has its inherent law through all its processes, and the spirit goes out in thinking according to its conscious laws with the same joyousness. Indeed, with Hegel, thought is personality; and absolute thought, excluding all nature's hindrances but not its own inherent laws, is true freedom. The conception of free thought is thus this very conception of free will, a spontaneity of spiritual activity going out lovingly according to its own law. There is conceived no law as an imperative, and thus a joyousness in the spontaneous obedience of moral rectitude; but solely a law inherently directive, and the spirit gladly going through the process which its inner law fits it for.

Other modifications of the conception of a will might be given, but the foregoing are among the most prominent of such as are deemed to be but partial and thus erroneous, and these may be sufficient to introduce us to the next enquiry.

SECTION II. WHAT IS A COMPLETE CONCEPTION OF THE WILL?—The susceptibility, as we have seen, prompts to an executive act in the attainment of its end; if the object is agreeable, the prompting is to attain it, and if disagreeable, to avoid it. But thus far, the action is wholly of the susceptibility, and is mere feeling. Beyond this prompting of feeling, the animal life may go out to get the object and gratify the want; and there is found in this, an activity which is out of and beyond the susceptibility, and is no more a feeling but an executive act to satisfy a feeling. This may be termed brute-will; animal-choice. But it is really animal impulse; a living activity impelled by sense; and not at all a will in liberty. It acts when the susceptibility prompts, and as this prompts, and can change its action only by a change of feeling in the susceptibility. When two conflicting feelings prompt, that which it is deemed will give highest gratification must nullify the promptings of the weaker, and the executive act is unavoidable. The occasion for an alternative act is not given. There may be the faculty of judging, from apprehended consequences, what will give on the whole the highest happiness, and thus what action is prudent; and if the higher gratification of self-love, on the whole, come in competition with only the lower present gratification, the prudential impulse must prevail, inasmuch as the less impulse is no alternative. And in the same way, the faculty of judging what will make others most happy may determine for us what action is benevolent; and if this appeal is to a susceptibility which, in gratification, is highest happiness on the whole, the kind impulse must overcome and take the action in that direction. In any way that highest gratification is judged as attainable, in that direction the executive act is unavoidable, for there is no alternative presented to it. The whole of animal being is bound in the necessity of nature, and all that we may say of brute-will must still include in its conception, the fact that the issue is unavoidable. Nature knows no liberty, and the animal being is wholly within nature. The conception of will involves within itself something supernatural.

The true conception of a responsible Will is in a capacity to originate, from the spirit itself, an act in contravention of the animal impulse. It is a power that may counteract the executive agency which gratifies natural want, and in this give a sovereign master over the animal being. This must be wholly a spiritual capacity, that it may originate action completely regnant over all natural appetite. This capacity for spiritual origination gives the competency to suppress animal gratification, and thus opens a proper alternative in permitting the animal executive act to go out in gratification, or putting forth the spiritual act which shall preclude it. Nature may be suppressed by the free action of the spirit. There is a freedom not only in the fact of unhindered activity, for this is true of the execution of appetite by the animal, but a freedom in the start; a beginning, and not a projection from something behind; a true origination in the spirit, and not an impulse from the sense. In this capacity for free origination, there is complete condition for a proper *libration* between the happiness of gratified want and the duty of secured worth, and which is truly will in *liberty*. That the spirit can, from itself, so act in controlling the sense, secures a valid alternative to sensual gratification, and thus the freedom of avoidability.

Looking, thus, at the human mind, which combines both animal and rational being, we say, that a conception of will must involve something else than mere executive agency to gratify want, even spiritual origination of action in restraining and controlling gratification, and thus full capacity for alternative agency. The animal can have no will in liberty, since however free from prevenient hindrance in gratification, it is impelled by constitutional nature *a' tergo*. The angel, as purely spiritual, may have alternatives in spiritual ends towards which he may originate action, and may thus stand between spiritual wickedness and spiritual holiness, and take on demoniac malignity or maintain angelic purity; but man must be studied as only in the flesh, and whatever soul-guilt he may contract, there will always be blended with his sin the inworking sensual lusts, and thus the human will must be conceived as capacity for avoiding sensual gratification by the claims of the reason. The Absolute Reason is above all occasion for alternatives to perfect rationality, and is free, in the absolute acceptation of spiritual origination with no conflict. Deity cannot be tempted with any alternative to right, except as the divinity becomes incarnate; but, as our psychology is human, we have only the human not the divine will to investigate.

Election may be used in a different sense from *selection;* the last being only a particular taking, but the first a taking with an alternative. All natural causes select their ends in their effects. The magnet selects steel-filings from saw-dust; the fire selects stubble from stones; electricity selects metals from glass and resin; and in all this taking to itself, there is no capacity to the alternative. But election is the taking of one, when it might have been not the taking of that, but some other. No animal can do more than to select; a spiritual being only can properly elect. With this apprehension of the meaning of terms, the definition of the human Will is a *Capacity for electing.*

In the more complete conception of this definition, the following considerations are all important.

An act of will must have its end.—The capacity for willing can no more go out into act without an object, than can the capacities for knowing, or for feeling. Even the brute-will must have an end in acting, or it would involve the absurdity of executive action with nothing to execute. A rational spirit cannot originate an act without an end for the action, for an aimless action cannot be rational. We may as well eat with nothing to be eaten, as choose with nothing to be chosen.

This end must have also an alternative in kind, and not merely in degree.—In order to all responsibility there must be avoidability, and every action is inevitable where no alternative is offered. With purely one object, the act is not that of election. The one object may present the alternatives to take, or not to take; to take part, or all, etc.; but to strictly one object, all *alter* is excluded. Nor can there be any proper alternative in the willing, except as the ends differ in their *kind*. One gold eagle and ten silver dollars present no alternative in kind, for in pecuniary value they are the same. One gold eagle and five silver dollars give alternative only in degree, and as end in the will, this is no proper alternative. The sole end of acting being for pecuniary value, the action must be for the greater when to this only the less stands opposed. The part of the same thing is absorbed and lost in the whole, so far as all occasion for choice is given.

To be an alternative in kind, there must be an end in the reason.—No matter how different may be the animal susceptibilities to be gratified, they offer no distinction in kind, but only in degree, as end of willing. The end, in both cases, is the gratification, and the two are really but one thing as motive to will, and that which is the greater has no alternative to it. Only as the prompting of an animal susceptibility has set over against it the claim of a rational susceptibility, can there be any proper alternative in the human will. An occasion being given, for the origination of an act in the spirit that it may suppress and control some lust of the animal, there is in this a full alternative in kind, and the fair occasion for an action in liberty.

The animal may crave, but the spirit may see that the claims of *taste* forbid the gratification, and the end of beauty in the reason may control the end of appetite in the animal. The artist may disdain to sell his product for any mercenary consideration. In the field of art is freedom, for the originations of the spirit can here counteract the clamors of appetite, and there is a fair alternative. So also the claims of *science* may forbid the offered happiness, and the end of truth be an occasion for the spirit to originate an act that is to suppress the execution of animal desire. Some Galilleo may resolutely say of the earth, "but it does turn," though he die for it. Philosophy is thus free, for it puts a dignity in the spirit as alternative to any craving for happiness. But more especially, the *moral* claim may be an alternative to any other end of action. The self-knowledge of the reason — clearly apprehending the excellency of its own spirituality of being, and thus knowing what is due to itself as against happiness, or above the claims of art and science, and in this conviction of duty possessing a conscience — may give a spiritual origination that shall suppress all action which is in conflict with right. And when this self-knowledge is also connected with the knowledge of God, and the insight of the finite spirit determines that its highest worthiness is in loving and adoring the Absolute Spirit, there is an alternative in man's *religious* being, which makes every action colliding with it to be thoroughly avoidable.

In this complete conception of an end in the spirit, which may countercheck all ends in happiness, is there occasion for free, pure, spiritual origination of action. Not because an outer object appeals to appetite, and awakes a want, and thus impels to greatest happiness; but solely because in the spirit's own being there is a claim for its own sake, and thus in itself alone originates the act, whose only end is that the spirit may *be* as worthy of all moral accepting as it is due to itself that it *should* be. The capacity to the alternative action is in the *super*natural only. So far as nature reaches in man, all is without avoidability; his spiritual being is capacity for true will in liberty.

CHAPTER II.

MAN EXERCISES SUCH CAPACITY OF WILL.

In the foregoing Chapter, we have attained a completed conception of a will in liberty; and now it is to be shown, that the human mind is endowed with such capacity, and that man actually so wills. It has already been made manifest that the human mind has susceptibility like the animal not only, but also that man's rational endowment capacitates him for feelings quite above, and other in kind than any animal can possess. Man is not left under the domination of appetite, with no alternative to the estimated highest happiness; he has the interest of taste and science, and may free himself from the bondage of the animal in the open spheres of beauty and of truth.

But quite above all, he is competent to know himself, and thus to find the rule within himself that determines the ground of his duty to himself, his fellows, and his God. In this moral imperative, there is attained the spring to a possible election of righteousness against any and all other interests. Taste or science may control happiness, and virtue or piety may control all. The spirit may keep all natural craving in subjection, and in the end of its own dignity in taste and philosophy, and more especially in ethics and religion, it can originate acts subjecting all of happiness to its own moral worth. All the elements, necessary to the capacity of a will in liberty, belong originally to the human mind. The evidence, that man puts in exercise such a capacity, is found in the following direct inferences from facts in consciousness, and is a direct fact in consciousness itself.

1. *Consciousness of personal responsibility can stand only in a capacity of will in liberty.*—The conviction of personal responsibility for personal character and action is in every consciousness. Speculative theories and delusive conclusions may often beguile the logical judgment to deny such personal accountability, but no speculations of the logical understanding can make the reason to belie its own insight. The spirit knows what it behooves itself to do for its own worthiness' sake, and that it must take in its own being the dignity of its virtuous, or the infamy of its vicious action; and while speculation may err, the conscience must hold true to its own claims. No man, in the honesty of his rational apprehension, ever doubted the fact of his moral accountability. The tribunal and the judge, the witness and the executioner, are all consciously within himself, and if he speculatively deny his God, he cannot dethrone the authority of his own reason. He must acquit or condemn himself, and be consciously elevated or degraded in his own eyes.

But the consciousness is as clearly explicit, that for unavoidable results there can be no moral accountability. Power may crush in hopeless misery for actions that had no alternative, but no power can make the spirit see its own sin in that which it could not avoid, nor feel guilty desert for an act that could not have been otherwise. The soul goes quite back of all speculation on both sides, and not from any deductions in the understanding, but from an insight into its own being, decides that it is responsible for personal deeds, and is not responsible for anything that is not voluntarily in its own personality. Power has nothing to do with such convictions; omnipotence itself, must go in accordance with them, and be judged conformably to them. Not arbitrary infliction, not even infallible testimony from another, can wake the feeling of responsibility in the spirit, except as that spirit is conscious of character and deeds of its own, which might have been avoided by it. A thousand *liabilities* to suffering there may be, which to the sufferer are wholly inevitable, but no such sufferings ever awoke the spirit to recognize any moral *responsibilities*.

These conscious facts make the conclusion valid for a capacity of human election. Man knows himself responsible for his character and actions; he knows himself not responsible for anything to him utterly inevitable; he has thus both a character and a life, that lie wholly within the capacity of a will in liberty.

2. *The distinction between brute and human will is in this very point.*—The animal is not rational spirit, and thus has no capacity for self-knowledge. To the brute there can be no insight of rights and claims due on its own account, and thus no moral rule to direct a moral life. There is no element of the ethical; all is perpetually the natural only. Experience teaches it in many things its highest happiness, and hence the animal learns the law of prudence; yea, experience sometimes teaches the animal what is kind, and so far the brute is pathologically

benevolent; but in all this, the animal never awakes to see the right, and feel the claim of moral obligation. The executive act goes out under the impulse of the strongest prompting, and appetite can be controlled only by arousing a stronger passion. Nothing can originate from within itself, but all the animal is, and does, has been determined for it in a previous condition. All is bound within the law of cause and effect in nature, and the brute can never lift itself above this bondage. There is no aspiration after freedom; no dreaming of a spiritual world above the senses; but an entire resting in the gratification of its own appetites. Satisfy want, and the brute is contented; the whole capacity is thereby filled; and the strugglings of a free spirit to reach some higher station are never known. Its whole end is happiness, and there is no quickening spring to rise to moral worthiness.

But from all this, man wholly differs. In his animal wants, he is like the brute, and prompted to highest gratification, and quiet when animal craving is satiated. But in his spiritual being there is that which no sensual gratification satisfies. Even as depraved, and the spirit basely subjected to the desires of the flesh, he knows that the claim is strong upon him, to crush his appetites in subordination to his rational worth, and restrain all their gratification by what is due to his spirit, and thus stand out again in all the dignity and manliness of a good will that masters passion. He cannot make himself to lie down at rest, with the brute, when animal craving is satisfied. There are the imperatives of conscience to fulfil; the dignity and worth of moral character to sustain; the approbation of his own and other's spirit to secure; and though the means of fullest gratification were given, this cannot content him. There is a conscious wrong to himself, a foul debasement and degradation of his manliness, if the behests of his spirit are not recognized and asserted against all the clamors of sense. He cowers in secret beneath the reproaches of his own conscience, and stands self-abashed and speechless before the rebukes of his own spirit, and well knows that he can not hold up his head among his fellows, nor keep the blush of guilt from his face when alone, if he has sacrificed his loyalty to the right, and allowed gratified want to usurp the control of imperative duty. On the other hand, he knows that he can bear all suffering, and permit all that is animal within him to be crushed and die, and go to his spirit in its integrity for support; all of which no brute can recognize, and in which nothing that is animal can participate. There is, to man, an alternative to his whole animal nature, and that he should live under the law of highest happiness, like the brute, is clearly avoidable. He has a capacity of will in liberty.

3. *It is only in this capacity of will in liberty, that man can discriminately determine what is personally his.* All of man's constitutional being is conditioned in its own nature, and in the connections of surrounding nature; and the supplied conditions bring the actions out with no alternatives. They really belong to nature, not to the man, except only as the onward causes in nature have wrought them out within the field of his consciousness, and made them necessarily to be a part of his patholo-

gical experience. That I am hungry and desire food, or cold and weary and desire warmth and rest, are no acts in which my proper personality participates; they are what nature is working in my constitution. Nature comes in and works upon me, and leaves its effects in my constitutional being, as the winds blow and the shadows pass over the landscape, and the sun shines and the showers fall upon it. These are not willed by me into act and being, and I never call them mine, as at all belonging to my proper personality All such events are linked into the connected successions of nature without an alternative, and the chain that they compose is a unit, whether the linked events be of matter or of mind. The tones have been struck upon me: they have not come up from the depths within me, and thus *sounded through* all my being as *personal* to me. In my constitutional nature, nothing is mine; all is put there by another. I am never to value myself upon it, nor to charge myself with it.

But, of all the originations of my spiritual activity, I am quite conscious that they sustain a very different relation to me. They are caused *by* me, and not merely caused *in* me; they are the product of an election, and not an unavoidable coercion; and I know them to be mine, in a sense that will not allow that they should so be appropriated to any other personality, human or divine. That ideal beauty; that poem or song; that completed system of science; each belongs to its author, as neither can be owned by any other. My disposition; my plan; my habit; my purpose; these are wholly mine and not to be referred to nature, as is my hunger, my thirst, or any other appetite. And so, also, that assent to temptation; that enticing allurement; that dishonest transaction; that plan to defraud; that direct falsehood, of which I may be conscious in my own experience; these have been wrought by me, and come back directly upon me, and fix themselves inalienably within me, and forever belong to me, and not to nature, nor to my neighbor, nor to God. They were avoidable by me, and yet originated from me, and belong solely to me. I alone, in my own person, am responsible for them. And thus, too, that act of virtuous self-denial; that fixed decision for the right; that firm stand in duty; these are mine, and no other personality in the universe, than me the doer, can feel any self-complacency in them. Influences from other quarters and agencies may have come upon me, which belong responsibly to their authors; but these are products of my electing agency, and have originated in my capacity of will in liberty, and are thus my personal deeds exclusively. Only because of this capacity of will, can I detach what is mine from all else, and see myself and my deeds to stand out together, wholly discriminated from all other beings or facts in the universe.

4. *Reciprocal complacency in moral character stands wholly in this capacity of will in liberty.*—Most animals are more or less gregarious, but their collection in flocks and herds is from constitutional propensities. The working of nature within them brings them together, and not that there is any reciprocal moral complacency between them. So, also, there are various associations

among men, which are induced by considerations of business, amusement or social enjoyment; and indeed a large proportion of human attachments that go under the name of friendship, and even take on the form of conjugal connections, are based on no higher considerations than kindred pursuits, common interests, or congenial temperament; and in all such cases, the bonds that hold them together find all their strength in constitutional nature alone. They are merely joint-stock partners in attaining happiness; held in connection only from the prudential consideration that they are useful to each other; and they never rise to the elevation of that social communion, where the attachments are all induced and perpetuated by the reciprocal congenialities of moral character.

But, one good man loves another, and all good men love God, from the congeniality of spiritual dispositions, and their reciprocal complacency is solely through the righteous character that each recognizes in the other. It is like communing with like, in free personality; and each heart beats in sympathy with the same ultimate moral rule, and glows with the same moral sentiments. Their spirits are all disposed to the same end, and thus the whole spiritual susceptibility, in each, is thoroughly congenial. They are kindred in spirit, and not merely held together as each can use the others for his highest happiness.

God may be pleased with man in his constitutional being just as he is pleased with all the other works of his hand in nature, solely in the light of original adaptations, and as he sees man to be fitted to the uses designed;

and he may pronounce man on this account as he did nature at the beginning, to be "very good." And in the same way, man may be pleased with God; and, viewing him merely as a means to be used for his own advantage, in that by him he gets propitious providences, fruitful seasons, a healthy body, and a happy heaven at last, man may say of God, in all the attributes which he cannot afford to lose, "very good;" his omnipotence; his wisdom; his foresight; his steady arrangement of nature; all "very good." What ends the man could not get, these attributes get for him; and he cannot do without them. They are all put to an excellent use, in governing the universe for man's happiness, and are just as much a greater good than the sunshine and the shower, as they subserve a more important end in gratifying human wants, and securing greater happiness. But in all this, there is no reciprocal complacency between God and man. Not thus does a good man love his God; not thus does God love good men. There is a mutual delight, each in each, as objects of simple contemplation. An intrinsic excellency of moral character is seen, and on each side loved for what it is, and not for what it can be bartered away for. The whole spirituality of each person is fully set on righteousness, and for no selfish considerations will the good will turn from its steadfastness; and in this solely is their communion, and not because they see that they are each necessary to the other's happiness. Take away from man the capacity of spiritual origination, in the election of highest worthiness above all happiness, and he can commune with his fellows only on the same basis as the animals herd together; and God can have complacency in him, only as he is pleased with the adaptations and uses of nature. Reciprocal complacency in character can possibly stand in nothing else, than the free originations of congenial moral dispositions.

5. *Only in this capacity of will in liberty can the current of constitutional nature be resisted.*—Constitutional nature works on, and I am hungry: in this condition I am conscious that the craving for food is unavoidable. I am weary; and in this condition I cannot exclude nature's desire for rest. Let only this prompting of the appetite be given, and there is no alternative to the executive act in gratification. Let only conflicting appetites crave, and there is no alternative to the act which goes out after what is deemed the highest gratification. A smaller amount of happiness can be no occasion for carrying the executive action against a greater. A calculation of consequences, and in this an attainment of the rule of prudence, can only appeal to a susceptibility for happiness, and whether considered as an aggregate of all susceptibilities, or as one generic susceptibility, the only occasion given is that for the simple estimate of higher and lower *degrees*. All is completely conditioned in constitutional nature, and my prudence is as much a pathological law as my hunger or my weariness. The stream is one, and as it floats me onward in the direction of greatest happiness, I can work the rudder against no counteracting force in the current that carries me. Nature is thoroughly all in and around me, and I can

seize upon nothing to steady myself against it, nor work my way upward in resistance to it. I myself am nature, and can only execute the promptings of my nature within me.

But, I am conscious, in my spiritual being, of the possession of supernatural agency. When appetite craves, in weaker or stronger measures, I can see in my spiritual being another law than highest happiness, and feel the claim of spiritual worthiness; and I can put this over upon the weaker appetite against the stronger, or over against all appetite that is in collision with it, and I have in this an alternative, in *kind*, to all that nature may present; and a spring to throw myself against nature, and work my way upward in resistance of it. The desires of the flesh may be aroused to their most passionate excitement, and all circumstances may favor the indulgence; prudential considerations may seem to lie on the same side, and even the promptings of kindness may also concur; and thus, the unbroken current of nature may tend towards gratification; but if I also see, that such indulgence would degrade and debase my spirit; I shall, in this claim of my rational being, have a full alternative to all of nature's promptings. Let constitutional nature do her best, or her worst, I may still stand in my spiritual integrity, regardless of either the happiness or the suffering that weighs itself against duty. There is, in this capacity of the spirit, that which is out of and above nature; a measure and a test for nature; a determiner when gratification may be, and when it may not be, with honor to the soul; and in the alternative of worthiness to happiness, thus opened, no alluring temptation from constitutional nature can ever come upon man, and be truly unavoidable. It is the right of the spirit to control and use the sense for its own highest excellency; and it is due to itself to put the flesh to any sacrifice and endurance which may preserve or exalt its own true dignity; and thus in its own behoof, the spirit may contemn all enjoyment, and all suffering, that nature can give.

6. *Individual consciousness is clear for this capacity of will in liberty.*—We do not say that any man is conscious of "the power of contrary choice," as it is called, in the sense that he can take a less degree of happiness when only a greater degree stands over against it. If only happiness appeals to a susceptibility, all consciousness is, that the greater must be taken; for there is literally no reason for anything else, and thus no alternative. But in all men there is a deep consciousness that, somehow, there is an alternative to present disposition and character, and thus an avoidability in all voluntary action. They may not be able to analyze the fact, so that they can represent it clearly in its conception to themselves, or to others; but they all know, that there is responsibility for their radical disposition of soul, and thus that its disposing is not without its alternative. It is not all the freedom a wicked man is conscious of, that he may change his action *if he please.* That *pleasing* is in his spiritual, and not in any constitutional disposition; and he knows the bond is on him that he *please* to change; and that his sin is in this very disposition which is *not*

pleased to change; and that, in this responsibility of disposition, the present evil one is avoidable. This fact may be made to stand out more perspicuous, by a comparison with other activities.

The Intellectual Capacity is consciously without any alternatives in its activity. In all conditions of knowing, the knowledge must be as it is, in the given condition. When the occasion is given for perceiving a house, there is not the alternative for perceiving, not it but, a tree. To the intellect, in that condition, the perception of the house, and just that specific house, is unavoidable. So in the concluding in a judgment; with the conditioned facts, the specific judgment must be as it is. We can not say we can change the knowledge if we please; for our pleasure has no control over it. All is determined in nature, and not at all in any spiritual disposition. So, also, is the constitutional susceptibility without any alternative, in its activity. When nature makes me cold, I cannot change the feeling to warmth; nor can I repress the desire to be warm; and when I hear that my brother is sick, I cannot change the feeling to that which is induced when I hear he is in good health. The feeling is determined in the condition; and all men are quite conscious, that, in order to change the feeling, there must be a change of conditions. To the constitutional susceptibility, all its activity is without an alternative; and every specific feeling is, in its given condition, wholly unavoidable. Not if we please, can we here feel differently, for all these feelings are wholly in nature, and not at all in a spiritual disposition.

But when I bring my capacity of will within the light of consciousness, I know that in precisely this point there is a wide distinction. I feel that my act of will was not bound, in its given conditions, without an alternative. I know that I could have done differently, if I had pleased; and I know, moreover, that if I was pleased to do wrong, that pleasing to so do was not inevitable. It was not determined in the conditions of nature, but wholly in my spiritual disposition; and to that, there was a full alternative. My spirit was bound, by the conscious claims of its own true dignity, to dispose its entire activity to a different end; and I am fully conscious that the way was open to it, though it did not take it. The question of the *certainty of fact* in liberty will hereafter be investigated, but now the only question is of conscious *avoidability;* and we have only to mark the conscious contrast, in this point, between the acts of the intellect and the acts of the constitutional susceptibility, and those of the will, and we find a clear decision. The last is with an alternative, and consciously avoidable; the two former, we know, are conditioned in nature.

7. *Universal consciousness.*—There is a full opportunity to appeal to universal consciousness, on the question of capacity for election, or of will in liberty. And this is affirmed, notwithstanding the fact that the speculations of the logical understanding must conclude against it. The operation of the understanding must be wholly within nature, and can possibly have no recognition of a supernatural. It can only *connect* conceptions, and can never *comprehend* the process, in an absolute beginning and

end. Thus, to the logical understanding, there can be only the conditioned, and never an absolute. There may be one circle enclosing all that has yet been, but not one that is absolute for all that can be. There may be a mounting up from effect to cause indefinitely, but not to an absolute first; for the understanding can only connect, and in its highest cause is still obliged to conceive of something higher that conditions it. The great first cause, to the logical understanding, has still its imposed conditions within itself, and can develop its activity in only one way. It is as much nature as any succeeding cause, only that it is assumed to be a first one. But common consciousness has always testified to the conviction that there is an absolute first cause, though the understanding can never find it, nor even have a conception of it.

Even so with liberty. The logical understanding can neither find it, nor get a conception of it. Absolute origination is to this faculty an absurdity. The originator finds already within himself that which conditions his products, and he can choose only as he finds himself *pleased* to choose, but can make no alternative to this *pleasing*. He finds his disposition already within him, and does not himself originate it. The conception of his changing his disposition would involve a previous *pleasing* to do so, and conditioned in this, a choosing to do so; and thus, endlessly, the choice must be conditioned already in some preceding given disposition. So, we say, the logical understanding *must* go. It is faculty for connecting, and not beginning; for conditioned producing, and not absolutely originating; for knowing nature, and not at all the supernatural; and if we have no higher faculty, we cannot possibly conceive of a God, whose disposition is in any other sense his, than that he finds it already originated in him; and then, that this determines all his acts of election, without alternative or avoidability. Nature itself thus runs upward through all the activity of the Deity, and both the finding, and the conceiving, of an originating will in liberty is an impossibility, and an absurdity. But the common consciousness never acquiesced in these speculative conclusions of a logical understanding. Universally, the common mind has recognized a God, whose disposing of his whole spiritual activity was his own, and not that he found it already disposed, and must condition all his choices by it. Though they may not have discriminated between the faculties of the understanding, which must have its *media* for connecting, and that of the reason, which has its *compass* for comprehending; yet, have they always testified to the convictions of the latter, against the speculative conclusions of the former. No thoroughly labored system of a will, conditioned in its antecedent grounds of preference, has ever satisfied the common conviction. That has always mounted to the source of all pleasing and preference; to the radical disposition itself; and affirmed that this was at the man's responsibility, and that it had ever its alternative. All human language, all legislation, all the history of man, speaks out what mankind in all ages have consciously felt, an alternative and avoidability to their inmost disposition.

The speculation of the understanding may at any time be counteracted, and corrected in the insight of the reason. While the understanding always finds a law imposed upon, the reason sees one inherent in, the agent. One holds to an end without an alternative, and is physical law; the other binds by the imperative of duty, admitting an alternative, and is ethical law. When the fact is clearly apprehended, that the spirit of man has the prerogative, which the animal nature has not, of knowing itself and its intrinsic excellency, and thus reading its duty in what is due in its own right, there is in this seen a full occasion for its own disposing of its activity, and not waiting for highest gratified want to determine it. There is capacity for originating an act in the end of its own worthiness, and for electing between this and any gratified want that may come in competition with this. And even, when a perverse disposing of itself has been effected, and a sinful and depraved disposition contracted; the conscious claim, of what is due to the spirit in its own right, has not ceased to press, and the alternative is open, however it may be certain as a fact that it will not be taken, for the spirit to break from its bondage and obey the imperative to secure its highest worthiness.

CHAPTER III.

THE DISCRIMINATION OF THE ACTS OF THE WILL FROM ALL OTHER MENTAL FACTS.

IN the attainment of the complete conception of a will in liberty, we are prepared to make an accurate discrimination between its acts and all other mental phenomena; and such discrimination is necessary to a correct psychology. A self-active being, which has its law within it, and not imposed upon it, must go out in its activity as no other agency can; its acts are its own originations, and not productions from it by an outer causality working upon it. When put forth there was an alternative, and thus an avoidability, and these are characteristics of all acts of will exclusively. In most cases, the acts of the will are readily distinguished from other mental facts. Intellectual acts are not liable to be confounded with voluntary acts; knowing is so little similar to willing, that cognitions never become mistaken for volitions. But other mental activities are sometimes misapprehended as from the will, and not unfrequently common speech confuses both volitions and other actions under the same word. We will notice some particulars in their order.

SECTION I. SIMPLE SPONTANEITY IS SOMETIMES CONFOUNDED WITH WILL.—Spirit is inherently self-active, and in given occasions goes out towards its ends spontaneously. We have already attained a number of such facts of simple spontaneity, as in the production of the General States of mind. The self-agency, on occasion given, goes of its own accord into the intellectual, emotive, or willing states; and though the occasion for this may sometimes be that the will is exerted, yet, as in memory, this willing is not directly in the production of the fact, but rather the putting of the mind in a fitting occasion for it. The remembering is not itself a volition, nor is the general state of either the knowing, feeling or willing, a volition, but is a spontaneous movement of the mind into the given state, as capacity to know, feel, or will.

And, here we observe, that such spontaneous outgoings of mind are sometimes mistaken for volitions, especially if they occur on occasion of their being consciously wished for. Such has been more particularly confounded with volition, in the facts of observation and attention. Cousin directly ascribes attention to the will, and makes it evidential of personality. But the thorough analysis, which attains to what an act of attention specifically is, will at once determine its purely spontaneous, and not voluntary origin. When a discriminated sensation is given, the operation of constructing or defining it, so as to give its exact limits in either space, time or degree, is of the intellect and not of the will. The will may be an occasion for it or not; but in any way, the intellectual movement, which limits and thus gives form to that which is in the sensation, is purely spontaneous and not willed directly. It is often quite beyond the reach of the will, inasmuch as the will sometimes cannot prevent its being done, and at others cannot secure its being done. I may wish to construct an object, but cannot; and I may wish not to have it definite, but there it is, in full form before me.

And precisely so, of an act of observation. I may wish to get an object distinct and cannot, or may wish not to have it distinct and cannot help it. Neither observation nor attention are of the will, but from mere mental spontaneity. The difference is in this; all acts of spiritual will in liberty must come within an alternative of worthiness and opposing gratification, and constitute an election; but pure spontaneity has no alternatives of imperative and appetitive, and merely a simple *ultro*-motivity to its object.

SECTION II. THE MERE EXECUTIVE OF APPETITE IS OFTEN MISTAKEN FOR WILL.—When animal susceptibility is excited, and the act goes out in attainment of the object for gratification, it is often spoken of as choice, and considered as truly an act of will. Indeed, with most, as a speculative conception, no other apprehension of will is attained. It is not apprehended but that the brute has as complete a will in liberty, and as truly an election, as man. A choice between degrees of happiness is no proper election, inasmuch as no true alternative is presented; the taking of the highest degree is unavoidable; and this is all of will that any animal nature can know. When, in any way, the conception of will is confined to the executing of some anterior pleasing, and thus unavoidably conditioned by it, such conception is incomplete and erroneous in its deficiency, and amounts to no more than mere brute-will. It is wholly in nature, and one of the conditioned links in its chain of causes and effects, and it does by no means take it out of this chain, to call it by the names of morality or spirituality. Its conditions are not *reasons*, for it has no rationality. It knows no self-law in the light of its own excellency, and thus no *reason* why it should not float on in nature's strongest current.

When I am hungry, or thirsty, and nothing but gratification is the condition for acting, I shall both eat and drink, and of that which will gratify my hunger and thirst the most; and the brute will do the same. If some greater happiness is to be secured, or danger avoided, by not eating; the prudential appeal will be the strongest, and I shall yet restrain my appetite; and the brute will do the same. There is in this no proper self-denial, but a real self-indulgence; I am gratifying my strongest appetite. There is no election in the case, but an action unavoidably conditioned. But hungry and thirsty as I may be, and prudential in highest happiness as a given gratification may be, and I possess also spiritual, rational existence, that sees in my own excellence of being what is worthy of me, and as such rational spirit, I hear the command from the absolute, "whether ye eat or drink, or whatsoever ye do, do all to the glory of God;" I shall in this have a *reason* for denying appetite, and discarding prudential highest happiness, which no animal may ever know. Not at all the awakening another and higher prudential want, in the eternal happiness or suffering that governmental retribution discloses; but the opening of my spiritual eye upon the guilt, and the debasement which disobedience to God will fix in my consciousness. That I shall thus make the spirit unworthy, is sufficient occasion for an alternative countercheck to the act that would make the appetite happy. The certainty which will be taken is no matter of consideration here; let that question be as it may, an alternative of kind, and not merely in degree, is here opened, and a proper election occurs, whether the act in certainty go out for sensual gratification, or for spiritual worthiness in seeking God's glory. In neither case was the act unavoidable. The man can stand here and elect; no animal can reach this station. The brute must execute the conditions of his nature, for to the brute there is no supernatural reason to take hold upon, whereby it may resist and overcome nature. We may call the animal executive a will, but it is a long way distant from a spiritual will in liberty.

SECTION III. WILL AND DESIRE ARE NOT UNFREQUENTLY CONFOUNDED.—Desire is the mere craving of the animal susceptibility directed towards its object of gratification, and is thus the occasion for an executive act to go forth in attainment. The executive act, we have already seen, is not from a proper will, much less then can the mere craving which prompts it be an act of will, and yet often is the mere desire taken as a volition. Indeed, in common speech, the word desire is sometimes put for will, and the word will is sometimes used for a mere desire. The two facts widely differ, and a correct psychology demands a clear discrimination, and no equivocal terms should be allowed to confound distinct things.

In the following examples, we have the word will put for desire. "Not my *will*, but thine be done."—Luke, xxii, 42. This is the memorable prayer of Jesus to the Father, in the hour of his agony in the garden. Should we take the word will here for a proper election, we should have not only the impiety of a will in Christ opposed to the will of the Father, but also the absurdity of a will opposed to itself. The prayer expresses Christ's real will, and yet it is that his will may not be done. Manifestly, the will here is desire, the mere craving of the animal susceptibility. Christ, as human, had truly the animal nature, and this reluctated all suffering and he desired to escape it. But the will in the prayer is, that the Father would disregard the desire of the flesh, and carry out in him his own desired ends of human redemption. The same changed use of the term occurs in Lam. iii, 33. "For he doth not *willingly* afflict nor grieve the children of men." Speaking after the manner of men, it is not a congenial feeling, as desire, to afflict mankind; but superior considerations induce the purpose, as will, to do so. So also it is said of God, "Who *will* have all men to be saved, and to come unto the knowledge of the truth."—1 Tim. ii, 4.

Again, we have the word desire put for will in the following examples. "They *desired* Pilate, that he (Christ) should be put to death."—Acts, xiii, 28. "And he (the Ethiopian eunuch) *desired* Philip that he would come up and sit with him."—Acts, viii, 31. "One of the Pharisees *desired* him, (Christ) that he would eat with him." —Luke, vii, 36. "Then Daniel went in and *desired* of the king," etc.—Dan. ii, 16. In all these cases there is more than a feeling in the susceptibility; a craving for an end; there is truly an election, as will.

The appetitive craving is one thing; the electing its gratification is quite another; and no matter how common speech may interchange words, philosophy must accurately discriminate facts.

SECTION IV. THE SPIRITUAL AFFECTIONS MAY SOMETIMES BE CONCEIVED AS VOLITIONS.—We are held responsible for our sentiments. Our spiritual feelings are the subject of commands, and come within the reach of legal retributions. Love and hatred, joy and sorrow, in the sense of spiritual affections, are enjoined upon us in reference to certain objects. This may very readily induce the conviction that they are themselves volitions. But their distinction from all direct acts of the will is manifest in the utter impracticability to immediately will them in or out of being. In a given condition, no act of the will can secure them; and in another condition, no act of the will can exclude them. In one disposition of spirit, I cannot will love to the right and sorrow for sin into exercise; and in another disposition, I cannot will them out of exercise. There is a susceptibility to feeling that takes its rise, and is altogether determined, in the spiritual disposition; hence we have termed it the spiritual susceptibility. Its exercises are properly feelings, affections, not at all volitions. The election is altogether in reference to the spiritual disposing, and not at all to the susceptibility and its feelings when the disposition has been taken. It is only because the disposition has its alternative and is avoidable, that the man is responsible for the affections which are conditioned in it. The disposition may be termed a state of will, but the affections are the exercises of the spiritual susceptibility.

In all cases, an open alternative, and thus an avoidability, will characterize all acts that are properly of the human will, and this will discriminate them from all other mental facts.

CHAPTER IV.

THE CLASSIFICATION OF THE ACTS OF WILL.

THE will, as capacity, is the power of election, and thus an avoidability in the origination of the act will characterize every proper volition; yet, in other respects, the acts of the will may have permanent distinctions among themselves, and there are many advantages from having them classified according to their inherent peculiarities. One great benefit from it is a clearer apprehension of the point of responsibility, and of the fountain of moral character.

SECTION I. IMMANENT PREFERENCE.—Preference is an actual putting of one thing before or above others, and this may be done in the spirit's own action, without any overt manifestation of it, and as thus lying hid in the mind may be termed an *immanent* preference. An act of the judgment may decide which of two sources of happiness is the greatest in degree, and of worthiness and happiness which is the highest good in kind, but such distinction of estimate in the judgment is not a preference. And so also one desire may go out towards its object more intensely than another, or one imperative may awaken a deeper sentiment of obligation than another; but no difference in degrees of awakened susceptibility should be termed a preference. There must be a proper election, a voluntary setting of one before others, or it is not a proper act of preference. Want of occasion, or countervailing circumstances, may preclude this preference from manifesting itself anywhere on the theater of active life, and thus the act of preferring never pass over from the mind; yea, the intention through all the duration of the preference may be, that it shall never come out in open action; yet is there in it a real commitment of the spirit to the end preferred, and such inward election is a personal willing, which to the eye that searches the heart has its proper moral character. It is fully within the person's own consciousness, and the conscience accuses or excuses accordingly.

As examples for illustration, there may be mentioned the declaration of the Savior, "Whoso looketh on a woman to lust after her, hath committed adultery already with her in his heart."—Math. v, 28. "Whoso hateth his brother is a murderer."—1 John, iii, 15. And quite prominently, the tenth commandment—"Thou shalt not covet," etc.—Ex. xx, 17. In a good sense we find this immanent preference in the case of David, who would have built a temple for the Lord, but was prevented because as a warrior he had shed much human blood. "It was in thine heart to build an house to my name, thou didst well that it was in thine heart."—1 Kings, viii, 18. As a general application on both sides, good and bad, we have Solomon's declaration of man, "As he thinketh in his heart, so is he."—Prov. xxiii, 7. This *thinking in heart* is a real *electing purpose.*

The immanent preference of objects and ends must widely affect the entire personal character, though the action towards the object externally be always restrained. The whole inner experience of the man is modified by it, and all his habits of meditation and silent reflection become tinged with the color of his secret preferences. It is easy to see what was the inward preference of David, when he said of the Lord, "Whom have I in heaven but thee, and there is none upon the earth that I desire beside thee."—Ps. lxxiii, 25. And while this induced pious meditations on his bed in the night-watches, the effect upon his entire character would be in strong contrast to the impure and debasing thoughts springing from the immanent preferences of the sensualist. The inward influence must soon so far affect the whole man, that the outward life will be colored by it, through all its communion and conversation, though the specific preferences be still restrained to the heart.

Section II. Governing purpose.—The spiritual activity may dispose itself towards an end, that may demand many supplementary acts before it can be attained; in such a case the general election of the end is a purpose, and inasmuch as it prompts the executive acts and guides and directs them to its own issues, it is properly termed a *governing* purpose. The executive acts are solely that the general purpose may be effected. Such governing purpose may be more or less comprehensive, proportioned to the number and complication of the means and agencies used to complete the end, and so far as it reaches it governs the process and is, to that extent, a governing purpose. A purpose to visit a distant place will govern all the actions necessary in preparation for, and prosecution of the journey; but such a purpose will not be so comprehensive nor engrossing as that which fixes upon the main end in life.

The governing purpose has this peculiarity, that it is continuous and prolonged through all the process to the consummation. An act of election is at once, and may wholly cease in its instantaneous energizing, and in this point of view volitions are transient and fleeting; but when the election has been of an end that is to be attained only through a long succession of activities, the electing act does not die in its outgoing, but the spirit fixes itself upon its object and remains in a state of energizing towards it. That it has taken its distant end removes all the uneasiness of hesitation and suspense, and there is no farther place for choice, since the mind is already made up; but the action, as will, has not terminated in the choosing; it flows on in a perpetuated current towards its object, and the spirit may be said to be in a permanent *state of will* for the accomplishment of that end. A purpose is thus a perpetuated will from an election. A person may not always retain the consciousness of having made the distinct and deliberate election; nor indeed, be conscious how deep and strong the current of his purpose has become. An absorption of all the mental energy may already be in a purpose to acquire and amass riches, and yet the distinct election of such an end may have no place in the memory; and the purpose itself may have strengthened so insidiously, that the man has no conception what a very miser he has become; but there needs only to be suddenly interposed some threatened danger to his wealth, or some obstacle to any farther gains, and at once the perturbed spirit manifests the intensity of its avarice. His will has yielded to passion so readily, that it has not known the strength of its bondage.

As the governing purpose is enlarged in the comprehensiveness of its end, and the control it holds over all the mental energies, it comes to be known as a permanent disposition, and while a fixed and comprehensive purpose in business would not be termed the man's disposition, yet when found so engrossing as to merge all else in the end of getting and of hoarding money, we should not hesitate to say of such a purpose, that it is the man's disposition. It goes so far, and is so controlling, that it gives character to the man. When we have an end so comprehensive that it includes all the action, and controls all the mental energy, we have in this the radical disposition, and thus the true moral character of the man. If the spirit is disposed towards happiness as its chief good, and puts that as end to the exclusion of its own worthiness, it has become radically and thoroughly depraved, and its disposition is totally sinful. If, on the other hand, the end of the spirit is the attaining and keeping its worthiness of its own and other spirit's approbation, and is denying every conflicting appetite for it; so far as such a disposition supremely controls, it is righteous, and the moral character is pure and virtuous. Out of this radical disposition springs the spiritual susceptibility, or heart, of the man, from which flows all pure or depraved affections.

The governing purpose is, in this way, distinguished from all the choices or volitions that are subordinate to it. They exist for it, and find their whole determination in it. They may change according to circumstances, and often the good and the bad man's end may induce to the same outward action. A wordly end may sometimes be best attained by putting on the semblance, and performing the ceremonials, of piety; but the character of the subordinate act is to be estimated, not from the outward seeming, but solely from the governing purpose which it is designed to execute. The radical character can be changed by no change in the choices and volitions of the man, but only in a change of the radical spiritual disposition.

Section III. Desultory volition.—An election of some comprehensive end may have induced a permanent state of will in a governing purpose, and this may still continue unrenounced and unchanged, and yet this governing purpose may not be so energetic as to preclude the sudden and strong awakening of some constitutional susceptibility, to carry out an executive act in gratification of it, against the direction of the governing purpose. Such turning aside from the main end, while the governing purpose towards it is not renounced, is what has been termed above a desultory volition. Observation and experience constantly give such facts, where a passionate impulse comes suddenly and strongly in, and the action for a time is carried away from the main object before this counter-impulse of sudden feeling. But inasmuch as the governing purpose which it thus counterworks has not been discarded, the desultory impulse must at length subside, and the old unrenounced purpose again bear sway. The passion is satiated and subsides, reflection returns, and the main end again comes in clear view, and the governing purpose controls the subordinate acts again for its attainment. The man chides himself for his folly and weakness, and hastens on more determinately towards the predominant object.

A familiar illustration of the intrusion of a desultory volition will make the conception distinct. I learn that a dear friend is dangerously sick in a distant city, and I take the purpose to visit him. This controls all my volitions in arranging for the journey, and from the start, onward for several days travel towards the place. Then an intensely interesting incident suddenly occurs, and my feelings are at once powerfully excited and attention absorbed by a surprising curiosity, or convivial opportunity, or chance for pecuniary speculation; and I give way to this desultory impulse and lose sight of my main end for some hours. But at length this impulse becomes exhausted; the main end and purpose of my journey comes vividly up; and conscious that they have never been renounced, though inexcusably suspended, I hasten on to the prosecution of my intention; reproaching myself for my weakness, and fearing that all may now be in vain, and that during my delay my friend may have died. And so once more, where the governing purpose rises to a permanent disposition,—an exceedingly avaricious man may be taken as an example, whose purpose fixed on gain may have made him a very miser in all his feelings and habits. There may suddenly come to him an appeal, from some interesting sufferer, that shall rouse his pity, and induce the gift of some of his idolized gold in relief of this deep distress. But his governing disposition has not at all been changed in the intrusion of such a desultory volition, and very probably, in a few hours, all this constitutional sympathy will have passed away, and he be chiding himself as a fool for his weakness, and more firmly resolving not again to be so overcome as thus to be cheated of the object of his ruling passion.

The real character of the man is in his radical disposition, and if this is not changed, no desultory acts affect his true character. A good man may have sudden and strong temptations, in appeals to constitutional appetite, and the impulse bear him away in sinful action; but if the good disposition has not been renounced, the tempting influence will at length fade, and the man come back from his fall with bitter tears and self-reproaches; a repenting backslider, but not a deliberate apostate. Against both a bad and a good governing purpose, such sudden impulses may induce desultory volitions, which are quite in contradiction to the main direction of the spirit, but we are not to estimate the man's proper character by them. If the bad man do a good deed, only through the impulse of constitutional feeling, all we can say in his favor is, that his depraved disposition was not too strong for some transient traits of humanity; and when a good man so does a bad deed, he is a sinner in that act, and should feel debased and humbled by it, and repent of it; but the real character of neither the bad nor the good man was in this way at all changed. The strength of character is in the decision and firmness of the radical disposition, and to be perfect, this should be so strong in the right that all desultory impulses should be resisted; but no man is safe in supposing, and no man can at any time be conscious, that his governing purpose is so strong, that all desultory volitions against it shall forever be excluded.

FOURTH DIVISION.

THE COMPETENCY OF THE HUMAN MIND TO ATTAIN THE END OF ITS BEING.

GENERAL REMARKS ON THE TRUE END OF THE HUMAN MIND.

We have now attained the facts, general and particular, of the human mind, and their classification in an orderly system, according to the testimony of universal consciousness; and have thus the conception of the human mind as a whole, and may thence determine what it is competent to execute. This is of much importance in many directions. All systems of education, and more or less all questions of responsibility in morals and religion, must be determined from the true view of the capabilities of the mind in its varied faculties. Merely to know what mind is, ought not to be the conclusion of our psychology. Taking it as it is, what is designed to be attained by it? and how competent is it to fulfil such design? These are enquiries yet to be prosecuted and settled. A farther reference to human consciousness, a careful observation of the facts which come within human experience, and fair deductions from all facts which have been above attained, are the sources from whence our answers must be derived.

The end of the human mind is its own perfection. Every claim that can come upon it, and every righteous wish that can be held for it, is fully satisfied, when every faculty is working completely according to the law of its adaptation in its place in the whole mind. When intellect, susceptibility, and will are in complete conformity to the SUMMUM BONUM, *the highest good* of the man, then is the great end for which the human mind exists consummated. It may thus hold on its way in eternity, and in its action every faculty augment in energy, and thus the whole mind rise in efficiency and inherent dignity indefinitely; but at any one point in such perpetual progress, this conforming activity in the whole mind to the highest good is then and there in its consummated degree, and a higher could not have been attained at that point, and only by passing through it and beyond it. What then is *the highest good*, to which the action of every faculty must be held conformable? This can be conclusively answered from the data already found in the conscious facts of the human mind.

The highest good of the *animal* portion of our nature is the gratification of its highest wants. An immediate gratification of a present want may be far counterbalanced by a present denial, and attaining the coming gratification of a future greater want. The perfection of the animal would thus be found, in the cultivation of the sense to perceive, and of the understanding to judge, the most accurately in reference to such objects and such constitutional susceptibilities as, when brought together, shall secure the greatest gratification. Such estimation of greatest happiness would induce the strongest craving want, and this would direct the executive agency accordingly, and the consummation of animal being would be found in the waiting for, and finally attaining, that highest happiness. It might so be found, that in the long run of experience, the gratification of kindness or benevolence would give decidedly the greatest happiness, and then this would be the greatest want and control the activity which must energize to satisfy it. It would be prudent to be kind; and the perfection of the animal is in knowing it, and feeling the strongest craving for the happiness of kind action, and thus doing and enjoying it. Its highest good is highest happiness, and its perfection is in knowing where to find it, and then it must go out conformably to get it. The mere animal can propose to itself no higher end, nor by any action reach a higher consummation.

But the *spiritual* in man can see an intrinsic excellency and dignity in spiritual being itself, which will not allow that any want shall stand in competition with its own worth. It can see its relationship to the animal, and that this, with all its wants, must be subservient to it, and not it to the wants of the animal. It can see its relationship to other spirits, and that in the excellency and dignity of their spiritual being, they have rights and claims upon itself. But no such relationship, either to the animal or to the spiritual, can be an ultimate ground in which the man can find his highest good, but solely in this, that in all relationships he has looked to the law written in his own spiritual being, and conformed to the claim of its worthiness. Other spirits, God, and God's revealed law, all stand in a certain relationship to him; but the last and highest question is taken to his own soul— how, in this relationship to other spirits, and to God, and to God's revealed law, shall I so stand as to make my own spirit the most worthy of its own approbation? No other spirit, and no legislating sovereign, can approve of my spirit, if it has not sacredly and solely done that, and been that, which made it the most worthy of its own acceptance. Not that somehow I shall get, or God may give me, greater happiness for it; for if I have looked at the happiness as end, I shall have in that said, that my worthiness is nothing but a means to happiness, and that if I can barter it away for greater happiness, or get the happiness as well by something else, then my worthiness of spirit is nothing to me. That I may see myself to be worthy of my own spiritual approbation is my highest good, and I shall know that God and good angels can approve, only when my whole activity is in conformity to it. In this is *conscience;* an insight into my own spiritual being; knowing my ultimate rule in connection with the very fact of knowing myself. The susceptibility awakened by the knowing of this rule of right, is the source of all feeling of obligation, and is wholly in the spiritual man and can never be induced in the animal constitution. The feeling of obligation, thus induced, was designed to control in opposition to all other feelings whatsoever, inasmuch as the gratification of any and all other interest, in conflict with this, would compel self-reproach, for which no possible gratification in happiness could compensate. To know myself to be worthy of my spiritual approbation is my highest good, and to be and remain so is my highest end.

This cannot be effected in any succession of specific volitions, for such particular volitions must be in execution of some general purpose terminating in a final result, which gives its character to the general purpose, and through that also to all the subordinate volitions. The supreme controlling purpose must then be found, which holds sway over all the volitions of life. This is only reached in the radical spiritual disposition; the bent of the spirit itself, as it goes out in its spontaneous activity. The man can be worthy, and thus attain his highest good, only in the possession of a radical spiritual disposition fixed in conformity to the claims of his own excellency. He obeys neither man nor God, ethically, except as he directly sees that the proper dignity of his own spirit demands it of him; and that spirit, permanently disposed on that end, is a righteous spiritual disposition. That the human mind may attain the end of its being, it must be competent to attain and maintain such a spiritual disposition.

It is quite manifest that such righteous spiritual disposition is not within us, nor in our fellow-men about us, with the first openings of our conscious moral activity and onward in life. Our own consciousness, our constant observation, and the whole past history of man, testify to the depravity of the radical disposition of man, as a race. It is not necessary to say, that without consciousness, but that without any remembrance of the origination of the fact in consciousness, the spirit has disposed its activity to the end of sense-gratification in happiness, and not to the end of its own right in worthiness. When we awake in self-consciousness, and reflect on our acts and our ends of action, we already find a carnal and not a spiritual mind or disposition. We may need the light of revelation, and it may thus be a theological doctrine which determines the occasion and the origin of such universal human depravity; but we need only the testimony of consciousness and observation, and it is thus only a psychological phenomenon, in which is determined the fact of the perverse and depraved disposition of man. It is as plain a truth in the book of human experience as in the Bible, "that men go astray as soon as they are born." With the opening dawn of consciousness, we find the spirit already has its bent, and is permanently disposed to self-gratification, not to self-dignity. The mind has already lost the end of its being, and is wandering after ends that are self-destructive. Theology must account for this, and also for the rectitude of the Divine government in either effecting or permitting this; but psychology has nothing to do with the doctrines of original sin, and the justification of God's character in the permission of sin. We must here only take the fact of human sinfulness, and enquire how this fact bears upon the one point of man's capability to attain the end of his being. The end, he finds with his first self-consciousness, is already lost; the enquiry thus is, what is man's competency to regain it?

Here there should be allowed no side ends to come in, and perplex and confuse the investigation. Not at all, how can he be forgiven for the past? how stand justified before a legal tribunal? how avail himself of any provisions of a gracious Divine influence? All these are within the religious sphere, and appropriate only for theological speculation. But, taking the facts of mind, just as experience gives them to us, how competent is man to stand forth among his fellows, and in his own consciousness and to the observation of others, manifest a spiritual disposition, that controls the whole mental activity to the grand end of spiritual worthiness? This is properly and wholly within the psychological field, and must be found as a fact in mind from conscious observation; and which, when we go to revealed theology, will be found to have been already settled, and the fact itself taken for granted. A range of collateral investigation somewhat extensive is necessary to this question, and we now pursue it through the several remaining Chapters.

CHAPTER I.

THE TRUE CONCEPTION OF CAUSALITY.

We have found the mind to be self-active, and the source of various states and exercises which spring out from it, and thus that the mind is a cause for various specific effects. But we have given no distinct attention to this fact of causality, that we might attain a complete conception of it, and discriminate fully between all varieties of it that may present themselves. We have the operation of causes in the world of nature about us, and in our own constitutional nature, as well as in the spontaneous activities of our spiritual being; and, while all without and all within is kept in ceaseless flow and change by these acting causes, it is important that we attain a correct and complete conception of what causality is, and that, in attaining its varieties, we may clearly discern how causes in matter and causes in mind may differ from each other. Such conception and discrimination is quite essential in the investigation on which we now enter. We cannot proceed a step, intelligently, in settling the fact of the mind's competency to attain its end, till this has been effected. To this end we devote this entire Chapter.

Causes and effects stand to each other, in time, as sequents; the cause is the antecedent, and the effect is the consequent. Even when we have the effect as instantaneous upon the operation of the cause, we still conceive the cause to be first and the condition for the effect, and that the effect is wholly conditioned by it. And it is in this point of the connection between cause and effect, that all the difficulty is found, and about this one point have all the theories for conceiving and explaining causality been made to turn. In common acceptation, there is what is termed *power* in the antecedent, and this power in exertion is that which constitutes the antecedent to be cause; making or effecting the consequent, and determining all its peculiarities. This conception of power is thus made the connecting medium between the antecedent and the consequent, and is really the conception which contains all the mystery. The whole difficulty in the conception of causation will be found, in reference to this interposition of power as the connecting medium between the sequences.

What, then, is the true conception of *power?* Power itself is never phenomenon, and can in no way be brought within the light of consciousness. One fact precedes, and another succeeds, and these successive facts are given in consciousness, and as distinguished and defined become clearly perceived in the sense. But no reflection upon the antecedent, no analysis nor generalization, no comparison nor contrast, no combining nor abstracting, no mental elaboration whatever can lay open this antecedent phenomenal fact and make its inherent power to appear, nor take the fact itself and make power, as a phenomenon, to come out of it. Power is wholly irrelevant and insignificant to the sense, and can thus be made in no way a sense-conception. As in sense, we have the qualities and not the substantial thing in which they inhere, so in sense we have the successive events and not the causal power on which they depend. And this is as thoroughly true in the internal sense as in the external. It may be deemed to be a phenomenal fact, that when I energize in thinking or willing, I really become conscious of power, and that here power becomes a proper phenomenon. But the feeling, which accompanies muscular or mental exertion, is by no means the power itself that goes out into effect, and is only a fact that appears in us when we energize, and as a phenomenon, wholly dependent upon the exertion and is not the power exerted. It is a phenomenal effect of our energizing, but is neither the efficiency of causality itself, nor anything that can be made explanatory of it. When our power goes out in effects, we have such phenomena in our experience; we feel ourselves energizing; but we do not feel nature in her energizing, nor deem that nature so feels herself in her ongoing of efficient causes and effects. This phenomenal feeling accompanying personal power is not the power, nor anything that at all helps to explain what power itself is. The sun shines upon me, and I perceive warmth; the mind goes out in thought, and I perceive the exertion; but in neither case do I perceive the power warming, nor the power outgoing. Power is thus no possible object for either the external or the internal sense. It never appears in consciousness, and is not at all phenomenal. We have gained much, when we have learned that neither sense, nor any reflection upon what sense may give, can help us at all in attaining any conception of power.

Power is wholly *notion*, and not *phenomenon;* it is altogether *thought* in the understanding, and not at all *perceived* in the sense. When any change occurs, and thus a new fact *comes out*, we term it an *event;* and we *think* that some modification has been made in the ground which gave out the old fact, and that this modification has introduced the new fact. The successive facts we perceive, but the modifying power we do not perceive; it is only *thought;* and this notion as a thought we put between the two facts, and judge that it connects them as cause and effect. Thus, we perceive the sun shining upon the solid ice, or the yielding clay, and we find the new facts that the ice has liquified, and the clay has indurated; we think the shining sun has so changed the two substances that they now give out their altered qualities, and we thus judge that there has been an efficiency, or power, in the sunshine, that has made the new events, and, as effected by it, we say, that they stand connected as cause and effect. The notion of power is thus conditional for the connection. Take it away, and the understanding could not make the connection; there would be nothing in the first on which the last depended, and thus no possible judgment of cause and effect could be formed. We cannot think in a judgment of connected cause and event, without this intervention of the notion of power; any more than we can perceive a shape by the sense, without the surrounding outlines of space. We think the power, and connect the antecedent and consequent by it, and could not form any judgment of cause and effect without it; but can never bring it within consciousness, that we may perceive what it is.

The validity of this notion of power is, thus, nothing that concerns us in Empirical Psychology, and can only be established in the conclusions of a Rational Psychology. Experience must take the revealings of consciousness unquestioned, and can only answer the sceptic by going into a higher science; so also, in thought, that which is essential to all connections in judgments must be admitted, and all question of its validity must be referred to the sphere of a rational science. Power itself cannot come into experience; but the conviction that power is, though no experience can explain what it is, is essential to all confidence in experience itself. Without it, we could not at all connect the phenomena of sense, in any judgment of an ordered succession of events. In our thinking, and thus in the conviction of the understanding, our conception of power is that of an efficiency in the antecedent which produces the consequent. Not power itself appears in consciousness, but through a process of thought in the understanding, the *conviction* that there is power comes within consciousness, and this conviction in experience must stand, in an Empirical Psychology, as valid for the fact of power itself. We need not attempt the enquiry here, what power is? Enough that we have the conviction, that it is.

This full distinction, that power cannot be phenomenon and must be notion; not appearance in sense but only thought in the understanding, will prepare us at once to detect the many fallacies that have prevailed in the different conceptions of causation. It is conditional for all connection of phenomena in successive events, and we cannot think an ongoing of nature without it, and thus cannot have a connected experience except by means of it, and must therefore assume its truth as the very ground of all knowledge in experience. Though we cannot perceive it, we must think it, or our very experience would be baseless. The conviction, that it is, is the force of thought; the perception, what it is, cannot from the nature of the case be effected. That there is an efficiency in the antecedent, which makes the consequent to be as it is, is the very conception of power, and this connection of antecedent and consequent by power, is the very conception of cause and effect; and the valid being of such power, and of such connection of causes and effects must be assumed in experience, and can be demonstrated in a Rational Psychology. With this discriminate view, it will be of much importance to look over the different theories of causation and see the very point of their fallacies; and then, with the true conception of cause, classify all its different varieties.

SECTION I. FALLACIOUS THEORIES OF CAUSATION. *The doctrine of "occasional causes."*—The Cartesian order of philosophizing is to distinguish all existence into two kinds, matter and spirit. The essence of matter is extension, and the essence of spirit is thought. Extension and thought are so heterogeneous, that there can be no communion between them, and no mutual influences and reciprocal activities, one from the other. Each, thus, standing in its own isolation, may have reciprocal action and reaction between its own separate portions, but neither can be a cause for producing effects over in, and upon, the other. When any occasions for such interchange of activities and influences occur, there must be a direct divine interposition, and the communion be effected by a direct act of the Deity. Such divine interpositions, in all needed cases, were termed "occasional causes;" and the separate worlds of matter and mind were thus connected only through the medium of the great First Cause.

The true conception of causality might in this case have been possessed, and the impossibility of its application between matter and mind be only in their complete isolation of being; but the error will be found in the denial of the inherent power of spirit to act on matter, and of the power of matter to modify spiritual action; and then in the absurdity of helping out from the difficulty, by an interposition which falsifies the very basis of the theory. If it can be supposed that the Absolute Spirit works in and upon matter, then there is no difficulty, in the case itself, that finite spirit should, in its degree, do the same. The whole need of "occasional causes" is placed in the essential contrariety of extension and thought, matter and spirit, and as these are in necessary exclusiveness and opposition one to the other, no augmentation of spirit to the absolute, can at all eliminate the difficulty of interaction, which had been placed in the contradictory essences of the two sole existences.

The doctrine of "sufficient reason."—Leibnitz analyzed all existence up to atomical being, and the atoms, as "indivisible," also became the "undistinguishable." As having nothing outer or inner distinguishable one from others, a faculty of representation was given them, and thus each one could represent or envisage all others, and was a little world in itself. Each microcosm was thus a monad; and the monads, of which matter is compounded, represent others in unconsciousness; those, of which animals are compounded, represent in partial consciousness; and those, of which man is compounded, represent in clear self-consciousness. God is the *Monad monadium;* representing all else, but himself irrepresentable, perfectly, by any. Inasmuch as no external communion is possible, and only by a mutual representation, so no efficiency in one atom can modify, or work changes in, any other; and thus, no conception of power or causality can connect one event with another, but all is mere succession of representations. Wolff so modified the system, in this point, that the unconscious and self-conscious portions, matter and mind, could only mutually represent or envisage each other; but, in both views, it was necessary that the mutual representations should harmonize, and such harmony of representation was originally established by God. A pre-established harmony has so arranged the representations that they occur orderly and constantly. When the representation of sunshine is given, then that of warmth immediately and regularly succeeds; when the representation of a volition is given, then the corresponding locomotion at once follows. One has not any efficiency causing the other; a pre-established arrangement makes one correspond with the other. One does not produce, but only tallies with the other. There is no causality, but the harmonized representation is a "sufficient reason" for the orderly succession. The unnumbered mirrors are so arranged as always to reflect in complete harmony.

Here is an admitted exclusion of all proper causation. God so handles all the reflectors, that their images make an orderly experience. The only causality is in the hand that arranges the envisaging monads. The last absurdity, and self-contradiction inheres in this ultimate point. All causality is excluded below, but surreptitiously admitted at the beginning. God is only Absolute Monad, envisaging all things; and yet it is assumed, that God is also efficient regulator and arranger of all things. If the essential being of a monad excludes all efficiency to outward causal activity, then the Absolute Monad must also be incapable of outward causal regulations.

The doctrine of an induced belief in causation from habitual repetition.—When the philosophy is made fundamental, that all knowledge is through sense, or reflection upon what is given in sense, there comes at once the difficulty of accounting for all pure notions, in the understanding. Among many others, is the enquiry, how attain the notion of power, or causality? Hume takes this, the then universally prevalent philosophy, and gives the only philosophical theory for any belief in the causal connections of nature.

Sense, direct, gives us "the impressions" of things; and reflection upon these, gives us the semblances and off-shoots of these impressions, which are called "ideas." Impressions and ideas are the essence of all human knowledge. Power, or causality, is no direct gift of any sense; it cannot be put among our primary "impressions." It must come from reflection upon the impressions, and be thus "idea." But no legitimate analysis or combination, comparison or contrast, can get the idea of power, causality, necessary connection, from mere antecedent and consequent. The sequences are all that sense gives, as primary "impressions;" no logical reflection can get the "idea" of cause; inasmuch as we have it in our belief, there must be some way of accounting for it. Its genesis is wholly illegitimate; and it is thus a spurious production, and can put forth no title to be accredited as knowledge. It is utter credulity at its highest strength. There is nothing but antecedent and consequent; there cannot be known anything in the antecedent, why it should have that consequent; it simply has been thus so often, that we have come to believe the connection necessary. The sequences have been together in that order so many times, that merely by dint of repetition and habit we have yielded, and credulously believed it must be so, and have called it cause and effect. It is neither "impression," nor "idea," which would be knowledge; it is wholly made up by our own credulity, and is thus truly fiction, though attaining universal "belief." The philosopher must be sceptical in reference to it, and to all deductions and conclusions derived from it.

That this method of accounting for the fact of our conviction of causation is not true, may be seen at once in this, that it does not always, nor often, require a long repetition of the sequences to induce the conviction that they are connected by a causal efficiency. The child, once smarting from the sting of a bee, will recognize the connection of cause and effect here, as thoroughly as after twenty repetitions. But it is true, that with only a philosophy of sensation and reflection, all accounting for the genesis of the conception of cause is wholly impossible. That it is a fiction, in some way surreptitiously enforcing belief, must be the philosophical conclusion; and the manner of Hume, in accounting for it, will be as plausible as any. The great error is, in at all attempting to account for it through sense. It is wholly notional and not phenomenal; and, as conditional for all connected experience, is to be assumed valid in an experimental psychology. The exposition and demonstration of it belong to a rational science alone.

The doctrine of "invariable succession," as resolved into the constitution of the human mind.—Brown dispenses with all notion of power, as giving any necessary connection to the sequences, and includes all there is in the conception of cause within a bare fact of "invariable succession." The notion of power, as some third thing between the antecedent and the consequent, is wholly a delusion. That the common mind has formed to itself some phantasm, called power, which it interposes between the sequences, as if it helped the conception of their invariable succession, may be accounted for by a reference to various illusory influences; but it is, in fact, a mere chimera, and must be utterly discarded. It helps nothing if you have it, and only interposes another difficulty; for this third thing, called power, must be only another phenomenon added to the antecedent and consequent, and itself just as difficult to be apprehended in its connection with either, as would be their connection together without it. It, in truth, makes all the mystery, and when wholly excluded, the whole conception of cause and effect is thoroughly perspicuous. All notion of power being discarded, there remains simple invariableness of succession in certain sequences, and this conception of invariableness is the peculiarity of the succession called cause and effect. If the succession might sometimes fail, then would the conception of causality be excluded, but when the sequences are deemed to be unfailing, then is it the connection of cause. To say, that a certain degree of heat in a metal is invariably followed by its liquescence, expresses the same thing as to say, so much heat is a power to melt the metal, and both are tantamount to saying the heat is the cause of the melting.

But, if nothing efficiently connects the antecedent and consequent, the enquiry must arise, whence can come the conviction of this invariableness? We must not attempt to interpose the notion of power, which may make the consequent to be a production from the antecedent; we must wholly exclude such notion; and hence the query —whence is this conception of invariableness possible? How can we think invariable succession in the absence of all efficient production? This knot is cut, with no attempt to loose it. All is resolved into the constitution of the human mind. We are so formed, as to anticipate infallibly, in the appearance of some phenomena, the sequence of their respective fellow phenomena. We do not need a repetition; but instinctively, if one comes, we forecast the other. It is "an internal revelation, like a voice of ceaseless and unerring prophecy."

If there is nothing in the antecedent efficiently to produce the consequent, then is it as philosophical to refer the conviction of invariable connection to a peculiar mental conformation as any way. But it will not reach to the real conviction which we find has some way come into the consciousness. Simple invariable succession is not our conviction of the connection in cause and effect, nor at all like it. Night invariably succeeds the day; one o'clock invariably succeeds twelve o'clock; one fixed star invariably succeeds another fixed star in crossing our meridian; but none of these invariable successions is our conviction of causal connection. If we assume two pair of wheels, one of which has each wheel separately driven, so that the cogs in their periphery exactly match in every revolution; but the other pair is so constructed, that, one wheel being moved, its cogs drive the other; there will be alike invariable succession in each case; but we must carry the mind quite beyond the fact of invariable succession, to some efficiency in an antecedent that produces the consequent. No conception of simple succession, no matter how invariable, is our notion of cause. The sequences belong to the perceptions of the sense, and perpetual perceptions cannot give connections in a judgment of the understanding without the notion being thought; the notion of power must be there, or the invariableness of succession comes from a void.

The doctrine that causality is only a regulative conception in our own minds.—Kant assumes the phenomenal sequences to be real; but what the substances as things in themselves, of which these phenomena are only qualities, truly are, can never be known by human intelligence. The mind, as a regulative principle for its thinking in judgments, is obliged to use the conception of causality, and bring its sequences into connection under this category; but this notion of causality is altogether subjective; a mental conception for regulating the mind's own thinking; and we cannot say that the phenomenal realities have any such connections in the things themselves. The mind has such original forms, as pure conceptions, from itself; and, in thinking, it fits these forms on to the real phenomena, and brings them into orderly connection thereby; but it is the mind which makes the connections, and not that the connections are in the things themselves, and that they make the mind to know after their conditions.

SECTION II. THE TRUE CONCEPTION OF CAUSE.—It may be said here, that it is competent to demonstrate in Rational Psychology, that the subjective notion of causality must have also its objective being in things themselves, or the human mind could never determine the passing phenomena to their successive periods in a whole of time; and that because we do so determine successive phenomena in our experience, therefore nature is truly successive in her causes; but such statement, and especially such demonstration, have here no relevancy. Experience, as such, must rest on her own conditions, and cannot itself question and examine that which must first be in order that itself should be. To it, the notion of power, and efficient production in causality, must be valid; and an Empirical Psychology is not to be disturbed, by anything that lies out of and beyond experience. If any such questions come up, they must be wholly ignored here, and referred over to their proper transcendental sphere. In experience, the conviction plainly and universally is, that nature has its powers; that an efficient working goes on in both mind and matter, and produces, in each realm, its changes, which manifest themselves in perpetually passing phenomena; and the true conception of cause can be equalled in nothing, that does not put an efficiency in the antecedent, which makes the consequent to be its conditioned product. Experience founds on nothing short of this; and for an Empirical Philosophy, this foundation must be unquestioned. We are not to say, the phenomena come in succession, and habit makes us deem the successions necessary; nor, the conformation of our mind makes us to predict them as invariable; nor, that a subjective conception of cause regulates our thinking of these phenomena together; but we are to say—our conscious conviction of causality is a power in the antecedent to make the consequent. They are not mere sequences, but one springs from the other, and is thus *event;* one is the product of the other, and is thus *effect.*

With this conception of causality, we are now ready to discriminate different causes.

SECTION III. CLASSIFICATION OF THE VARIETIES OF CAUSE.—It will be more conclusive if we also give a place to all distinctions of succession, and thereby show, in one view, the gradations from simple succession up to the most perfect causality. We shall draw the lines rapidly, though still distinctly, between the varieties.

MERE SUCCESSION may be given in two varieties. *Simple succession* is when one phenomenon follows another casually; occurring once in that order of sequence, but no probability or expectation of a repetition. There was a cause for each fact in the sequence, but their causes are not regarded, and they are viewed only as independent occurrences, and which we say, somehow so happened to come in succession; as "he went out into the porch, and the cock crew."—Mark, xiv, 68. *Invariable succession* gives the same sequences at all times, while both phenomena are the results of independent sources of appearance. Thus, of the invariable order of the seasons; of day and night in alternation; of one place on the earth invariably passing under the meridian consequently to another that is at the eastward of it; etc. In all such cases of succession, though the sequence be invariable, we have only concurrence, not adherence. The sequences have no connection as cause and effect.

QUALIFIED CAUSES are destitute of all proper efficiency, and yet stand more intimately related to their consequents than in mere succession. They are familiarly termed causes; but, since they involve no conception of efficient production one of the other, they have their qualifying adjuncts to mark their distinction from all efficient causes. *Conditional causes* are such antecedents as must be given as occasions for the consequents. The efficiency, which is in the proper cause, cannot work in the production of the effect, except on the condition that this qualified cause is also given. This may be *the removal of a hindrance* to the efficiency—as, the withdrawment of the support, and the fall of the body resting upon it; the shutting off of the moving force, and the stopping of the machinery; the taking away of life, and the corruption and dissolution of the animal body; etc. In all the above cases, no real efficiency for the consequent is supposed in the antecedent; it is only the taking away of an efficient counteraction to the power which is to produce the consequent. In another form, there may be *the direct supply of an occasion*—as, in bringing the fire and gunpower in contact; or, the flint and steel in collision; or, the presence of some object to the sense; in which cases the explosion, the spark, the perception, are effects, not directly of these antecedents, but only by occasion of them. Such cause was known by the old schoolmen as *causa sine qua non*. *Final causes* are the terminating ends of actions, and are viewed as the objective motives to the act, or as the consummation for which the work was designed. Thus sight is the end for which the eye was designed; and happiness the end for which the animal acts; and virtue the end for which the spirit is given; and as such inducements to the being of the means, the ends are called causes, yet as they are not the efficients in producing the means, they are causes in only a qualified sense, and are known as teleological or final causes. They are that for which the efficient cause is exerted.

We now come to those sequences which are properly causes and effects, and though differing among themselves in other particulars, they will all agree in this, that the antecedent is efficient in producing the consequent, and herein will they all be distinguished from the foregoing.

MECHANICAL CAUSE is an applied force for directly counteracting other forces, chiefly that of gravity. Its action is the push or pull of some mechanism. They may be considered as modifications of two simple mechanical powers—*the lever*, including the proper lever, the flexible lever or pulley, the wheel and axis, and the cog wheel and loco-motive-wheel; *the inclined plane*, including the simple form, the wedge, the spiral plane or screw, and the arch. Here, also, may be placed, as a mechanical force, all direct action by impulse.

PHYSICAL CAUSES are the forces inherent in nature, and which are perpetually in action to make the successive changes of the material universe. They are other than mechanical impulses, and include all the primordial forces which belong to material being, and which are giving unceasing motion and change to matter, both in its forms and localities. Without assuming very exact delineations, we may recognize them as gravitating force, including repulsion as well as attraction; bipolar-forces, magnetism, electricity, galvanism, and perhaps as bipolar, combustion, illumination, chemical affinities, crystalization, etc. They may all be conceived as simple acts in different directions of counteraction, and in their commingled working, showing their effects in the planetary motions, and producing all cosmic changes, pneumatic, hydrostatic, or telluric.

VITAL CAUSE is a living force inherent originally in the germ, and in its activity producing an organic development of all the rudimental elements. It may be viewed as a simple activity, producing itself and thus ever advancing; stating itself and thus ever abiding. The life of the plant ever produces itself in the advanced bud, and also ever states itself in the permanent stock; as does the life of the animal advance in the assimilation of new elements, and remain in the incorporation of the old. Life has two aspects in its activity, viz. that of development, as above, in which the vital cause goes on to its maturity in the parent stock; and then, that of propagation, where, through the medium of sex, the life passes over into a new germ, and by refusing to state itself and thus posit itself in the old stock, it thereby separates itself from the parent, and is the organic embryo of another being after the old type. Vital causes thus work on from age to age, maturing the present and propagating the future being.

SPONTANEOUS CAUSE is the originating from itself some thing wholly new, and not a mere production of itself into another. In all mechanical, physical, and vital causes, the cause itself is caused in its action, and produces itself into its effects; in spontaneous cause, the activity originates in and from itself, and creates that which is other than itself produced. It is solely the prerogative of spiritual being. Nature, neither as material, vegetable nor animal, has any proper spontaneity. There is ever causality, *a' tergo;* securing only a production of what is, onwards to another form of the same in the becoming. Nature, thus, from first to last, has no new originations, but only a change of what already is, into another form, and which is only a propagation. New animals, and new men, exclusive of their spiritual being, are as much propagations of the old stock, as new trees, new herbs, or even new wine from the old cluster. What comes from nature is itself *natured;* what comes from spirit is a spontaneous origination. So nature came from the hand of its Creator at first; a spontaneous origination, not something already in being, and only pushed forward in another form by a conditioning nature still behind it. So rational thought, and spiritual feeling and volition, are new originations, and not old existences produced in new forms. The whole consenting spirit, of its own accord, *sponte*, originates the new thought, the new affection, or the new purpose; and these are altogether its own creations, and not nature's, nor another spirit's, nor God's workmanship.

But mere spontaneity is still conditioned in its occasion. It truly originates, with no conditioning nature working back of it, but is cause for origination only in given occasions. The reason's eye must see the necessary and universal principle within the reason itself, and the intellectual movement goes on in glad accord under its guiding light, and thus the free *thought* is consummated; but the spirit is cause for thought only in such occasions; and with such occasions, only in that one direction. So with the *affection;* the object must be in the spiritual vision, and the whole according soul assenting, and in such occasion the affection embraces its object; but the spirit is cause for that affection only in that occasion, and can have no alternative. The thought and the affection are free from all conditioning in nature, but they have open to them only one direction by conditions within the spirit itself.

CAUSE IN LIBERTY is not only spontaneous, but with an open alternative. It is the capacity of the spirit, knowing its ethical rule in knowing what is due to itself, to hold firmly by it against all the colliding appetites of a lower nature. It may spontaneously dispose its activity in this direction, though another direction be also open before it. In the disposition, unlike the thought and the affection, there is an alternative, and an occasion given to either course; and the spirit is potential for a right disposition, and responsible to its own tribunal and to God, that it effect and maintain such a consummation. As spiritual intellect and susceptibility, the soul is cause for spontaneous origination; as spiritual will, the soul is cause for originating one result, when there was also an open way to another. Cause in liberty is will, and is the highest conceivable causality, supernatural, and ethically responsible. In man, though fallen, the alternatives still lie open; and the self-conditioning of the spirit only, and no necessitating condition of nature, perpetuates the depravity. In all holy beings, the spiritual disposition is maintained in its integrity, though to such the alternative in perversion is still conceivable.

CHAPTER II.

THE GROUNDS OF CERTAINTY.

SOME sequences have no connection by a direct efficiency; some stand in the nature of the case itself, without any interposition of power; and others are connected by a direct efficiency in their production. Even where efficient causes make their effects to be, there is a wide difference of degree in the clearness with which the efficiency reveals itself, and the grounds on which it can be determined beforehand that the causal efficiency will be exerted. The certainty of events must, thus, stand on quite different grounds, and one be certain because of this, and another certain because of that interposition. This whole ground of certainty needs to be examined, in order to the settlement of the question, how far the human mind is competent to gain the ends of its being? We need not attempt any explanation of the mode of knowledge, or ground of certainty, to the Absolute Mind, save that to God knowledge cannot be mediate and derived; but we enquire only for the grounds of certainty in reference to man, and the connections which stand in our human experience.

From the comprehensive view already taken of the successions of phenomena, and the different connections of causal efficiency, we are prepared to attain and accurately discriminate the different grounds of certainty, in reference to all the sequences in human experience. We will find these grounds of certainty in the varied order of connected events, and show the bearing of each upon the certainty of the fact itself, and upon the knowledge of the fact, as made to stand in the convictions of our own consciousness.

SECTION I. THE NEGATION OF ALL GROUND OF CERTAINTY.—For all that has been, is, or will be, there must be some ground on which the certainty of the being of such facts rests, and without which no such certainty could be predicated; and thus for all facts, past, present and future, there are positive grounds of certainty. But some assumptions may be made of the origin of all facts, which would do away with all ground of certainty in reference to any fact, and which need first to be presented and their absurdity exposed, in order that we may proceed intelligently and confidently on the conviction that all facts have their grounds of certainty. These negations of all ground of certainty are perversions of the very laws of thought itself.

The assumption of chance.—A common use of the word chance is in reference to such events as occur without a recognition of the causes inducing them. Because we were quite ignorant of the operating causes, and the event has come unexpectedly up in our experience, we say, 'somehow it has so happened;' or, 'it chanced to be.' So, because the connections, which link events in their series, are not recognized, we say that "time and chance happen to all."—Eccl. ix, 11.

In the turning of dice, or any form of casting lots, we also speak of leaving the event to the determination of chance; but the real meaning in all is the same, viz. that we withdraw the mind from all recognition of the acting efficiencies that must secure the event, and because we exclude all control ourselves, and leave unseen causes to control, we say we have left it to chance.

But the philosophical conception of chance utterly denies all causation. All efficiency is excluded, and something comes from nothing. Not as creation from nothing external to the Creator, but creation exclusive of the Creator himself; origination from an utter void of all being. Such a conception, were it possible, would of course annihilate all ground of certainty. There is no ground for the being itself, and can, therefore, be no ground for any certainty about it. It comes from nothing, exists in nothing, and goes out in nothing, and can have no determination in any possible certainty. But such negation of all causality is impossible to the human understanding. It is not merely a ghost which appears without substance, and may be a phantasm made by the mind; but a ghost that has no maker, subjective nor objective; inhering in nothing and adhering to nothing. The understanding can connect it in no judgment, nor bring it within any possible form of thought. It is that about which the mind cannot reflect, and concerning which it can deduce nothing, and conclude nothing; and which is thus the absurdity of being understood, without its coming at all within the understanding.

To exclude all ground of certainty in chance, is thus wholly to exclude all causality. If we merely ignore the cause, while we yet do not deny that there is cause, we leave all its ground of certainty, both that it must be, and what it must be, and only exclude the certainty from our cognition. The common use of chance excludes nothing of certainty; the philosophical meaning, which is a negative of all causality, is, in that, a negation of all ground of certainty. The human mind cannot so connect in any form of judgments, and cannot, therefore, exclude from its facts their grounds of certainty.

The assumption of fate.—The common acceptation of fate is that an event is made inevitable, and the issue bound in its connections beyond entreaty or resistance. But with this view, the ongoings of nature would be fate. The determinations of infinite power and wisdom would be fate. This is *destiny;* an event destined by omniscience, and executed by omnipotence. There may sometimes be added the conception of arbitrariness, as if the sovereign disposer consulted only his own will, as in Mahomedan predestination; but this still is not the proper meaning of fate. In all the above, there is a ground of certainty, and this of so fixed a nature as to be inevitable.

But the true philosophical conception of fate is that of blind causation undirected and undeterminable by any conditions. In all natural causes, the thing on which the cause works is as determinative of the effect as the working of the cause itself. The sun-shine, as cause, is conditioned to one effect by the nature of the wax, and to another effect by the nature of the clay, and by knowing the cause working, and the substance on which it works, there is the ground of certainty in reference to the event. But the conception of fate, is that of cause merely, without any conditions. It is positive of an efficiency to produce, but negative of all conditioning in that which is to be produced. There is an acting efficiency to originate something, but there is nothing to react upon that efficiency to give to it any qualification. The blind giant will work, but he has no directory; neither end nor aim; no pity nor fear; no rule nor restraint. There is nothing to heed prayer; and thus nothing to pray to, nor to pray for. There is no destiny to work out, for no result is destined; and no consummation to reach, for no end is proposed. There is simply a power fated to work on incessantly, but nothing in nor out of itself to determine the direction or the product of its working. Heartless, aimless, lawless; man is placed beneath it, and it is his wisdom neither to hope nor to fear, but patiently to endure. The old Stoic philosophy put both gods and men beneath such a blind power, and thus required the patience of hopelessness and the fortitude of despair, and made it the highest evil to be disquieted by anything.

There is here ground for certainty that something will be, for there is causality working; but there is no ground for certainty what the effects will be, inasmuch as there is no conditioning of this blind and senseless efficiency. But such a conception of blind, naked causation is as impossible for the human understanding as chance. Physical causes must have their reaction from the substances on which they act, or the understanding can connect no causes and effects in a judgment; and moral agents must have a reflex bearing of all their acts upon themselves, or they can be brought within no judgment of moral responsibility. That any power should be wholly unconditioned is inconceivable. It would require the understanding to be as crazy in its thinking, as the fatality is lawless in its working.

SECTION II. THE POSITIVE GROUNDS OF CERTAINTY.—Under this head is included all connections of phenomena which are held in *necessity*. They are opposed to chance, inasmuch as there is a ground of their being, and they are opposed to fate, inasmuch as they are conditioned to be what they are. They are of several varieties.

By necessity, in common acceptation, is meant an event that occurs in the face of all opposition and hindrance. The cause is conceived as overcoming a counteraction. *Individual* necessity is a cause overcoming in that particular case; and *universal* necessity is when the cause must overcome in all cases. But this conception, of opposition and resistance overcome, is not essential to the true meaning of necessity. It is more properly *impossibility of prevention*, and is only one species of necessity.

In a philosophical acceptation, necessity is inclusive of all that which has no alternative. Whether opposition be conceived or not, if there is no alternative to the event, it is necessary. The word necessity should be used in no other application, when philosophical precision is designed by it. It cannot admit of alteration, for there is no *alter;* it can admit of no negation, for a negative would itself be an alternative. When, therefore, an event is grounded in necessity, its certainty is infallible, in the sense that no other event can then and there be. In as many ways as we conceive of connections without an alternative, in so many ways may there be events grounded in infallible certainty, and it is important that we be able clearly to distinguish each in its own peculiar ground.

Absolute necessity is when in *the nature of the case* there is no alternative, and thus the result lies beyond the reach of all efficiency. It is not the product of power, and must thus be unconditioned by power. Power, or causality has no reference to it, can neither unmake nor change it; but the truth stands out unalterable in its own absolute being. All such truths are given in the insight of the reason. Such is the certainty of the Deity, and of all his perfections in connection with his being. God is, and as he is, from no causal efficiency. His ground of being stands beyond the reach of all power, finite or infinite, and as thus absolute, its certainty is absolute. In the nature of the case, there can be no alternative to his being. So also, with all necessary and universal truths. Their certainty is grounded in the nature of the case, and no conception of an alternative in their case can be possible. All mathematical intuitions are of this kind, and their certainty is absolute, because grounded in the very nature of the case. The radii of the same circle must all be equal; any three points must lie in the same plane; the two acute angles of a right angled triangle must together be equal to a right angle; etc. An alternative is inconceivable as it would involve an absurdity. So, in the same way, of necessary physical principles; they have an absolute certainty in their own ground. Matter must have place and dimensions; must be divisible and impenetrable; force must involve counteraction; action and reaction must be opposite and equal; etc. If the conception at all be, the very case contains these truths; and all conception of an alternative would make a wholly different case. Here is absolute necessity.

Physical necessity is grounded in the efficiency of *physical causation.* In the ongoings of nature, the antecedent conditions the consequent, and the whole series is truly determined in the first link. If only nature work on in its causes, there can be no alternatives, and all change must be effected by a supernatural interposition. There is a ground of certainty in each link what all its successors must be, inasmuch as the causal efficiency that is to produce future changes is wholly contained within it. Any new originations of efficiency in nature cannot spring out from nature, inasmuch as the addition would be wholly from a void, and all nature may have sprung by chance out of a void as readily as that additional portion. A power above nature must put all new things in nature, so that nature alone must work on through all her processes with no alternatives. Her inward efficiency necessitates her processes, and the certainty what they must be is grounded in this efficiency, and the events are as inevitable as the ongoing of nature. They are only not absolute, because an alternative can be conceived through a miraculous interposition. Nature is unalterable in her course to all but a supernatural efficiency.

Hypothetical necessity has its ground in the originations of *spontaneous causality.* Pure spontaneity is always supernatural, for it originates new things of its own accord, *sponte;* and thus, it is not a mere production of somewhat that already lay back in nature. Nature is always caused cause, and never spontaneous cause. What we term spontaneous production, spontaneous combustion, etc., is still nature acting according to her inner conditions, and producing in another form what already is, and not any origination of wholly a new thing. It is spontaneous, only as no efficiency is supplied from some foreign causality. But rational spirit originates from itself new things, in its thoughts and emotions. They are not productions of somewhat that already is, and only an old thing put forward in a new form; they are really new creations. They come into nature, as something not at all of nature; but as wholly born of the spirit. A poem is a new creation, a thing made by the spirit of the poet, and added to nature, as truly as that poet's spirit is put into nature by its maker. And so with a science; a philosophy; an idea; they are spontaneously originated from the rational spirit.

But all such originations are hypothetical. They differ from the causality of nature, in that they are not conditioned by something back in nature; they do not come along down through nature's connected series. They involve a superinduction upon nature, of that which is not of nature. A spiritual existence must be, and must be so placed in relation to nature that it may operate in and upon nature, and find the occasion for its thinking or feeling through nature; and then, with such an hypothesis, the effect is necessary. The spirit, as cause, is as efficient as nature, and, on such occasion, is cause for such origination and for no other; and, therefore, the occasion being given, the cause must go out in action, and the particular thought or emotion is necessary. The freedom of thought and feeling is not at all will in liberty; it is only causation free from nature, and acting in its own spontaneity; but still, cause in that occasion for only that one thing. With such occasion, it must be thought, and such thought; and with another occasion, it must be emotion, and such emotion. It is cause, in that occasion, for that one thing, and has thus no alternative in its occasion; on that hypothesis the event is necessary. The ground of certainty, thus covers both the efficiency of the spontaneous cause, and the occasion for it, and is certain without alternative if the efficiency and its occasion be; and is only not absolute certainty, inasmuch as such hypothesis may not be fact. The certainty is grounded on an hypothesis becoming a fact, and is then a certainty from necessity; for, to the event there is then no alternative.

The term hypothetical necessity is sometimes applied in physical causation, where a conditional cause must intervene. On condition of contact, fire explodes gunpowder; and on the hypothesis of such contact, the explosion is necessary. But with mere physical causality, there can be no such hypothesis. What already is must condition all that shall be, and the contact and explosion are already determined in the present conditions of nature. Not so with spontaneous causes. Nature can not determine their being and relationship to itself. There is here a genuine hypothesis, depending on the interposition of some supernatural author. A spirit must exist, and stand in certain relations to nature; and this nothing now in nature can determine, but must depend upon the working of a supernatural efficiency; and only so, is the event certain with no alternative.

And now, in all the above varieties of necessity, we have grounds of certainty which differ in reference to their truths and facts as the necessities themselves differ. They are all without alternatives, in their respective cases, but the exclusion of all alternatives is from quite different sources. In absolute necessity, no alternative can be from the nature of the case, and no conception of any application of power could make an alternative. In physical necessity, no alternative can come from nature, nor from that which does not counteract nature, and thus only from a supernatural being. In hypothetical necessity no alternative can come from anything, provided the hypothesis be fact; but nature can neither secure nor hinder that the hypothesis be fact. The highest certainty is grounded in absolute necessity, for no application of power can demolish it. The next in order is physical necessity, as a ground of certainty; for nature already is, and is working out her conditioned processes, and she reveals nothing that is about to counteract her working. Hypothetical necessity is the least certain to man, for he has the least data for determining the validity of the hypothetical fact. But all are alike inevitable in their own grounds, for the ground being given, they have neither of them any alternative.

SECTION III. A POSSIBLE GROUND OF CERTAINTY IN CONTINGENCY.—Contingency is used, in common acceptation, with much the same latitude as chance. An event is said to be contingent, when it is supposed to happen without a foreseen causality determining it. Especially is that event denominated contingent, when it is supposed to depend upon some other event which is yet indeterminate. It has been used with a more precise definition, as "something which has absolutely no ground or reason, with which its existence has any fixed and certain connection." This can hardly be made to differ from the true conception of chance, which is origination from nothing. But all conception of contingency, as a happening, chance, accident, fails to reach the precise meaning. It is an event which comes *with a touch.* It hangs in suspense, and a voluntary touch determines it.

The true philosophical application is to an event that has an alternative. It is the converse of the word necessity, not in the sense of uncaused, but of being avoidable. A contingent event has its efficient cause, and also has its occasion for the efficiency to work, but the working is not shut up to one issue. At the same time that the touch brought that event, the alternative was open to touch and bring in another event to the exclusion of the former. When the touch was given, it was not inevitable; not a necessity; but had an open alternative. All physical causes work with no alternative, and thus in necessity; all free cause works with an alternative; an avoidability; a liberty; and thus contingently. The word truly applies only to an event that depends upon a will. It stands opposed to necessity solely in this sense, that it always implies avoidability, while necessity is inevitable.

And, here, the point of enquiry is, has a contingent event any ground of certainty? The very definition excludes the certainty that is unavoidable; necessitated; is there then an opportunity for predicating any certainty of a contingent event? The answer to this is made plain, only by a clear conception of what is a will in liberty, and the occasion of its action. To the human mind, which must attain its knowledge through some media, in all facts of future existence, there can be no ground of certainty in the mere efficiency. The will in liberty is cause for either alternative, and may dispose its activity for the right of the spiritual being against the sensual appetite, or it may yield to natural inclination and make carnal gratification its end; and simply, that it has a capacity for these alternatives affords no ground of certainty, which event will come out. When we know a cause which has no alternative, the cause itself is sufficient means for determining the event. The ground of certainty is in the efficiency of the cause itself. But when we know a cause which has an alternative, the cause itself is no ground for determining which alternative will come. No ground of certainty can be found in the bare efficiency. But, if that cause has already conditioned itself by a previous action, we have in this some thing more than the bare efficiency, even the conditioning which its own directing of its activity has already given to it, and this may now be taken as a fair ground for determining the certainty of its future action. What is the ground of certainty given by this conditioning of itself in a previous act?

When the spirit has already gone out in its activity towards an end, there is in that a disposing of itself in reference to that end; and as all ends must ultimately resolve themselves into worthiness or happiness, this disposing of itself in reference to any end truly gives to the self-active spirit a radical disposition, and which is virtuous or vicious according to the ultimate end towards which the activity is directed. If then, this disposition be now considered, there is in it a condition which gives its ground for certainty in the events to come. That it is a virtuous disposition will give the stronger confidence, that it will not turn back on itself and go out after appetite; or that it is a vicious disposition will give the less hope, that it will convert itself to the end of its highest worth, and resist appetite. The confidence of the one, and the hopelessness of the other is each proportionate to the strength of the disposed spiritual activity towards its respective end. This may be to such a degree, that we shall have no hesitation in affirming what the event will be, nor in risking any interest upon the issue. At the very strongest degree, it will not rise to necessity, for the alternative will still be open; the event will be avoidable; but there may be the certainty that though avoidable it will not be avoided, and thus the event may be infallible.

But the disposition is not the only conditioning that should be regarded. The constitutional susceptibility may itself be more or less readily and intensely excitable, or the objects appealing to it may be of more or less motive-influence; and accordingly as these may concur with the disposition, will the certainty of the event be augmented. The stronger virtue with the less temptation, or the deeper depravity with the stronger temptation, in the absence of the contrary influences in each case, will proportionally strengthen the grounds of certainty: yea, if it be apprehended that, at the point of beginning spiritual existence, strength of subjective susceptibility and objective influence be all on one side, or very largely predominant; this may even be a ground of certainty, how the spirit shall dispose its activity and give to itself an original and radical disposition. In none of these cases is there at all an exclusion of the open alternative, and the event is thus wholly contingent, and yet it may be certain that the touch will be on one side. To an insight so keen and comprehensive as to detect all the conditioning of temperament and applied motive, and especially the direction and strength of radical disposition, it might be no difficult thing to predict infallibly what events were coming from the efficiency of free causes. The certainty differs in its ground from all certainty in necessity. In necessity the event must be, and there is no alternative; in contingency there is an alternative, and it can never be said that from the very efficiency it must be, but only.that in the conditions it certainly will be. To mark this distinction, the first is sometimes called *physical* certainty, and the last *moral* certainty; though each may be infallible.

It should be understood that all these grounds of certainty are in reference to human forms of judgments. Without such grounds, it is not possible that we should connect events in any judgments, nor can we conceive of any other forms of thinking in judgments except through the series of conditions and conditioned. But we know that, to the Deity, some other form of knowing, altogether inexplicable by us, must be possessed. His knowledge cannot be mediate, through organs of sense and connections of substances and causes. He must know things as they are in themselves, immediately, intuitively, thoroughly. The future and the past must be wholly irrelevant to God's mode of knowledge, though he knows what quality and succession are to us. To God, there is no cold nor heat; no nervous pain nor muscular weariness; no phenomenon of sensual appearance; and hence, no thinking of them in connected judgments; but to him all things in themselves are plain and naked. As he knows what a guilty conscience is, immediately without experience, so he must know what all our sense and understanding-cognitions are without experience. God does not think, and conclude; he must know by immediate insight. Grounds of certainty, thus, are all irrelevant to God. He knows the things that are future to us, and needs not to look through their conditions to determine them. Man knows the future conditionally, God knows it absolutely.

SECTION IV. DIFFERENT APPLICATIONS OF CERTAINTY.—There is, as the primary and most comprehensive application of certainty, that of *infallible* being, and which may be termed *the certainty of truth.* It wholly excludes all regard to the grounds on which anything is certain, and also to the knowledge of the thing or its certainty, and is only the truth of that thing in itself. That a fact is, and that the fact is so conditioned that it may be known, are two quite different things. And so also, that a fact will be, or has been, is quite different from the fact that some being knows it. The certainty of truth is wholly independent of all grounds on which that certainty may be determined. Though no intellect knew, the certainty of being would not be thereby at all modified; and no matter on what ground the certainty rests; necessity or contingency; that there is certainty makes both alike infallible. The future, that shall be, is equally certain as the past, that has been; and the whole stream to come has its truth, as fully as the stream that has passed by. What events, all future actions of free causes shall produce, can have no greater certainty of truth when they shall already have come, than they have now. We may thus exclude all grounds of certainty and all knowledge of the fact, and may yet conceive that an event is infallible in its true being, and which will be the conception of certainty of truth.

Infallible truth of being may be somehow known, and we have in this, *certainty of knowledge.* As already said, to God, this knowledge is independent of conditions. That there is the certainty of truth is enough that, to God, there should be absolute knowledge. But the human understanding can know facts only mediately and conditionally. Phenomena must be given in the sense, and connected in the notions of substance and cause in the understanding, or there can be no determined experience; and such experience must have its conditions, or we can judge nothing in reference to any future events. Our certainty of knowledge must, thus, rest upon the apprehension of the grounds of certainty. That there is the certainty of truth will be of no help to our knowledge, except as the conditions which form the ground of certainty come into our apprehension; and then the certainty of the knowledge is as the infallibility of the ground on which the facts rest. Thus, I may know that the radii of the same circle will always be equal to each other, but it will be certain knowledge only as I apprehend the ground of its certainty in the nature of the case; the very conception of the circle itself. I may foreknow the certainty of natural events, but only as I know their ground in the connection of physical causes. I may know spontaneous events, but only as I know the hypothesis, which is to be their occasion, to be also an actual fact. And so, lastly, I may know the future action of free beings, but only as I know the conditions of their action in their disposition, temperament, and circumstances. Certainty of truth will not give me certainty of knowledge, unless I also apprehend the grounds of this certainty; and my knowledge will be wholly modified by these grounds. Certainty of knowledge cannot be the same in necessity as in contingency; and of that grounded in necessity, there must be a difference of certainty between absolute, physical and hypothetical necessity. Though in all, there may be infallible certainty of truth; yet in certainty of knowledge, the degree will vary as the apprehension of the grounds of certainty vary.

When the grounds of certainty are apprehended by another, and we depend upon his testimony, we may have *the assurance of faith.* The highest assurance of faith differs from knowledge, in this point; that knowledge has the grounds of certainty in its own apprehension, and faith is always through the medium of another's testimony. Confidence in the testimony may rise to what is termed the faith of assurance, so that there is no hesitation in resting the most important interests upon it; but it is still faith, and cannot be knowledge. God may foretell the future, and the confidence in the prediction may be so strong, both from his knowledge, his power, and his veracity, that it may exclude all doubt; and the faith may thus be "the substance of things hoped for, and the evidence of things not seen;" yet the man can still only say, "I believe," and have no need to say "help my unbelief;" while he cannot strictly say, I know, until his faith is actually "swallowed up in vision."

Thus we have certainty of truth, when the event is infallible *in re;* the certainty of knowledge, when the ground of certainty is apprehended; and assurance of faith, when the confidence in the veracity of the testimony is unquestioned. Absolute truths, physical facts, and spontaneous events stand on different grounds of certainty; but all in necessity, because all in their way are without an alternative, and unavoidable. Contingent events may have their infallible certainty, and may be foreknown in knowing their conditions; but they never come within the sphere of necessity and ever stand upon the ground of responsibility, for they have their open alternative, and thus their avoidability.

CHAPTER III.

NATURAL AND MORAL INABILITY.

The animal body has its gravitating and chemical forces working within it, as in the case of all other material being; and also its vital forces, like the rest of animated existences; and has thus a physical efficiency as a component part of universal nature. But this physical efficiency, in working its effects, is as much of nature, and as little of the personal possession, as any of the ongoing causes and effects in the world around us, and does not need to be examined, in connection with the enquiry for man's competency to attain the end of his being.

We have found the human mind to be a peculiar causality; a self-active, spiritual existence; competent to originate wholly new things, and not merely to take on conditioned changes in what already is, as the causes and effects in nature pass onward. It is a supernatural existence, and has thus a power independent of nature, and competent to work in, upon, and against nature. It can originate an efficiency, that shall awake and direct muscular activity, and through the use of its own bodily members can modify matter, and make changes in the physical world. It can also hold communion with other minds, and from the originations of its own plans and purposes within, can throw its influence upon the mental world, and work its modifications in other spiritual existences. But all this power of the human spirit, over matter and mind, has its limits. It is conditioned within its own sphere, and which is very limited compared with the omnipotence of the Absolute Spirit. This conditioning and limiting, of the supernatural causality of the human spirit, may be from obstacles in outward nature too powerful for its counteraction; or, it may be from hindrances within itself, which come from its own neglect or from its positive perversion. This spiritual efficiency it is, that we need to examine in its entire capabilities and hindrances, as it is only this efficiency which is concerned in the attainment of the end of human existence.

If we confine the attention to the one point of the limitation of spiritual efficiency, we shall gain all we need the most directly, since by an undivided attention we shall get clearer views of the limitation of human power; and having thus a complete view of human inability, from all sources of mental limitation, we shall in that have also the most completely within our vision, the whole field of human ability and direct personal responsibility. How is the human spirit limited in its efficiency? And what bearing has this limitation, upon its competency and responsibility in attaining the end of its being? It has already been said that the limiting of spiritual efficiency may be from obstacles in nature out of the spirit, and from hindrances which the spirit puts within itself. Both may be an infallible prevention to the attainment of many ends for which the spirit might act, but the first hindrance will be from without itself and thus excluding all moral accountability; and the second, being wholly from itself, will stand wholly chargeable to its own account. The end of spiritual being can be gained, notwithstanding all outward hindrance to efficiency; it is only the subjective hindrance, that can exclude the spirit from completely consummating the end of its being. The obstacles to efficiency in the first will give a *natural inability;* and the subjective hindrances will be a *moral inability;* both of which will be here adequately investigated.

SECTION I. NATURAL INABILITY.—The way is fully prepared, in the results of the preceding Chapter, to make an exact and universal discrimination between the two kinds of inability, natural and moral. The distinction is not at all of degree, but of kind; the two differing as two distinct things, having each their own separate and peculiar identity. One cannot displace the other, nor be at all equivalent in meaning to the other. Natural inability is a limitation of spiritual efficiency by *necessity.* When, in any case, an alternative is excluded and the event is unavoidable, it is an obstacle necessitating the spirit in its efficiency to one event, and making a natural inability to any other event. In every such case, there is a complete exclusion of all personal accountability. This may stand in each ground of certainty in necessity, as before attained, and will in each constitute a variety of the inability, but all of the same kind as natural inability.

Spiritual efficiency may be hindered by absolute necessity.—Universal and necessary principles stand out quite beyond the sphere of efficient causes, and cannot be brought within the conditioning of any efficiency. The principle must control power, and not the power control principle. That, in which all power is from the very nature of the case limited, must subject to a necessity that is absolute. The spirit, as rational, is limited to the measure of its own reason; and, that it should be able to nullify its own principles, would be the absurdity that reason should make itself to be unreasonable. As mathematician, the spirit cannot modify its own axioms; as philosopher, the spirit cannot condition its own scientific laws; and as moralist, the spirit cannot abrogate its own imperatives. The spiritual efficiency is thus necessarily held to all ultimate truth.

The spirit has the capacity of will in liberty, only because, in knowing its own intrinsic dignity, it finds its ultimate rule, and is thus competent to hold itself against any end that may conflict with it. This will cannot, then, change its ultimate rule, for only in the apprehension of such rule is there the capacity of will at all in being. As spiritual being, also, the spirit's own intrinsic excellency legislates, and this legislation is absolute, for the spirit goes to no authority out of itself; as spiritual activity, the spirit's competency to exclude all ends but its own legislation becomes a capacity of will, and is responsible to the legislator; the will, as subject, cannot, therefore, rise above the absolute sovereign and meddle with his immutable laws. Both in the very nature of will, and also in the necessary subjection of will to respon sibility, there is a *natural* inability to modify the foundations of immutable morality.

The will may be limited by physical necessity.—The human will, inasmuch as it is spiritual activity, is supernatural; and as such, it is a capacity to resist and modify nature. It is higher than nature, and cannot be crushed by nature; but becomes servant to nature, in no case, except by its own consent. Still, though it cannot be coerced by nature, and may hold on to its own ends in spite of nature; yet cannot it become the sovereign arbiter of nature. It can exclude nature from its own sphere, but cannot bring all of nature within its own sphere, and hold it there in subjection to its own purposes. It may use nature in many things for its own purposes, but such use is comparatively limited, and such limitation is necessitated in physical causation.

Nature is the product of supernatural efficiency. It is; and, through all its incessant changes, it still goes on, ever the same identical existence in its real substantial being. Its ongoing adds nothing to itself, and drops nothing out of itself, but only perpetually varies the modes of its being. If anything is either new created or annihilated in the successions of nature, it is a miraculous event, and must have come from a hand which holds nature in its power. Now, man may originate, and in this sense create new thoughts, new emotions, new purposes; and these may in various ways make their modifications of nature, but they do not become incorporated into nature. They are still the offspring of the human mind, and perpetuate themselves only within the realm of the spiritual, and make no additions to, nor subtractions from the realities of nature. Human efficiency is not competent to create nor to annihilate anything of nature, and has thus a natural inability to counteract any inherent law of nature.

In the various modifications which man is competent to make in the ongoing of cause and effect in nature, it is rather by supplying occasions for nature to act differently upon herself, than that his own efficiency is the producer. He puts one power of nature to act upon a different material, or in a different direction, from that in which the natural course of events was tending, and thus manages and combines and uses the powers of nature for his own ends. But in doing this, he must himself conform to nature, and cannot make nature serve him in opposition to its own laws. And many powers of nature cannot be at all managed by him, but stand out wholly beyond the reach of all his efficiency. He may study and learn new and surprising ways of subjecting natural powers to his service, but he will ever find physical causes still too mighty for his control. In all such hindrances there will be cases of natural inability.

And even in cases of direct muscular action, and the combination of all practicable mechanical operations, by which immense masses of matter are detached and displaced, the power of man soon finds its limit against the gravitations and cohesions of nature. He may move certain things and not others; to a given degree and not beyond; and though he may think how, with given engines and their place to stand, he could move the world, yet must his actual execution come far short of his ideal projections. His physical efficiency is weakness compared with the overwhelming forces of nature.

Thus, in all creations and annihilations of nature; in all modes of bringing nature to act upon herself; and in all direct counteraction of nature's forces; man soon finds a limit to his efficiency, and comes to events that to him have no alternative. The efficiency of natural causation shuts out his volition in necessity, and he stands helpless from natural inability.

The will may be limited in hypothetical necessity.—The spirit is self-active, and a cause for originating thought and sentiment as wholly new products. On occasion being given, spontaneously the spirit thinks and feels. But its spontaneous activity as knowing and feeling is conditioned by appropriate occasions. The spirit does not always think the same thoughts nor always feel the same emotions. Specific occasions, which lie in both the subjective state and the objective circumstances, must be supplied, or the spirit is not efficient for given thoughts and feelings. The occasions do not think and feel, nor do they cause the spirit to think and feel; the whole efficiency is from the spirit; but this efficiency does not become a cause for such products, except as the occasions are given. The spirit cannot conclude in a judgment without the requisite *data*, nor put forth a particular affection without the presence of the appropriate object; but when the occasion is given, it is the spirit which is the sole cause of the judgment or of the affection. In such occasion it spontaneously originated the new product, and was cause for that, and for nothing other than that. While spontaneous, it still has no alternative. It is a cause causing, without being a cause caused; but the presence of one occasion and the absence of all others, gives no alternative to the originating, and to the origination of just that product. All is hypothecated to the presence of the appropriate occasion, and when that is, the spirit is efficient for such a judgment, or such an affection, and the product is given in complete spontaneity. The conditioning is solely through the occasion, and not at all by a physical causing; it is thus unavoidable and in necessity, and the event without alternative, and thus to the spirit there is a natural inability to any other issue.

The above covers all the varieties of necessity, and thus all the grounds of certainty in which there is no alternative, and in this comprehends all possible cases of natural inability. The event is strictly unavoidable by the spirit, and thus entirely beyond the domain of will in liberty, and in this view is wholly destitute of all personal responsibility. So far as the occasion depends upon a volition, in hypothetical natural inability, there is indirect responsibility; but this responsibility is solely at the point of the voluntariness, and where there was an alternative; when that point has been passed, all merges in necessity, against which there is a natural inability, and under which there is no ethical responsibility. Natural inability cannot come within the constraint of an imperative.

SECTION II. MORAL INABILITY.—This is always a hindrance within the sphere of a complete contingency. It knows nothing of any form of necessity, and has, in its strongest hindrance, a full and open alternative. The event is not excluded because its exclusion was unavoidable; but solely because, from some hindrance within the spirit itself, the event was not secured though it might have been. We need not attempt to give all the forms of moral, as before in the case of natural inability. They all come within the one form of contingency, and find their hindrance within the spirit itself, and their modifications need only to be illustrated by some prominent examples.

The spirit may be hindered by a strong desire.—When an agreeable object is presented to the animal susceptibility, a craving, as a desire, is awakened, and the impulsive prompting is direct to an executive act in gratification. Such impulse may be of any degree in strength, from some faint appetite up to the strongest passion. Were there nothing but the animal nature, there would be no alternative to the strongest impulse, and what was deemed the highest happiness must govern the action in necessity. In such case here could be no moral accountability.

But in the human being, the spirit may apprehend a direct prohibition to this animal gratification, in the claim of its own excellency, and thus the rules of greatest happiness and highest worthiness may seem to be in direct collision. To one who well knows all the conditions in which such a mind is placed, both subjective and objective, it might be foreseen, as a certainty that this man would gratify the desire and violate the imperative. Quite strong language might be here applied in expressing the certainty of the event, and the man may say of him; I foresee that his passion will overpower him; that under its power he cannot control himself; that he can not resist such a temptation; but in all such expressions, we mean only to include the certainty of the prevalence of passion, and not that the gratification was unavoidable. We recognize a full and open alternative, though we speak so strongly of inability, and feel no impropriety in any application of terms expressing guilt and moral responsibility to the sensualist. The spiritual end in worthiness *ought* to have ruled, and we know *might* have been taken; and no matter how high the passion, and the certainty in his case that it would prevail, nor how emphatically we say he *could not* resist it; we never mean by it that an alternative was shut out, and that the guilty gratification was a necessity. The inability did not stand in any ground of necessity, and was only a moral inability, as wholly a different thing from all natural inability. A regard to human infirmity may induce us to palliate an offence committed under strong temptation, but in our strongest apology we shall not speak of it, nor judge of it, as of an event that had no alternative and was wholly unavoidable. If we allow ourselves to get a full view of all the truth, that the very force of the temptation gave an occasion for higher virtue, and more exalted dignity, in manfully resisting and expelling it; and that a thousand offered helps were near, making a way of escape that he might be able to bear it; we should be more likely, in our consciences, to hold him to a rigid responsibility than to plead for him apologies and palliations. The strongest desire against the claims of duty will never make a necessity; but, the very fact, that duty is set over against desire, opens an alternative; indicates a spiritual and not merely animal being; and installs a will in liberty, that should be, and will be, held accountable. Its highest certainties are in contingency, not necessity.

A hindrance from balanced desires.—Animal desires may often counterwork each other, and while the impulse from both is strong, and the two presented gratifications are of nearly equal degrees, there may be much hesitation. An exigency, in which great interests are so nearly balanced as to confuse the judgment, and yet where a prompt and decided conclusion must be formed, may very painfully perplex and very violently agitate the mind. The man may express his hesitation very strongly by saying, 'I cannot make up my mind'; 'I cannot choose between them.' Animal impulse is under necessity, and the strongest must carry, unavoidably; and, perhaps, if a perfect equilibrium of desire could be induced and kept up, it might be a necessity that the animal should stand between its objects of equal desire, and take neither. But not thus with a rational spirit. A reference of each to the end of his worthiness will bring in an ethical claim on one side, and reveal that one is imperative as well as desirable. Even if we could conceive of two objects of equal desire and equal duty, one only of which could be taken, then one only would be duty, and the indignity that the man should perpetually stand between them, and make himself an animal, would constrain him soon to cut short all hesitation and even blindly take either, rather than longer stand with none. No such position holds man in any necessity. The claim of his own excellency comes in and settles the object to be taken, or, that in the absence of sufficient grounds for a decision which, the mind make to itself a ground, and say 'first seen first taken,' and fulfil the duty in taking one, rather than, in the suspense, do wrong by rejecting both. All inability in such decision is moral inability, contingent and avoidable.

Hindrance to desultory impulses from the governing purpose.—When a purpose is fully fixed on the attainment of some remote end, there necessarily intervenes a great variety of subordinate acts in the fulfilment of the main purpose. When all the process passes on equably and uninterruptedly, the subordinate acts go out spontaneously under the control of the main purpose, and the general plan proceeds on to its consummation. But it may often happen that appetites and interests shall, in the meantime, be awakened in conflict with the main purpose. Great inducements may arise to turn aside from the grand end, and do that which is quite inconsistent with it. The strong desultory influence is to gratify this suddenly excited passion, and for the time forget the main end in view. But under the most impulsive passions and the strongest bribes to withdraw the attention and energy from the main pursuit, the governing purpose may be so firm and constant to its end, that the awakened passion does not take hold, and the will does not at all go out after it. In such case it may be strongly said, 'nothing can make him forget his purpose;' 'it is impossible to draw him aside from his chosen object.'

But it is manifest here, that the hindrance to nature is in the will itself. The appetite strongly awakened would at once go out in executive acts, and gratify the craving desire, but the strong will watches it, and guards against it, and thus hinders it from all interference with its own end. Not nature here hinders will, but will holds nature in check, and thus, of course, the strongest assertions of inability and impossibility can be only of a moral kind. That purpose can relax its tension; that watchful decision may become sluggish and careless; and thus appetite work the hindrance or defeat of the main purpose. It is only because the will has taken one alternative so strongly, that appetite has not before this conquered; the other side is still open, and a voluntary effort must constantly be made or that will be taken.

Inability to change the governing disposition.—In all cases of a settled governing purpose, there is a state of will directed to its main end; and then, many subordinate volitions to carry into execution this main purpose. It would be absurd to suppose, that the subordinate volition should change the governing purpose; that an executive volition should reverse a state of will; since the former, in both cases is only prompted and determined in the latter. The radical disposition is the spirit itself, disposed in a direction to an ultimate end of all action.

It must be comprehensive of all on one or the other side of worthiness and happiness; or, which is the same thing, of duty and gratification; God and mammon. When in the first direction, the disposition is righteous; when in the second, it is depraved. The radical disposition is thus a governing purpose, differing from other governing purposes in this, that it is ultimate and comprehensive, while the most general of others is still partial and concluded by a higher end. It would thus be the same absurdity, as above, to suppose that a radical disposition could be changed by any action of an executive will. The spirit itself, disposed on the ultimate end of its attainment, must carry all its executive agency in that direction.

There is thus a hindrance to all change or reversing of the disposition, in the very comprehensiveness of activity included in the disposition. The entire spiritual activity is directed to its ultimate end; and as righteous, the spiritual activity goes out in duty; or, as depraved, the immortal energy of the spirit bows itself in the bondage of making gratified appetite its end. The strength of this disposition may be of indefinite degrees, on either side; but on both sides, of whatever strength, it is comprehensive of the entire spiritual activity. If on worthiness; it is completely righteous, though not as perfect in strength as it might be: and if on happiness, it is totally depraved, though not as strong in its depravity as it may be. And now, this wholesoulness of disposition may be expressed in strong language, on both sides; by saying of the righteous, "he cannot sin;" and of the depraved, "ye cannot serve the Lord:" and may indeed be expressed by allusions to, and comparisons with, physical necessity; as when we say of a Washington, 'the sun may as well turn in his course;' or, of the incorrigibly wicked, "can the Ethiopian change his skin or the leopard his spots, then may ye also who are accustomed to do evil, learn to do well." But in none of these strong expressions, though likened in certainty to physical necessity, do we include a natural inability.

If we conceived the spirit to stand connected in the causalities of nature, and that its disposition was itself an effect of a physical efficiency wrought into it, then would it come within physical necessity and be unavoidable, and like all cases without an alternative, be a natural inability. Nature would have to turn itself back upon its old course, when nature is only causality going on in one course. But since we know spirit as the supernatural, and competent to originate its own disposing; we may well conceive that when it has its disposition, good or bad, there is still the alternative open to both, and neither the good disposition nor the bad disposition are henceforth inevitable. The good spirit has still its animal appetites, and the way is open to passionate impulses; the depraved spirit has still the conscious apprehension of what is due to itself, as spirit, and feels the pressure of obligation to reassert its own sovereignty over the appetites, and the way is open to do so; and hence, with all the certainty on either side, that both the righteous and the depraved will persevere in their old disposition, it is not a certainty grounded in any necessity, but a certainty in full contingency and avoidability, and hence admitting only of a moral inability.

The enquiry may here be made, Why apply this term inability to two so distinct cases? or, indeed, why apply the term inability at all to the mere self-hindrances of action, when it is plainly practicable that the hindrance the man himself makes, he himself can remove? We answer, that in the case of going against a radical disposition, or of changing that disposition, the deep consciousness of moral impotence in the human mind will never be satisfied to clothe its conviction, in any other form than that of directly expressed inability. A sense of great guilt, and of great danger, may press upon the spirit in the conviction of its perverse and depraved disposition, and the man may know and own his responsibility for every moment's delay to "put off the old, and to put on the new man," and yet be deeply conscious that his spirit has so come to love its bondage, and to hate its duty, that he can only adequately express his sense of his helplessness by emphatically saying 'I cannot change;' 'I find myself utterly helpless;' 'I am sold under sin;' 'some one else must help me, for I cannot help myself.' The deep conviction cannot rest in any weaker expressions.

And where strong, appetites, desires and passions, prompt to action, and the man speaks out from the fullness of his heart the difficulty he finds in restraining from gratification; or, when he is under the deep conviction of a depraved disposition and the obligation to return to righteousness, and he spontaneously utters the deep sense of his helplessness, he will naturally and certainly use the strong expressions of inability and impotence. It is no hyperbole, but honest, felt conviction. Inability may have its primary meaning in necessity, but when the deep hindrance to action is in the will itself, and the disposition reluctates all agency but in the line to its own end, and thus the inability is wholly of a moral kind, still the consciousness of weakness, in promptly effecting so thorough a reformation as the worthiness of the spirit demands, will infallibly secure the application of the terms implying inability to many cases of contingency only. Nor does the use of such language mislead us. The perceived nature of the case readily furnishes the proper interpretation, and we know at once from the subject given, whether the inability is in inevitable necessity or avoidable contingency. It would be a vain labor to attempt to preclude any fancied danger of ambiguity, by excluding all use of inability in cases of moral hindrance.

All books, the Bible itself, will give multiplied examples of such expressions, and except through some perversion of a speculative or dogmatic interest, there will be no liability to misapprehension. When God says to Lot, "Haste thee, escape thither; for I cannot do any thing till thou be come thither;"—Gen. xix, 22, we need have no fear that common sense will ever mistake it, as if God was denying his own omnipotence. So of the following, no mistake can be made. The brethren of Joseph "hated him, and could not speak peaceably unto him."—Gen. xxxvii, 4. "My children are with me in bed, I cannot rise and give thee."—Luke xi, 7. "I have married a wife, and therefore I cannot come." —Luke xiv, 20. And just as little will plain common sense mistake the following, and make them to be natural inability, grounded in necessity, without some previous perversion. "Joshua said unto the people, ye cannot serve the Lord, for he is a holy God."—Josh. xxiv, 19. "No man can come to me, except the Father which hath sent me draw him."—John, vi, 44. "Having eyes full of adultery and which cannot cease from sin."—2 Pet. ii, 14. The real distinction between the applications of inability is preserved by the qualifications of *natural* and *moral;* and the fact of necessity and irresponsibility in the first, and of avoidability and accountability in the last, makes the two to be permanently and consciously diverse from each other.

SECTION III. CASES WHERE NATURAL AND MORAL INABILITY ARE MORE EASILY CONFOUNDED.—In all cases of doubtful meaning, the ground of certainty is the criterion. If that be in any form of necessity, the case is one of natural inability; and if the ground of certainty be found only in the conditions in the spirit itself, and thus leaving an alternative open and the event avoidable, the most emphatic expression of inability is still only of a moral kind. The subject in hand will ordinarily determine, very readily, to which kind the particular case belongs, and yet in some cases there is much more liability of confounding the two from the want of a complete analysis of the mental facts.

The inability of constitutional and of spiritual susceptibility may be often mistaken.—Both the animal and rational susceptibilities we have found to be given, and their action determined, in constitutional nature. They are themselves conditioned in a previous fact, and can find no alternative. In such conditions the susceptibility must have such emotions, and the conditions are already given beyond any control of the mind itself. No matter whether the case be one of physical or hypothetical necessity, they are both alike unavoidable and the event stands beyond all accountableness in natural inability.

But the spiritual susceptibility is conditioned wholly in the spiritual disposition. The disposition being given, the feeling is as much determined in necessity as in a constitutional susceptibility, and is, in that point, held in natural inability. But the disposition itself, as a determining condition of the emotion, is not unavoidable. The person is held responsible for the whole disposing of the spiritual activity, and may thus be properly held responsible for all the feelings which are determined in it. It is natural inability no farther than being necessitated in the disposition, and no matter how intense the certainty that the disposition will not be changed, the fact that it may be, since there is an open alternative, throws the whole action of the spiritual susceptibility, which depends upon it, within the sphere of only a moral inability. The importance of this distinction is very great. Some feelings are necessitated, and the man should not stand accountable for them; others are necessitated only in a condition which is itself avoidable, and are thus as properly a matter of responsibility as the disposition that conditions them. When the man knows the line between natural and moral inability here, he will know also just where he is accountable for his affections.

Inability from constitutional temperament, and that from a spiritual disposition.—The constitutional temperament is determined in the physical organization, and gives its peculiar characteristics to the man permanently through life. Voluntary control may modify and restrain the promptings of the temperament, but no force of will can make the man of one temperament to be like the man of a different temperament. Peter's sanguine, and Paul's choleric temperament gave their peculiarities to each Apostle, and made them to be very different men through life. The whole action of temperament, except only in its watchful restraint, is in necessity and subjects to a natural inability.

The moral disposition, as already seen, is avoidable, and all the determination which is thus given to feeling and action is in contingency, and all the certainty connected with its events stands only in a moral inability. A miserly or an ambitious disposition may be in connection with a constitutional temperament very agreeable, or very disagreeable, but the whole demerit of his moral character is in his disposition, and his amiable or disagreeable temperament has no more connection with responsible character than the mildness of the lamb, or the ferocity of the tiger. A good man may have a constitutional temperament far less mild and amiable than some very vicious men, and yet this should never be deemed to detract from his real goodness, nor does the naturally amiable disposition of a bad man at all palliate the depravity of his moral disposition. The want of due discrimination in these respects leads often to very unjust estimates of human character, and on one side undervalues the virtue, and on the other, underrates the vice, of the radical disposition. There is a natural inability in the conditioning of temperament; the determining of moral disposition has only a moral inability.

Inability in changing character, and that of changing the outward conduct.—The true character is as the radical disposition, and can be changed, only in a change of the disposition. The outward conduct may vary at will, but the inward character be all the while unchanged. A moral inability only prevents the change of character or of conduct, but that any change of conduct should change the character is a natural inability. The conduct springs from the disposition, and must be estimated accordingly, and no merely executive acts can reach back and transform the disposition. The disposition must first be right, in order that the conduct may be morally approved, and not that the conduct, being constrained, will bring the disposition to be right.

A man may rob me by violence, or make a show of kindness to cheat me the more securely, and with the same disposition in each case. The devil is as truly malevolent in "transforming himself into an angel of light," as in "going about like a roaring lion;" for in both cases there is the disposition "seeking whom he may devour." Yea, the man may constrain the conduct, and control the whole outward life, from regard to reputation, from self-righteous zeal, or from the mistaken conception that he can so reform his character, and nothing but moral difficulties will be found in his way; but no such constrained action can at all modify character, for in the necessity of the case, the outward act can be no determiner of the inward disposition.

In the same way, desultory impulses may carry the outward conduct contrary to the governing disposition, and yet in such outer acting there is truly no change of character. A pirate may be touched with sudden sympathy for some interesting sufferer, and give in charity the very money which he has murdered others to get, and yet keep the disposition that will murder others for money to-morrow. And so, on the other hand, a good man may, perhaps, sometimes give from mere sympathy or from habit, or from policy, and in the act there may be no merit, because in it there was really no prompting of the righteous disposition. Yea, even a good man may, like Peter, deny his Lord through sudden fear, while his disposition is radically unchanged. There is great sin in the act, for the disposition should have been so strong as to overcome any colliding passion, but if the seed of the good disposition remains within, and the faith truly does not fail, he cannot sin as a rebel and an enemy, but only as an infirm and unstable disciple. The first look, that wakes the real disposition and draws out the true character, will bring bitter tears and godly sorrow. A bad man can do nothing truly good, for the evil disposition characterises all that springs from it, and whatever comes from impulses of humanity are without any moral root. A good man may do much that is wrong, but it will be his infirmity. He will condemn and loathe himself for it, and mourn over the weakness of his character, but he will still be conscious that his prevailing disposition has not changed. The wicked man should not say, 'I am delivered to do these abominations;' 'I cannot do good, and therefore am content to do evil.' Rather should he say, 'I can do nothing good with such a depraved disposition; here is a natural inability; I will therefore dispose my spirit anew, and attain to a righteous disposition, for to this there is nothing but a moral hindrance, and thus nothing to weaken the fact of constant obligation.' Nor should or will the good man say, 'I cannot change my character without changing my disposition, therefore I will be careless of all desultory impulses;' but rather, 'such impulses prevail through too yielding and infirm a disposition, and they stain and pollute the character with grievous offences, I will therefore set my spirit more firmly on the right, and deepen the current of my prevailing disposition towards godliness.'

Sometimes there may be mistaken the case of an absolute necessity, in an intrinsic absurdity, for a moral inability.—Thus the Apostle Paul declares, that "the carnal mind is enmity against God, for it is not subject to the law of God, neither indeed can be."—Rom. viii, 7. This may be often so misunderstood, as if the subjection to the law of God was an inability to the spirit itself; and might be interpreted as a natural inability in some form of necessity; or, by others, as a moral inability that is avoidable. But the truth is, that neither is meant, inasmuch as the avoidability of a carnal mind is not the point in view, but the great fact that a carnal disposition cannot be a loyal disposition. It is essential enmity, and whatever form it may take, while it is a carnal mind there can be no true subjection to God's law. If it obeys at all, it will be from fear or hope; from a selfish regard; and thus at the best mere legality and not loyalty. It is the intrinsic absurdity and thus the absolute inability, that carnality, which is enmity, should itself obey God from love.

So, again, the same Apostle says, "the natural man receiveth not the things of the spirit of God, for they are foolishness unto him, neither can he know them, because they are spiritually discerned."—1 Cor. ii, 14. The same mistake may be made here, as above; as if it were affirmed that there was an inability in the man to change from a natural to a spiritual state, and which some might affirm was a natural, others a moral inability. But the point is not whether a natural man can become a spiritual man, but the affirmation that a natural man, as such, can not have spiritual discernment; the intrinsic absurdity that he, who has had only carnal experiences, should know anything of the truly christian experience. Natural discernment cannot be spiritual discernment; an intrinsic absurdity, just as when it is said "ye cannot serve God and mammon." You cannot be, nor do, two opposite things at the same time.

The whole matter of human inability thus resolves itself into the two kinds of hindrance; one, in any kind of necessity, is a natural inability, without alternative, unavoidable, and wholly irresponsible; the other, always in contingency and avoidable, and thus wholly responsible, no matter how certain the events may be from the conditions within the spirit itself, and therefore a moral inability. The natural inability can interpose no hindrance to the man's attaining the end of his being; for the end of worthiness is solely for the spirit itself to assume; and to this, nature can oppose no barriers that become such, except through the assent of the spirit itself. The moral inability; which is a hindrance in the very spirit itself, and eclipsing all its dignity; making it to become unworthy; this only can keep the soul of man from reaching its goal, and attaining the consummation of that for which it has had its being.

CHAPTER IV.

THE HUMAN MIND AS AN AGENT.

THE single facts of mind have been attained, and apprehended in their connections and reciprocal relations, and have also been analyzed into their simple elements. We have, moreover, found them in their organic combination according to the revelation of consciousness in our own experience, and have thus the human mind as a whole, and may contemplate it as an entire being, in reference to the ends that are designed to be consummated in it. Farther, we have considered the whole subject of causality and efficiency; the grounds of certainty in reference to all events; and the distinctions of natural and moral inability in reference to human action. We are thus prepared to take the human mind entire as an agent, and know the whole sphere in which it is competent to put forth its activity.

That we may attain this the more completely, we will first look separately at the sphere of man's animal nature, and determine the peculiarities of its agency; then, to the sphere of man's rational being, and the higher agency there exerted; and lastly, to the whole in combination, as reciprocally modified one by the other. We may thus have both a distinct and comprehensive knowledge of human agency, and of the entire sphere which it was designed the human mind should fill.

SECTION 1. MAN, IN A CERTAIN SPHERE, ACTS AS THE ANIMAL.—We never find man excluded wholly from his rational being, and thus acting solely as a brute. In his most sensual activity, there is that which evinces the posession of higher faculties, and this higher prerogative always modifies the mere life of the animal. But the whole animal activity is still so distinct in its nature and end from the spiritual being of man, that it is competent to us to abstract the modifying influence of the rational, and regard man as solely animal agent. We may find him, in most particulars, above other animals in the perfection and strength of his faculties, and in all combined, that he is the most complete of the entire animal creation; but no augmentation of degree will at all take him out of the sphere of mere brute existence. He is still the fellow to the creatures of the stall and the stye.

In the intellectual capacity, as animal, there is the full provision given for attaining all the phenomena that belong to the sensible world. All the qualities which are perceived through any organ of sense, and all the mental phenomena, as the exercises of the mind itself, which may in any way come within consciousness, are wholly within the reach of the human mind. Some animals may have a quicker and keener sense than man, and some peculiar instincts are given to some of even the lower animals, but in general it may be said, that all the activity which belongs to animal perception is in its most complete degree the possession of man. And far more perfectly than any other animal can man exercise the connecting operations of the understanding. The experience of the man, in bringing the changing pheno mena of the sense within the concluded judgments of the understanding, must be far more orderly and extensive than any brute experience can reach. The deductions from past experience are far more conclusive and comprehensive than in the case of other animals. Brutes can, and do, draw general conclusions from objects of sense, and thus learn what is useful and prudent, but the generalizations of man, though of the same kind here as the brute, are much broader and clearer, and hence he may be a wiser and safer economist than any other animal. This capacity for perceiving, and judging according to what has thus been perceived in the sense, is the whole extent of the animal endowment as knowing, and in all this knowledge man is pre-eminent. He can thoroughly commune with the brute in all its ways of knowing, and is, thus, truly animal.

In common with the brute, man has the whole sphere of the animal susceptibility, and knows how to commingle feelings with the animal in all its appetites and their gratification. The social and dissocial propensities, the sympathies in joy and suffering, the natural affections which hold the parents to their offspring, all come out the same in kind on the field of human and animal experience. The feeling that appropriates possessions, and gives to animals an interest in things and places, and induces to the formation of habits, is more completely developed in man, though still of the same kind as in the brute. The sentient nature of man and animal is thus the same, and man is no more kindred to the animal in a certain sphere of knowing, than he is in a common sphere of feeling.

All this capacitates man for an impulsive activity. His sentient capacity opens in appetites and their wants, and the impulse of all appetite is to go out in action after the object of gratification. The sole end of appetite is satiety in the enjoyment, and then the whole activity rests, until nature again stimulates the appetite to repeat the same activity for the same end. The end of animal life is happiness, and the whole activity is a blind impulse, going out unavoidably in its conditions after its end. There may be deductions from past experience, which modify future action; and the animal, having learned to be prudent, may act quite differently in the same outward conditions. But this prudential consideration is a new condition, and itself just as impulsive as the appetite, and restraining and controlling it by the same law of highest happiness, and thus the animal goes after the prudent by the same law of necessity as before. The strongest prompting is already determined in the constitutional nature, and the objects awakening the impulse are conditioned in their order by the ongoing of surrounding nature, and thus, to the animal, there is no alternative to the order of its activity. Each event is, in its condition, unavoidable.

Man is, therefore, an agent, in his animal being, acting as the brute does solely for enjoyment; and though from his broader experience and wider generalizations, competent to take hold on higher prudential considerations than any other animal, yet is this a difference of degree only, and leaving the higher prudential prompting to be equally as impulsive as any other animal feeling. In this sphere of activity there is an entire exclusion of all proper will, and thus of all liberty and responsibility.

SECTION II. MAN IS ALSO A RATIONAL AGENT.—Superinduced upon the animal nature, in its capacity of the sense and the understanding judging according to sense, and which also has a susceptibility to all animal feeling, there is the high prerogative of a rational and spiritual existence. In the possession of reason, man is competent to apply necessary and universal principles, for expounding and comprehending all the perceptions of the sense and the judgments of the understanding. In this sphere he rises above the natural, and is truly supernatural. He not only knows what is given in experience, but attains principles which are prior to, and conditional for, experience, and thus can make experience itself the subject of his philosophy. He can, moreover, apply the principles of taste to nature, and determine how far nature is beautiful; and also the principles of science to nature, and determine how far nature is philosophical; and can thus make his reason the absolute measure of nature, in art and philosophy. In addition to all this, he can know himself, as spiritual, and determine therein an ultimate rule of right for his action towards others, and his claims on other's activity towards him, and in this comprehend the whole sphere of morals.

This capacity for rational knowledge is occasion, also, for a rational susceptibility, and man is competent to exercise feeling in the spheres of art, science, and morals. The emotions awakened by the beautiful and the sublime; the feelings inspired by philosophy; and the moral obligations and emotions which originate in the imperatives of conscience; all these transcend the highest experience of animal nature, and are possible to man only as he is a rational spiritual agent. In all these departments of knowledge and feeling he is competent, also, to find an absolute rule within himself, and thus to direct his action by his own law, and exclude all other ends from holding dominion over him; and in this self-direction he possesses truly a will in liberty, and has an alternative to all the impulses of nature.

SECTION III. THIS AGENCY OF THE ANIMAL AND THE RATIONAL IS COMBINED, IN MAN, IN PERPETUAL UNITY.—The animal, in man, does not stand in complete isolation, as mere brute; nor does the rational stand completely separate, as pure spirit; but animal and rational, sense and spirit, so combine in unity that both make one personality. One life is in the whole, and one law of development controls all, so that we say of man, both animal and spiritual, he is yet but one being. In this respect, the human differs, on one side from the brutal, and on the other side from the angelic life. They are so combined in unity as to be neither purely, but each is so modified by the other that the whole is a third thing not identical with either.

It might be an interesting examination, and yet, as it must be mainly speculation, not appropriate here, to determine the origin of this rational superinduction upon the animal. Is reason a propagation as truly as the animal being? Were all spiritual rudiments in humanity given in the first of the race, and are all souls a traduction from Adam? Is it not rather propagation only so far as the animal, and a perpetual divine superinducing, in each case, so far as the spiritual being is concerned? Must not flesh be born of flesh, and spirit be a spiritual superinduction solely? Is there not some help in the conception each way, in considering how the Lord Jesus Christ could be human and divine in one person, which would be truly animal, spiritual, and divine in one; and how man can be animal and spiritual, in one person? May not, yea must not, the rational be as truly a supernatural putting on to the animal, as was the divine to the human? But however such questioning may be solved, this is true, that the man can in no way act solely as the brute, any more than the Divine Mediator could act solely as a man. The two in union go to make the peculiar one, and any separation of the two at once annihilates the peculiar third thing. The conception of the two agencies separately, is not then, by any means, a conception of human agency. The personality of the man is the synthesis of both, and as human agent, he must be animal and spiritual reciprocally modified. Neither his intellect, susceptibility nor will, can be like either those of the brute or of the angel; his knowledge, feeling, and willing must be *sui generis*, that is, solely

32

human knowing, feeling and willing. We cannot speak of animal happiness for man, as if such happiness could be solely the gratification of appetite as in the mere brute. The man cannot make happiness his end, and gratify want, solely as an animal does. He has also a spiritual being, and his very spirit, as a reigning disposition and permanent will, enters into his appetitive cravings, and takes up their gratification as an end of life. The animal gratifies from natural impulse; the man goes after carnal pleasure as a chosen object, and puts the activity of his spiritual will into his voluptuousness. Nor, on the other hand, can we speak of angelic holiness or sin as belonging to man, for man cannot stand towards the ultimate rule of right, and come to its fulfilment or violation as the angel does. His subjection of the animal nature to the demand of his spirit necessarily enters into his virtue; and the bowing of the spirit in bondage to the animal nature necessarily enters into his sin; but the angel is not also animal, and cannot therefore have either holiness or sin in the forms of human holiness and sin. The moral character of the human must be peculiar, inasmuch as his constitutional being, and his attitude towards the ultimate rule of right, is peculiar—a compound of the animal and the spiritual.

Man cannot have purely soul-holiness, nor exclusively soul-sin; for his spirit can never act but as modified in its agency by "the law in the members." The reverence, and humility, and love, of the spirit, will participate in the animal feeling that is accordant with such emotions; and the pride, and envy, and malice of the soul, will be tinctured with a selfishness that has its sympathies in the wants of the flesh. Even in the spirit-world, the exercises of the human soul must still retain the modifications of its sensual experience, and the scripture-doctrine of a resurrection determines some kind of coporeal existence forever. Human worship will differ from angelic, and human blasphemy from the demoniac, for something of the animal must ever blend itself with the activities of the spiritual.

We do not need to examine the peculiar activity of purely spiritual being, because humanity is not, and is not to be, purely spiritual. Both with angels and especially with God, will in liberty must differ from human will. All spirit, finite or absolute, will know itself, and know the claim upon itself that all its activity be in the end of its own worthiness; but the colliding influences which hinder such direction to the activity will widely differ in man, angels, and God. An angel, from his finiteness, is open to appeals from ambition, and may greatly debase himself by seeking unduly to exalt himself, and thus "lifted up of pride, he falls into the condemnation of the devil." "God cannot be tempted of evil," for he is above all sources of influence that would urge to any activity in disparagement of his own glory. No inducement that he should disregard his own dignity, and thus "deny himself," can reach to him. His will is serene and tranquil, and never knows any colliding and disturbing motives. But quite otherwise is it with the will of man. His animal nature, even when brought into subjection, must be constantly guarded; for at any hour passions may rise, that unrestrained will lead to ruin. His spirit may have the temptations of ambition; because he, like an angel, is finite; but in addition to spiritual pride, he is open through all the senses to worldly pomp and "the pride of life." Spiritual ambition will have also its carnal desires, and demoniac malice will be accompanied by brutal lust. Not pure spiritual agency, finite or infinite, but human spiritual agency, is what we seek to know. What is the kind of activity which man may exert, and what is the field on which it may be manifested? This is essential in the enquiry for his capability to reach the end of his being.

Nature is working in him, and upon him, and were he only nature, he must obey her currents, and float as the stream should carry him. He is not only nature; he is supernatural. In his spiritual being he has a law of worthiness, and he may hold on to this imperative which awakes in his own spirit, and resist and beat back all the appetites which awake in his animal nature. He is not held in necessity to the bondage of the flesh; the alternative is open, whether he take it or not, to crush and keep the flesh at the foot-stool, and make it to serve and not to rule the spirit. Spiritual causality is above all natural efficiency. If it may not be able to hold muscular resistance against the powers of nature, it can still wholly exclude nature from its own sphere, and keep its own end, and hold itself steadfast to it, in spite of all the happiness or suffering which nature can give.

Man is, therefore, an agent who has the capacity of will in liberty, and is thus endowed with free causality.

To the question, Why does man choose between duty and appetite? the proper answer is, that he has both ends in his own being, the law of happiness as end of the animal and the law of worthiness as end of the spiritual being, and he must make his election. He must take one, and he cannot take both, and he is thus shut up to the necessity of choosing between them. And to the question, Why does he choose *thus?* Why take happiness as end against his spiritual worthiness? or, why change from one to the other? the proper answer is, that with full avoidability, the conditions within and without give a ground of certainty which it will be. Taking the whole being, animal and spiritual; the clearness of the perception and the excitability of the feeling, and the outer motives that come before him; there may, in these, be a ground of certainty which he will choose, and what permanent disposition he will form, though at the time there was an alternative, and thus a choice and avoidability in reference to the end chosen. When the disposition has already been made, that adds itself as a conditional ground of certainty for perpetuated choice of the same end, other things without and within remaining the same. With this given strength of disposition, and all else belonging to the being; a full knowledge of all the outer motives, and direct spiritual influences that may act upon him, may give a ground of certainty in reference to his change of permanent disposition. The conditions are not natural causes, nor at all excluding the capacity of his own free causality, but they give the certainty which end the free spiritual cause will take in the full alternatives of worth and want, duty and happiness. The spirit is supernatural cause, and its conditions are not themselves causes making the spirit's agency a *causa causata*, but in such conditions, the spirit truly originates a choice, and goes out to one when that was avoidable and a full alternative was open.

We here regard only the capacities of the mind as agent, and leave entirely to revealed theology the whole ground of determining the certainty of perpetuated depravity; the fact of original sin; and the interposition of Divine Grace to radically change the disposition and sanctify all the spiritual affections. These revealed doctrines will be in full accordance with the conscious facts of the human mind, but they will take these facts as already given, and assume the psychology without at all attempting to teach it. It may be legitimate to carefully deduce from the theological dogma, what is the assumed psychological fact; but quite surely, no scriptural doctrine will contradict the fact of avoidability in all responsible agency. There are, still, some direct objections made to the fact of such agency in liberty and which require a full and fair consideration. This we now undertake.

SECTION IV. STATE AND ANSWER FAIRLY THE PROMINENT OBJECTIONS TO LIBERTY.

1. Obj. *Like causes always produce like effects.*—The force of this objection is, that by an invariable law of causality, its action is uniform in like circumstances, and acting in the same conditions must ever produce the

same effects. This law must hold in the mental world, as well as the physical, and we are not thus to suppose that any mental acts can be different under the same conditions.

If there is nothing above nature, this objection is sound, for past all contradiction, physical causes operate alike in the like conditions. But if nature is subject to the control of a supernatural, then must there somewhere be a causality that is not itself caused by a higher efficiency, and which truly originates events from itself. If this supernatural cause has an ultimate rule of right in its own being, it is not only more than physical efficiency, but more also than pure spontaneity, since it conditions itself in its own ethical demands, and originates its effects intelligently and morally, and thus contingently and not necessarily. Such causality is not thing, but person, and as absolved from all causality above him, and all imperative except what is found within him, he is the absolute, spiritual Jehovah.

Just so far as man's spirituality reaches, he too is person, and possesses the capacity of origination in liberty. His moral acts are not the product of a natural causality necessitating them with no alternative, but are his own originations, on occasion of both the impulse of appetite and the obligations of duty; and which of these he takes is at his own responsibility, for the open way to the other made the taking of this avoidable.

We need not, thus, deny a certainty of like results in like conditions, but the certainty of natural and spiritual causalities are wholly different. Nature has no capability of origination from itself, and all its causes are themselves caused by an efficiency back of their own acting, and have thus no alternative; but spiritual causality is out of, and above, all nature's causes, and may begin action in itself and thus truly originate, and not that its acts shall be caused and thus necessarily determined by nature. How certain soever it may be, in reference to any action, what it shall be from its occasions; those occasions do not cause it to be, and thus do not exclude avoidability.

2. Obj. *Then all means are powerless.*—If the spirit can begin action in resistance to nature, then no matter what motives are presented, nor what means are used, the spirit can counteract them and the will go against them, and thus nullify all their efficiency.

True, all means are powerless, since they are not efficient causes operating on the spirit, and themselves causing the acts which come from it; else would the spirit be subjected to nature, and all its acts would be unavoidable, because grounded in necessity. But not powerless in this sense, that they give occasion for spiritual action, and throw a moral influence upon the spirit in the direction to a given action. Whether of the appetite towards happiness, or of the imperative towards worthiness, they are inducements in one direction, and hindrances in the other direction; and may be a ground of certainty which direction will be taken; but inasmuch as they are not physical causes, themselves causing the spirit to act, they constitute no natural inability to an alternative, and at the highest are truly avoidable. They have no power to make the spirit to be nature; they have influence which may give the certainty what a supernatural spirit will do.

3. Obj. *It denies that every event must have its cause.*—Here are acts of the spirit which are not connected in any efficiency with their antecedents; these antecedents may be of any kind, and they do not make their consequents to be after their kind; the antecedents do not cause the consequents, and thus the consequents are without cause.

Yes, the spiritual act is without cause in this, that it is not an effect from any of nature's causes. No antecedent in nature is its immediate antecedent, but it originates in a source wholly supernatural. It is wholly a new thing put into nature which does not come out of nature. Nature gets so much new, which was not in it before. All her consequents are only changes of what permanently has been, but the spiritual act is no change of what was in nature already. Still the spiritual act is not without cause. It does not come up out of a void. Its proximate antecedent, and thus its immediate cause, is the spirit itself. Nothing out of the spirit, and especially nothing back of the spirit in the realm of nature, has caused it; the spirit itself has originated it, and henceforth that event, whatever it may be doing in nature, belongs to the spirit, and can nowhere find for itself another author.

4. Obj. *This cuts off all spiritual action from the possibility of foreknowledge.*—The act is contingent and may be avoided; it has no necessary connection to any thing that now is in nature; it may therefore be avoided,

and nothing that now is can determine that it will not be avoided; it is thus impossible to be foreknown.

True, it is not now given in anything yet within nature, and cannot thus be foreknown by looking through any successive changes in nature; but this does not deny that the Absolute Spirit may have the certainty of it. Must God foreknow, only as he can look through the necessary sequences in nature! Yea, it does not deny but affirms, that any spirit, which might know all the inner and outer occasions in which the agent shall be, might find a ground of certainty in these very facts. These occasions will not cause the spiritual event, but may give a ground of certainty that what is in itself wholly avoidable yet will not be avoided. This is always the only ground of moral certainty, and yet with our limited means of knowing the occasions, we often trust the highest interests on our convictions of certainty what free agents will do; a perfect knowledge of all the circumstances might give perfect certainty which alternative would be taken.

5. Obj. *Such free origination is inconceivable.*—It supposes a causality which can go out one way or another, and that there is nothing back of it causing it to go in either, and that thus it must go the way it does for no cause or reason whatever. This is the absurdity of choosing without choice, and is inconceivable.

It is admitted, and affirmed, that it is inconceivable by the logical understanding. A liberty in physical causation is an absurdity. On one side, we cannot conceive that the causality can have an alternative, for that would involve that a conditioned cause might rise above its conditions, and would be the absurdity of action from nothing. On the other hand, a will, already determined in its cause and going out with no alternative, is the absurdity of unavoidable choice. Physical causality can have no alternative; action in liberty can be only with an alternative; and thus an understanding, which can only connect by conditions, cannot conceive of a liberty in causation. A logical understanding can conceive of no beginning, and of course can conceive of no originator. But we are obliged by our reason to demand a first, and thus to attain a conception of an author who has no cause before him conditioning either his being or acting, but in whom action originates. This is the very conception of spiritual being; an entirely supernatural existence; a being not bound in nature, but competent to originate uncaused by nature; and till the reason gets this conception, entirely distinct from all the efficiences in nature, it knows neither a God nor a soul, and must confine all things within the linked succession of a series, to which it can give neither an origin nor a consummation. Liberty is a necessary attribute of spiritual being, and is fully conceived in an existence that can hold on to a law of duty within itself, against any end of action from without itself. It lifts the conception at once out of nature to that which can work against nature, and is both self-action and self-law.

Such we must conceive to have been the creative act of God. It must have originated in himself, and gone out self-directed; for any conception of previous conditioning, that made the creative act to be, and to be such as it was, would demand a necessitated series of conditions running up in the bosom of the Creator without an original. The same conception of agency, as an endowment by God, originating acts within the finite sphere of man's efficiency, is both possible and actual.

6. Obj. *All analogy is opposed to it.*—All the causes in nature are conditioned in some higher causality, and go out into effect without an alternative, and thus from analogy we should conclude that it is so with mind, and that all its acts have their previous determining causes.

To this it might readily be answered, that analogy is of no force against a matter of fact. Where a fact can not be brought within experience and thus to the test of consciousness, a fair argument from analogy is legitimate, but conscious experience cannot allow itself to be contradicted by any analogical argument. But were analogy admissible, we should derive from it the strongest support in favor of action in liberty. No physical causality is held at all responsible. It lies confessedly outside of the entire sphere of ethical activity, and can be subjected to no imperative constraints; it may, therefore, at all times be conditioned in its antecedents, and be doomed to work on without an alternative. But spiritual agency is responsible agency, and on this account is excluded from conditions of all physical causation and all analogical deductions therefrom, and demands just this agency of free origination and alternative election.

7. Obj. *All surprise for the most rash and unreasonable conduct is wholly without foundation.*—All spiritual action is contingent, and thus wholly avoidable, and may

just as well be against reason as with it, and even against interest as for it; thus there is no ground for expecting one act rather than another, and no occasion for being surprised at any man's action.

But, occasions for action are necessary to all free causation, and these occasions give inducements or hindrances to the act, and may supply a ground of certainty what the action will be, though they do not fix it in unavoidable necessity; certainly then, these moral occasions may furnish strong grounds for expecting the act, and reasonable surprise if not exerted, or if some quite different action be put forth. But this objection may much more forcibly be retorted upon the objector himself. With him all is made unavoidable in the previous conditions. As the case is, there is no alternative; one event alone can be. All surprise at the event must thus be wholly from ignorance. I should feel no more surprised at any human conduct than at the bursting of a steam-boiler. Neither could have been otherwise in the conditions, and the surprise is alike in both, viz. ignorance of the reason why they could not help it. But actually, my surprise for the human conduct is, why the man did not help it.

CHAPTER V.

THE COMPETENCY AND IMPOTENCY OF THE HUMAN MIND TO ATTAIN THE END OF ITS BEING.

THE end of animal nature is happiness; the end of spiritual being is worthiness; and as man is both animal and spiritual, he has both of these ends for his attainment. Speculatively, it might be held as true, that the attainment of either, completely, is incompatible with itself except in the attainment of both. It may be presumed that the animal nature will be unhappy in the debasing of the spirit, and that the spirit will feel an indignity in yielding to any uncompensated unhappiness in the animal. So, also, ethically considered, it might be argued that providential allotments should make the most worthy, to be the most happy. But all speculation aside, experience will not be competent to determine, in all cases, where the greatest ultimate happiness can be gained; and every man will find himself in circumstances, where he can maintain his spiritual worthiness only by sacrificing animal happiness; and in all such cases, the conscious conviction is, that the worthiness should be maintained whether the sacrifice in happiness be ever compensated hereafter, or not. The ultimate end of man is the integrity of his spirit at the hazard of whatever loss to his gratification, and he may cheerfully leave the end of happiness to its own issue, if he has kept himself faithful to the end of worthiness. So to dispose all a man's agency as to be most worthy of his spiritual acceptance, is to have a righteous disposition; and permanently to maintain such a disposition, is the end of his being.

The great mass of mankind reverse this order entirely, and live for happiness, not for spiritual worthiness; and thus sacrifice the end of their being. Yet this perversion of the highest law of existence, and thus a depraving of the race, is everywhere connected with the conviction of personal demerit in it, and personal responsibility for it, and thereby a manifest competency to avoid such perpetuated depravity, and that the man put and keep himself within the claims of his spirit. And yet, with all this competency manifest in the conscious obligation and responsibility, there is also the consciousness of irresolution to break away from this bondage, and of so succumbing in the spirit to the domination of appetite as proves also an impotency to regain the lost dominion, and to bring the body under. This conscious competency and conscious impotency to the same thing, exist as opposite facts, at the same time, in the same man. It is the great moral paradox in human nature, and can never be solved by any ignoring or eliminating of either element, but must somehow be harmonized by admitting the existence of both. What has now been gained is sufficient to put these contradictory facts in a light, which shows them to stand to each other in true consistency.

SECTION I. MAN IS NATURALLY COMPETENT TO GAIN THE END OF HIS BEING.—*He is capable of determining his highest law.*—The inner witness of what is due to the dignity of his spiritual being secures the perpetual working of a conscience, excusing or accusing. In the light of his own spirit man knows what exalts and what debases him; what sustains his true dignity, and what degrades him; and in this alone he is a law to himself. When no outward authority promulgates a positive commandment, he has the law written on his heart; and where positive laws are imposed, they must be brought home to his conscience, and in the light of his own spirit he must see that disobedience to them is a reproach and dishonor to him, or their sanctions can have no moral obligation. He needs nothing more than this rational insight into his own being, and in all conditions the law is legible.

His appetites crave; and where no claim of his spiritual being is infringed, he may virtuously gratify them, and to just the degree that the worthiness of his spirit will permit. Where the clear estimate of highest happiness gives a plain dictate of prudence, and nothing else comes up as a directory; in the light of his own spirit he will at once read his duty in this perception of utility, for his spirit would itself be dishonored, in bringing his animal nature to endure needless suffering or privation. Mere prudence is thus itself made a virtue. When others may be more happy by his self-sacrifice, the spirit will see in itself that its own true dignity is exalted in such self-denial; and thus, when only kindness to others is contemplated, the benevolence is seen to be a duty, and becomes a virtue because it adorns the spirit. But when, in any condition, the wants of animal happiness for himself or for others—the dictates of personal happiness or of social kindness—come in conflict with what is due to the rational spirit; then, the true dignity of the man is secured only in sacrificing both his own and other's happiness to his spiritual worth, and it becomes a virtue to be severe against his own flesh, and to close his ear to all the pleadings of pity for others. And when some positive claim is enforced from the authority of the Absolute Spirit, requiring prompt obedience without consulting any other want or claim whatever, the human spirit knows that its own dignity is maintained and exalted by implicit and unquestioning obedience.

There is no place where the spirit may not see the bearing of any action upon its own worthiness, and where, thus, the law that binds it may not be adequately apprehended. It is not necessary to ascend to heaven, nor to descend to the abyss; for the law is nigh to every man, and speaks out from the conscious imperatives awakening within his own spirit.

Man is competent to obey this law.—The human mind has all the capabilities necessary for knowing not only, but also for doing every duty. There may be strong conflicts of appetite and impulsive passion against the strict demands which the purity and integrity of the spirit imposes, and all the occasions and soliciting conditions of nature may seem to lie temptingly open to the indulgence of animal desire; but his virtue is found in the manly valor that beats back, and brings under, these unruly appetites, and which puts and keeps them in subjection to the intrinsic excellency that belongs to man's spiritual constitution. And this spiritual activity and energy is always present in the very being of the spirit itself, and the requisite control of the most turbulent passion can only be lost in the neglect to watch and suppress its sudden impulses. The contest with any single appetite may long last, and the warfare with all animal propensities may hold on through life, but the restraint for the hour is the victory for that hour, and the triumph is as perpetual as the prolonged ascendancy of the good will; and this may be effectual in restraining as long as there is a body to keep under and bring into subjection.

The right and authority, the throne and scepter, the executive force and prerogative are all the possession of the spirit, and it must be in treachery to its own sovereignty, if it lay them by, or give them over into the power of the enemy, and yield to the usurpation of any lust. In the contempt of every gratification, and the defiance of every torture that nature can get or feel, the spirit of the man *can*, as it *should*, hold itself steadfast in its own integrity, and go down to death with its high end and purpose unrenounced and inviolate.

When wrongly disposed, it is competent to change the disposition, and take again the end for which existence is given.—We are not concerned here with any grounds of certainty that the depraved disposition will or will not be changed, nor with any speculation or revelation how the once righteous disposition became perverse and depraved; but that in the depravity of the spirit, it is still competent to itself to renounce the wrong end towards which it has disposed its activity, and return to the true end of its being, and thus re-assert its dominion over those appetites under which it has slavishly been in bondage. Though the man has made the end, for which the brute lives, his end, and even put the immortal energies of his spirit in active chase after happiness, so that he pursues gratification as no animal can; never satiated; never resting; yet has he not thereby become the mere animal. Giving in to nature, and subjecting himself to serve nature as he does, yet has he not at all lost his supernatural being. He is rational spirit still, and well knows, and sometimes keenly feels, the deep degradation of his soul in living so beneath the intrinsic excellency which still belongs to it. The rational has most absurdly bent in servitude to the animal; the spirit has most unnaturally fixed its end in nature; but the reason sees the absurdity, and the spirit feels the indignity, and hence the wretched man cowers in shame and guilt before the upbraidings of his own conscience. He knows the alternative is open: the perpetuation of his shame and guilt is avoidable: that if he persist in his baseness, it will not be nature holding him down under any form of necessity, but that his spirit freely stays, as it voluntarily went down, in the place of its degradation. Every hour's delay, every fresh act of sensuous gratification, brings down another stroke of the whip of scorpions; for he is choosing carnal happiness, when he might be, and ought to be, aspiring after, and reaping, the immortal dignities and honors of his spiritual birth-right.

In many things he knows he is linked into the successions of nature, and that the connections of the antecedents and consequents are indissoluble; but not in the taking of the end for which he lives, nor in the perpetuation of that perverse and guilty disposition which is turned to folly. That is his work, and not nature's, nor God's. Nothing perpetuates it, but the perpetual free action of the spirit. But for him it had not been begun; only by him can it be perpetuated; and the responsibility is on him that it cease immediately. No matter how strong the tempting inducements without; no matter how ready the consenting appetites within; the spirit must willingly take, or it is not defiled by them; and it must willingly persist, or its guilt is not perpetuated in them. The worth and the reward are in the spirit's own resistance to these forbidden indulgences, and the battle and the victory is in meeting and treading down every lust. No matter how stubborn and severe the contest; the obstinacy of the foe gives more sublimity to the battle, and more dignity to the triumph; and the very occasion for so heroic a contest, is also an opportunity for so glorious a victory. Within the entire domain of the spiritual, the will reigns sole sovereign, and nothing forces it to serve the flesh; nor, when it has basely been doing it, does anything, without the spirit itself, bind it in its prison-house. It has no natural inability; it comes within no necessities of nature; with no hesitation or equivocation, we say that the spirit disposed on happiness should avoid, yea, is competent to avoid the perpetuated guilt, and stand again disposed on the end of its own worthiness.

SECTION II. MAN IS MORALLY IMPOTENT TO GAIN THE END OF HIS BEING.—Universal observation establishes the sad fact that man is depraved from the first. With all that is tender, trusting, and amiable in childhood, still the innocence of youth is only comparative. The child is not so stubborn and hardened in vice as is the old transgressor. But when the strict rule of ethical obligation is applied, that the whole spiritual activity should be permanently disposed to the end of worthiness, and not of happiness; that the animal nature should be utterly subject, and the spiritual in man completely regnant; we do not find either in youth or age that the mass of mankind can sustain such a test. The end of gratification, in some form, is universal, and it is only in very special cases that we can affirm "the law in the members" is rigidly held subordinate to "the law of the mind." So soon as we can ascertain by its working the disposition of the man, it is found that his spirit has already turned to seek happiness, and has become delinquent to the end of its highest worthiness. Nature as truly as Revelation, affirms that "all have gone out of the way."

Now we cannot, in psychology, help out our ignorance of the source of such universal depravity, by any statements from revelation; and can only say, the history of the race evinces, so high as we can trace it, that humanity is in a fallen condition, and that it is not, and has never been, supremely disposed to attain the grand end of a spiritual life. If there are exceptions, they have always been under such conditions as to prove the general rule of depravity. Inasmuch as this perverseness of disposition appears from the first, and its origination is truly back of all personal recollection in each case, we are left without any explanation of it from experience. If this original disposing act of the spirit was in consciousness, the memory has not so retained it that it can at any subsequent time be brought up for careful and intelligent reflection. The ground of this certainty of human delinquency cannot, thus, be made subject to human investigation through any experience. From our conscious conviction of guilt and responsibility that we have now such a disposition, it will be safe to assume as a theory, that at no point is such a disposition unavoidable; that it is not, and does not continue, from any natural inability and because there is no open alternative to it; but that it is ever the spirit's own, and solely and righteously at its responsibility. All the impotency, therefore, at the first, and at any subsequent period, that the spirit should not take on and perpetuate such a perverse disposing, is of a moral kind, and from within the spirit itself, and not forced upon it in any necessary connections of nature. The first instant of such disposing was as truly the spirit's own, as at any subsequent moment of its existence, and we can no more say, it could not avoid sinning at the first, or avoid being sinful, than we can at any point of subsequent activity. But, that there is a moral impotency in each case, at the first disposing, may well be assumed from the universality of the result; and we can only leave it on such proof, since we cannot carry up any conscious recollection to the examination of what was then our experience.

We are, however, much more competent to examine the fact of our impotency to break off from all depravity, and to stand out, in all our daily experience, in the full perfection of having attained and kept the great end for which our spiritual being is given to us. This change has not been made, and when the man is summoned to it, and even when he essays to effect it, there is a sense in which he honestly says, 'I am unable to do it.' Let us endeavor to know precisely what this impotency is.

The gratification of animal appetite is agreeable, and the immediate impulse of the whole animal being is towards happiness, on every offered occasion. Were man only animal, it might be said on all occasions of presented happiness, that he has no alternative to the going out after the highest degree. He could not help going out after the strongest desire; and in this we should mean that there was a natural inability. There is no alternative to the end of happiness, and that which causes the taking of happiness at all must, thus unhindered by any alternative, cause the taking of the highest offered degree. If denial in one direction will give greater happiness in another, then denial is on that account most desirable, and the impulse must be accordingly. To the animal, prudence will be as impulsive as appetite, and the strongest impulse cannot find its alternative in any lower degree. All is really the same thing; happiness; and the animal is naturally unable to hold himself back from it. There is no disposing, as of a permanent state of spiritual activity, or will; there is only the inclination of constitutional nature. We cannot here say anything about moral impotency; the conception is wholly irrelevant. The whole inability is grounded in necessity.

But the man is not all animal. He feels the impulse to happiness, and, in the consciousness of what is due to his spirit, he feels also the obligation to consult first this ethical claim of highest worthiness. Here is an end of wholly another kind, and which will not admit of comparison with happiness in degrees. No degree of happiness can give moral worthiness; and no satisfaction of appetite can fulfil an imperative claim. There is in this ethical end, a complete alternative to all happiness, even the highest and the eternal. It is one thing to be worthy of spiritual approbation, and quite another thing to be enjoying the applications to every appetite; and no matter how high the appeal to animal nature, while the mere brute cannot resist, the human being can. He has that within his reach which he can sieze as a complete and sufficient countercheck to the strongest desire for happiness. A natural inability it cannot be, which keeps the man from renouncing happiness as his end, and taking that of spiritual worthiness.

The impotency is wholly found within the spirit itself, and is an exclusion of all hope of change, left to the spirit's own agency. It has given itself to sensual good, and discarded the ethical good, and thus the very agent that should dispose itself to its true dignity, has sold itself in debasement to the lower nature, and voluntarily put on the bonds of appetite. How, now, release itself from the bondage which it loves and chooses? How choose anew against its own choice? How lift itself out of the gulf into which its own impulses and activity thrust itself down? Its determined activity is in one direction, how shall the same determiner of activity put the agency in another direction? Is it said that the spirit may take to itself new influences and motives, and by their means change its direction? But what other motives can it take, than such as it already has, and has rejected? And if there were others within its reach, what hope that it will reach and use them, when it does not wish their intervention nor the end to which they tend? How use what is repugnant, to attain an end already discarded? How set itself to seek what it does not wish to find? and this, that it may turn itself about in a direction it does not wish to go? How, then, is the carnal disposition, which is simply the spiritual activity disposed on animal gratification, to change itself to the spiritual disposition, which is simply the spiritual activity disposed on the end of its own worthiness? If the carnal mind be left alone in its own action, it is most hopeless that it will ever change itself to spiritual-mindedness.

But is not then this impotency truly a natural inability? Does not the spirit subject itself to the necessity of nature, by subjecting itself to the service of nature? Having wholly gone out after the sense, has it not thus abolished the alternative of a return to its own worth? Is not depravity, henceforth, unavoidable to itself? It would certainly so be, if by disposing itself on an ultimate end, and thereby attaining a radical disposition, it became only a physical cause, and could now only go out in efficiency as it was caused to go out by some agency *ab extra* to itself. As it has disposed itself, so it must perpetuate itself; and nature might as well turn itself back upon its own course, as the spirit convert itself from the error of its way. It would henceforth be nature, and subject to the necessities of nature; and whether the disposition were depraved or righteous, in that direction it must so remain. But this would be wholly a false conception, and abolish utterly the true distinction between natural and moral inability, and identify again nature and spirit.

By subjecting itself to the bondage of nature, the spirit does not itself become nature. It is itself a free causality, and wholly competent to originate action in itself, without a cause antecedent to itself causing it to act. Whether in a right or a wrong disposition, the spirit is still a supernatural existence; having its law in its own being, and competent to steady itself by that law against all the impulses of nature. When holy, it is competent to renounce the end which makes it holy, without the necessity of another and prior efficiency to cause it thus to renounce; and so, when sinful, it is competent to renounce the end which secures it to be sinful, without its being caused thus to renounce. The peculiarity of its efficiency is by no means lost, whichever direction it may have given to its activity. That it has a sinful disposition, is still consistent with the conception that it is spirit thus sinfully disposing its activity, and not that it is nature moving in a current which a higher cause has determined for it.

This depraved spirit, going out after its appetites and not after its duties, has thus the full natural competency to originate in itself an act of renunciation of the carnal end, and an act of adhesion to the end of its own worthiness, and may justly be required to "put off the old man, and to put on the new man," for this alternative is so open to it; but still, all the attachment to the wrong, and all the repugnance to the right, is there in the carnal disposition; and what hope of its originating the great change from spiritual death to spiritual life? The man may, yea, he must say, 'I ought to change; I am under the strongest obligations to my own spirit that I debase and degrade it no more; and thus that I *can* renew my disposition and reform my life.' But he can and must, also, say, in another sense, 'I love and choose my carnal gratifications; I hate and reluctate all the claims of the spirit that restrain me; I *cannot* renounce the happiness I love, and choose the restraints I hate.' In the full possession of his conscious natural competency, he has as full a consciousness of his deep moral impotency. In the pressure of these alternatives—on one side the passionate impulses of appetite, and on the other the stern imperatives of his own dignity—the bad man may often say to his conscience, "hast thou come to torment me before my time;" and the good man may say to his lusts, "O, wretched man that I am, who shall deliver me from the body of this death?" When the wicked man will do evil, the prompting imperatives of his spirit are yet within him; and when the righteous man will do good, the lusting to evil is still present. Humanity is in self-conflict; the spirit is naturally competent to rein the animal in subjection; and yet it is often morally impotent to put on and pull up the curb.

Thus man is both able and unable to attain the end of his being, in holding all his activity wholly to the claims of his spiritual nature. But in this there is neither absurdity nor contradiction. He is able not in the same sense that he is unable. His ability is a freedom from all the coercions and necessities of nature, and his inability is a bondage of the spirit itself—self-imposed and self-perpetuated. His freedom from all the compulsion of nature leaves him wholly responsible, and utterly inexcusable, in his depravity; and his whole-souled subjection to his carnal appetites, and the fixed state of will on the end of animal gratification, render it utterly hopeless that the same spiritual will, left to its own way, is ever about to turn from that which it so loves, and fix anew upon that which it so hates. In such a condition, perpetuated depravity must have its perpetuated consciousness of degradation and guilt; and the recovery of the spirit to its original integrity awaits the gracious advent of One, who, by a spiritual regeneration, may seek and save the lost.

and arguments on the many points on which as an honest and independent thinker and teacher he was called upon to decide.—*Literary World.*

To say that it is a work of profound thought, nice in discrimination, forcible in expression, instructing the reader in the fundamental principles of right action, and in the application of those principles to the individual, to society, and to God, —suggesting even when it fails to instruct, and awakening where it fails to convince,—merely to say this, is to give no idea of one of the highest and best works in the department of moral science. Perhaps our notice will best answer the purposes of the publisher, if we say outright that every person who buys this book will make a safe and profitable investment of his money, that the student who ponders it will gain a valuable mental discipline, and a deep and comprehensive range of view, and especially that the minister will find in it volumes of thought upon topics with which his own mental activity is most conversant.

Its views of the Divine Government, with respect both to justice and to grace, give one of the very best expositions of the momentous doctrines of atonement to be found in the English language.—*The Independent.*

This valuable Treatise of Dr. Hickok exhibits and tends to cultivate a true manliness of spirit, a sense of personal honor, an abhorrence of pusillanimity. The author is independent in his reasonings as well as in his style. He has his own system, and he defends it in kind manner, but with an honorable self-reliance. It is, as all who know Dr. Hickok, may well suppose, an able Treatise, and deserves the study of all clergymen, moralists, and general scholars."—*Bib. Sacra.*

RATIONAL PSYCHOLOGY.

BY LAURENS P. HICKOK.

[Formerly published by Derby & Miller, Auburn.]

OPINIONS OF THE PRESS.

The attractions which it presents are of a purely intellectual, scientific character, arising from the singular clearness with which the author perceives the subjects of his investigation, the severity with which he gives the analysis of them into their primitive elements, and the philosophical closeness and precision with which he exhibits the conclusions that were attainable only after the most sustained and vigorous processes of thought.

It was not until the appearance of this volume, that we have been able to point to a work exhibiting a profound study of foreign authorities, and at the same time the power of original enquiry and construction in the same field. This remark indicates the estimate we place on the value of Dr. Hickok's production.

He is profoundly versed in the writings of the great Continental philosophers. He is so familiar with their thoughts, their modes of reasoning, and their phraseology, that their exceeding intellectual wealth is no source of embarrassment, but he handles and makes use of their treasures with the graceful facility of one who was born for their enjoyment. He has melted down the rough, rugged ore of German Thought in the crucible of his own strenuous, persistent intellect, till it flows forth in a clear, brilliant, translucent stream of refined and precious metal, ready to receive the original impress, which will give it value in the currency of all thinking men, Nor is he confined to this process of reproduction and purification. His work is essentially original. It is a uniform, consistent whole, which everywhere shows the characteristics of an independent mind.—*N. Y. Tribune.*

One who reads Dr. Hickok's work, as it ought to be read, will find, often, that it requires great steadiness and concentration to follow him; but he will also find that there is meaning there, and that when discovered, nothing could be more transparent. He will often, too, be satisfied that in no other manner could the thought have been presented without some deficiency, or some redundancy, or some less eligible arrangement of its parts, that would have detracted from its force, no less then from its significance. In these respects we do not deem it extravagant to compare him with some of the master minds of antiquity. His ... be studied and so must those of Bacon, of Plato, and of Aristotle.

Will rid your premises of bats free for the bats. AN. 14851.—*Adv. in Los Angeles Examiner.*

Refurbishing an old belfry?

—deeply impressed with a conviction of the value of the Book, we have attempted to convey that conviction and the grounds of it, to others. In doing so, we have endeavored also to discharge a debt of gratitude for the rich instruction received from its perusal. After weeks of intense study, we laid it down with the impression that it must be henceforth one of our few Books, to be kept as a settled standard for future thinking. We believe the same feeling of substantiality will be left upon the mind of every intelligent man, who will give it that close study which is the only worthy tribute to its intrinsic excellence.—*Dr. T. Lewis, in Bib. Sacra.*

We venture to say that Dr. HICKOK has made out a good *prima facia* case, that his processes of investigation appear original, based upon sure principle, and deserving careful examination. If it should appear that he has established some definite land-marks in the ever shifting sea of metaphysics, he will have rendered good service to all speculative enquiries.—*Christian Remembrancer, London.*

THE SIX DAYS OF CREATION:

OR

THE SCRIPTURAL COSMOLOGY;

WITH THE ANCIENT IDEA OF THE PLURALITY OF TIME-WORLDS,

IN DISTINCTION OF WORLDS OF SPACE.

BY TAYLER LEWIS, LL. D.

1 vol. 12 mo.

(In press; to be published about the first of April.)

The publisher would call the most favorable attention to the above work which, it is hoped, will be found of no little service, not only to the cause of Biblical Literature and Theology, but also to the general reader.

AN ELEMENTARY TREATISE ON OPTICS.

BY ISAAC W. JACKSON, LL. D.,

PROF. OF MATHEMATICS IN UNION COLLEGE.

This work contains 260 pages, 8vo., with many plates, &c., printed on the finest paper. It is adopted as a Text-Book in many of the most important Colleges and Universities in the country. Price, $1.50.

AN ELEMENTARY TREATISE ON MECHANICS.

BY ISAAC W. JACKSON, LL. D.,

PROF. OF MATHEMATICS IN UNION COLLEGE.

The above work contains about 200 pages, with plates, &c., uniform with the Optics. Price, $1.50.

www.ingramcontent.com/pod-product-compliance
Lightning Source LLC
LaVergne TN
LVHW020108110826
845151LV00001B/98

* 9 7 8 1 4 2 5 5 4 3 2 2 8 *